Powerful Profits from

KENO

Casino Magazine's Play Smart and Win
(Simon & Schuster/Fireside, 1994)

Casino Games Made Easy (Premier, 1999)

Powerful Profits from Blackjack (Kensington, 2003)

Powerful Profits from Slots (Kensington, 2003)

*Casino GambleTalk: The Language of Gambling and
New Casino Games* (Kensington, 2003)

Powerful Profits from Craps (Kensington, 2003)

Powerful Profits from Video Poker (Kensington, 2003)

Powerful Profits: Winning Strategies for Casino Games
(Kensington, 2004)

Powerful Profits from Casino Table Games
(Kensington, 2004)

Powerful Profits from Internet Gambling
(Kensington, 2005)

Powerful Profits from Video Slots (Kensington, 2005)

Powerful Profits from Poker (Kensington, 2005)

Powerful Profits from

KENO

VICTOR H. ROYER

LYLE STUART
Kensington Publishing Corp.
www.kensingtonbooks.com

LYLE STUART BOOKS are published by

Kensington Publishing Corp.
850 Third Avenue
New York, NY 10022

All Kensington titles, imprints, and distributed lines are available at special quantity discounts for bulk purchases for sales promotions, premiums, fund-raising, educational, or institutional use. Special book excerpts or customized printings can also be created to fit specific needs. For details, write or phone the office of the Kensington special sales manager: Kensington Publishing Corp., 850 Third Avenue, New York, NY 10022, attn: Special Sales Department, phone 1-800-221-2647.

Lyle Stuart is a trademark of Kensington Publishing Corp.

First printing: July 2004

10 9 8 7 6 5 4 3 2 1

Printed in the United States of America

ISBN 0-8184-0637-2

This book is gratefully dedicated to

Georgina S. Royer

"Veni, vidi, vici"—I came, I saw, I conquered.

—Julius Caesar

Remember this each time you go to a casino.

Contents

Foreword

Players who know where the big money is play Keno. They play Live Keno, called "Big Board Keno," because there they can play what is essentially a lottery, but play it much faster, and with group combinations unavailable in any state-sponsored lottery. They also play Video Keno—a much misunderstood game, but one offering some of the best machine pays around—for jackpots worth tens of thousands.

Although lottery players spend lots of dollars on state lotteries, where the odds are in the hundreds of thousands or millions to one against their winning (and then have to wait three days, or a week before the game is drawn), keno players spend less money in a game offering hugely better odds, with comparable payouts—and a game played every ten minutes. State lottery players can pick only one set of numbers and then are victim to the fate of the draw; keno players can play "way" tickets, and multiple "wheel" ticket combinations, often at reduced rates, allowing them to combine numbers in groups such as are not possible in any lottery. Not only does this enhance their odds of winning on the keno ticket, but it provides for significant moneymaking opportunities unlike those in other casino games, and certainly none in any lottery.

For example, many state lotteries use the Pick-5 game, a game in which the players pick five numbers, and they win if they draw all of them, or win smaller prizes for four hits, three hits, sometimes even two hits. The odds of hitting these solid five are about 160,000,000-to-1 against (actual odds depend on number of numbers in the choice field, tickets purchased, number of available players, size of areas of domain, and so on). For this, the payoff can be as low as $500 for the solid hit. Now consider playing a 5-spot keno ticket. Even if played straight up, meaning you mark only the five numbers in the same manner as you would on the lottery ticket, your payoff is generally around 810-for-1. Your odds of hitting it are around 1,550-for-1.

Now look at the video keno version, or compare both keno games to a video poker game, as an example. In Video Poker, the major jackpot is the Royal Flush, which normally pays around 800-for-1 (with max coins played), for the jackpot of 4,000 coins. Using the 25-cent game as an example, this is an investment of $1.25 for the maximum jackpot of $1,000. The keno pay of 810-for-1 is not only better, but it costs only $1, saving you 25 cents per play. Further, the odds of hitting a Royal Flush on a standard video poker machine are about 41,000-for-1, but the game pays only at 800-for-1. The odds of hitting a keno 5-spot are 1,550-for-1, and the payoff is at 810-for-1. You don't need to be a mathematical genius to quickly discover the staggering difference.

There is now a game in Nevada called "Nevada Numbers," which is a keno game played like a state lottery. Although lotteries are illegal in Nevada, the Nevada Numbers is not considered a lottery because it works as a multilink keno progressive, linking casino keno games throughout the state among participating casinos. The game is a Pick-5 game, drawn once per day. The jackpot *starts* at $5 million. Consider the odds of a state lottery versus a keno Pick-5. Consider the jackpot starting amount. Consider the frequency in which the game is played. Now you know why people who know play Keno!

Also consider the very popular 10-spot keno ticket. In

the Big Board Keno game, this ticket often pays $1 million for a solid 10-hit. On a video keno machine, this ticket can pay anywhere from $10,000 for the $1 bet all the way to several million for a progressive. Even nickel video keno games often pay over $100,000 for a 10-spot hit, for an investment of 4 nickels—20 cents. Even someone with a small bankroll can afford to play Keno and have a chance at winning big money. But that isn't the best news about this game. The best news about Keno, and the 10-spots, is that many of the frequent jackpots come as hits of 8-out-of-10. This pays $1,000 for a $1 bet. Again, consider the difference between this and Video Poker. While Video Poker in the quarter game will cost $1.25 per bet, with a jackpot of $1,000, the game faces the odds of around 41,000-for-1 for this hit. The lower $1 wager in Keno, however, faces odds of only 7,384-for-1 and still pays a $1,000 jackpot!

These are just some of the reasons why many professional and semiprofessional gamblers—and players "in the know"—play Keno and Video Keno as their games of choice, or at least as their supplementary games of profit. Among games with house odds against a win, but huge payoffs relative to the investment, keno games are much preferred by players who want to win. I play Keno and Video Keno almost exclusively, because that's where the money is. Up to now, these methods of play have not been made available to the general public. Most people misunderstand this game because they have never been shown what a great money-maker this game can be. Now you can find out.

Casinos offer the game, but they rarely promote it because of these same reasons. Although often described as a "house game" in the books now in general circulation, whereby it is often mentioned that the game "holds" anywhere from 25 percent to 43 percent for the house, the game has changed. Casino competition has made payoffs a lot better than before, and the newest variations on Video Keno have made the game vastly better than most of the slot machines and video poker machines now available. But casual players shy away from the game because it has never been explained, or explained in a way that shows not only how the game works, but *how to play it to make money*. These same players flock to the lotteries, but ignore a game that is identical to any lottery, but offers far better payouts and odds. Now, for the first time, I will reveal the secrets and methods of profitable play in Keno, using strategies and innovations never before revealed. My purpose in writing this book is to provide you with the *most up-to-date and current* ammunition for making money from a game that is essentially a lottery, but played with far better odds. It is a money-making game played by people who know what the game can truly provide. It is a game that anyone can play, and for small stakes, yet with huge profits.

The book is divided into two parts:

Part One is "Big Board Keno." This is the "live" game, played in comfortable lounges. The game uses the same methods for drawing numbers as those used in state lotteries. Anyone who has ever bought a lottery ticket will immediately know how to play this game. Even persons unfamiliar with casino gambling will be able to sit down and enjoy this game. Live Keno is a leisurely game, wherein each draw happens about every ten minutes—much faster than the three days, or a week, in state lotteries. The keno lounge provides sumptuous chairs for relaxation, free cocktails, and often even free food delivered right to you. The games can be played in most casinos for as little as 10 cents per way. The average price of a ticket is about $1.

There are many more combinations possible in Keno than there are in any state lottery. Although Keno is virtually identical to a lottery, here you can play "way" tickets and "wheels," such as are not possible in lotteries. These methods of play will not only enhance your experience, but will also provide for many frequent wins and very large jackpots relative to the investment. This is the first book that shows not only the modern game of Keno as it is now played in the casinos of the twenty-first century, but also the secret combinations that professional gamblers and keno players have used for decades—the same methods that have produced tens of thousands of dollars for their players, and millions of dollars even for a single hit. Casino Keno is a game anyone can play, even with little money. You can have a great time and often exploit it for very large wins.

Part Two is "Video Keno." Similar to Big Board Keno, Video Keno has been equally misunderstood. Although this machine is often among the best paying slots on the casino floor, many casual players have so far avoided this game because they find it intimidating, or because no one has ever explained what a profitable and enjoyable game this can be. With new advances in computer technology, many variations on keno games are now possible. Some versions offer simplified models of the Big Board Keno "way" tickets. Other variations are the popular *Four Card Keno*™, where one can play more than one ticket at a time, allowing for the perfect "wheel" game.

Many video poker machines pay an average of around 90 percent, allowing for casino programs and imperfect plays, but video keno games generally pay at around 92 percent to 93 percent. This is very comparable to the $1 reel slot machines, which generally pay around 94 percent, or 90 percent to 92 percent in some casinos. Most video keno games are available in the quarter denomination, and while quarter Reel Slots often pay back at less than 85 percent, Video Keno still maintains the average 92 percent payback, overall. And, while the odds of hitting $1,000 for the Royal Flush on the video poker machine are around 41,000-for-1 on an average quarter machine at an investment of $1.25, a hit of 8 out of 10 on a video keno machine brings the same $1,000 jackpot at an investment of only $1, and facing odds of only 7,384-for-1.

No book before this one has presented these gaming machines, and these playing methods, in a manner so powerfully profitable. As I stated previously, I play Video Keno regularly, because it is a moneymaking game. I have many methods and secrets to reveal. For example, did you know that grouping numbers is profitable, and why? Did you know that certain patterns in Video Keno are more profitable than others, and why? I will answer these and many other questions in this book.

Introduction

The game of Keno has been around for a long time. It was actually called something that we can translate to "the numbers." In fact, the "mob" used to "run numbers," and that's why Keno is even today still sometimes called "the numbers game." The real origins of Keno date back to the ancient Chinese people. About 3,000 years ago, they came up with a terrific game. However, the real truth of why this game was invented had little to do with either altruism, or the need of recreation, and even less to do with gambling. It seems the Chinese emperor of the time—some say it was Liang Wu Ti, but no one's really sure—needed to raise money for his army and to fund the building of the Great Wall. His already overtaxed people weren't willing to bear any more taxes, and any such imposition would have resulted in an open rebellion. Not wishing to spark a national revolt or a civil war, the emperor instead instituted what we would now call the very first state lottery.

Sound familiar? It should. Just about every lottery run in the world today is virtually identical to that game, originally invented by the Chinese so long ago. Back then the emperor kept 50 percent of the money that was raised; the other 50 percent was paid back in various prizes. The game became so popular that even people from countries far away would send emissaries to China to buy tickets. Of course, that huge popularity soon begot corruption. As with most things done on a grand scale, so was the grandious corruption that soon plagued the ancient Chinese lottery. Soon officials began to "cook" the numbers, meaning to alter the winning events. Then they sold the winning tickets only to themselves, or to their associates. Eventually the people revolted anyway, because no one except the lottery officials and their families was winning the prizes. In the end the lottery was discontinued by command of the emperor, the lottery officials were beheaded, and the emperor simply raised taxes and put down the revolt.

Naturally, there are other versions of this story. Some have similar core elements, and others do not. In the interest of fairness, here is another description of how Keno became known as "the Chinese Lottery," and how we came to play a game almost identical to it.

As this version of the story goes, the game we now know as "Keno" started out using 120 Chinese characters. It is said to have originated about 200 B.C. out of an ancient Chinese poem known as "The Thousand Character Classic." Rather than numbers 1 through 80, the first 80 characters of "The Thousand Character Classic" were used in the body of the keno ticket. "The Thousand Character Classic" was used in China as the second primer for teaching reading and writing to children. By putting 1,000 characters into a more or less coherent rhymed form, learning was presumably made easier and more interesting. It is interesting that no character is repeated. This poem was so well known in China that its 1,000 characters, arranged in order, were often used as a fanciful way of notation or counting from 1 to 1,000.

Many legendary stories exist about the origin of the poem. One story claims that the celebrated penman Wang Hi-Che wrote the thousand characters on a thousand separate pieces of paper. Emperor Liang Wu Ti then directed Chou Hsing-Szu to arrange them in rhymed sentences to convey a meaning. This task was accomplished in a single night, but such was the mental effort that the compiler's hair and beard were turned completely white before morning. The poem is read from top to bottom and from right to left. The table below shows its "keno" version—in 80 characters—in English, with corresponding numerals.

Sky	(10)	Earth	(20)	Mysteries	(30)	Yellow	(40)
Universe	(50)	Infinite	(60)	Vast	(70)	Space	(80)
Sun	(9)	Moon	(19)	Full	(29)	Declining	(39)
Stars	(49)	Lunar	(59)	Arrange	(69)	Widely	(79)
Cold	(8)	Come	(18)	Heat	(28)	Go	(38)
Autumn	(48)	Harvest	(58)	Winter	(68)	Storage	(78)
Intercalary	(7)	Surplus	(17)	Complete	(27)	Year	(37)
Musical	(47)	Instrument	(57)	Harmonize	(67)	Nature	(77)
Cloud	(6)	Ascend	(16)	Cause	(26)	Rain	(36)
Dew	(46)	Frozen	(56)	Create	(66)	Frost	(76)
Gold	(5)	Make	(15)	Beautiful	(25)	Water	(35)
Jade	(45)	From	(55)	High	(65)	Mountain	(75)
Sword	(4)	Label	(14)	High	(24)	Gate	(34)
Pearl	(44)	Called	(54)	Night	(64)	Shine	(74)
Fruit	(3)	Precious Plum	(13)	Crab	(23)	Apple	(33)
Vegetables	(43)	Important	(53)	Mustard	(63)	Ginger	(73)
Sea	(2)	Salty River	(12)	Salt	(22)	Less	(32)
Scales	(42)	Submerge	(52)	Feathers	(62)	Soar	(72)
Dragon	(1)	Teacher	(11)	Fire	(21)	Emperor	(31)
Bird	(41)	Official	(51)	Human	(61)	Sovereign	(71)

Although the use of these characters on a keno ticket is merely to represent numbers, some Chinese people select the character marked for the word's meaning. The words selected usually have a special meaning to them—pronounced the same as their name, an event that has happened to them, or a recent dream. Before the game left China, the number of characters was reduced to ninety. The game came to America with the wave of Chinese immigrants in the nineteenth century. These were mostly the Chinese railroad workers. About this time the game was reduced to eighty Chinese characters.

Although illegal, Keno thrived among Chinese immigrants, especially around big cities like San Francisco. It became known as "the Chinese Lottery." English-speaking Americans became interested in the game, but had difficulty understanding the Chinese characters used in the game. Around the beginning of the twentieth century, keno operators replaced the Chinese characters with Arabic numerals to entice more players.

Although Nevada legalized most forms of gambling in 1931, the legislature did not legalize lottery, and the Chinese Lottery was definitely a lottery. To get around this nuisance, operators simply changed the name to Race Horse Keno. Each number was deemed to be a horse. Today, many keno operations still call their games "races." When the U.S. government passed a law taxing off-track betting, the name was once again changed, this time to Keno. In 1963 the aggregate keno payout limit in Nevada was $25,000. In 1979 it was changed to $50,000. In 1989 the Nevada Gaming Commission eliminated the cap, and casinos are now free to set their aggregate limits as they wish.

Of all the lottery games, and various numbers derivatives, the game of casino Keno is actually almost identical to that Chinese game from more than 3,000 years ago, even though what we now know as Keno perhaps dates from about 200 B.C. In those times, the game consisted of a board of eighty numbers, divided into two sections—top and bottom—each containing forty numbers. This is exactly like the keno game played in today's casinos, both as the live Big Board Keno game and as the video keno games in machines. The only other similarity was the picking of the numbers. Here, however, the similarities end. In any lottery, you can pick only single numbers, called "straight up" picks. Whatever the number of numbers that the lottery allows, you must pick exactly those. For example, the California lottery plays a game called "Pick Six." This means that you must pick six numbers straight up, as single number selections. Although you can play as many tickets as you want, each ticket can only be marked with six numbers—no more, no less, and only singly. The most basic ticket in any live keno game can be made in exactly the same manner. For example, if you want to play six numbers—called a "Six Spot"—you will mark six numbers total on a ticket showing eighty numbers, from 1 through 80—all selections being "straight up," marked singly, just as in the lottery. This is called a "straight up" ticket with six numbers, all together called a "Straight Up Pick Six Ticket." It is the simplest method of selecting numbers in a game of Keno, and it exactly mirrors lottery principles.

There are, however, some very significant differences between a live keno game and a lottery. First is the number of available numbers. Many state lotteries have a selection field of only 56 numbers. Some have 42 numbers, some 47, some fewer, some perhaps more. In California, the state lottery has been playing a version of the Pick Six where the ticket is really a combination of a Pick Five plus a "super" ball Pick One. The base game Pick Five has a field of 47 numbers, and the secondary field has 27 numbers for the Pick One. The objective is to pick all 5 numbers from the field of 47, and then match these by also picking the 1 number from the field of 27 in the Pick One game. Together, this makes a Pick Six game with a combined field of 74 numbers. However, there is a great odds leap between the two, by first picking the 5, and then matching the 1. It's almost like a 6-spot "way" ticket in Keno, with a group-5 plus a King, as you will soon find out, although this is only an analogy because the odds of making the ticket in the casino keno game are far better than in the California lottery. Similar state lotteries spawn jackpots in the hundreds of millions of dollars, such as the Powerball games played as a multistate lottery.

In casino Keno, hitting a solid 6-spot is a little easier. To hit it, you will have to pick a solid 6 from the available field of 80 numbers, and match your selected 6 to those from among the 20 numbers drawn from the total field of 80. However, what is often not considered when statistics are compared is the fact that the lottery will *only* draw 6 numbers *total*, and you must match each of them *exactly*, often including the last number drawn such as in the California lottery, or the Powerball number in the Powerball Lottery (or whatever the expression may be). In Keno, the game draws 20 numbers out of the available number field of 80, and you only have to match 6 of those to win. So, in Keno, you are actually picking 6 numbers from an available field of 80, but then you only have to match 6 of the 20 numbers drawn in the game to win your Pick Six ticket. For this reason, the odds of winning a lottery are actually enormously higher than the comparable odds of hitting a similar numbers ticket in Keno. Of course this also means that the keno Pick Six won't pay nearly as much as a lottery Pick Six ticket. But which would you rather have? A chance of winning $10 million on a lottery Pick Six with odds of around 160,000,000-to-1, or $10,000 on a keno Pick Six with odds of only about 7,750-to-1 against? What if you could only win, say, $2,500 on such a Pick Six bet in Keno? Would you mind that? Well, what if you could only win $2,000, or $1,480 on such a ticket? Would that not be good? The point is—you can. You can win all of these amounts on exactly this same ticket on a keno Pick Six game, and even more if you bet more. You see, in Live Keno, you can bet more than $1 a game—something that you can't do in any lottery. So, while your potential wins rise dramatically with the amounts you bet, your odds do not. Each game faces the same odds against you—that same 7,750-to-1. So, while you can bet $5, $25, $50, or more, and your wins now start to approach really significant money, the odds against you are always the same, because each and every game is a completely independent event. Although we all agree that long odds are not a good thing, and while we also agree that Keno can often hold upward of 25 percent for the house, here we are comparing the odds of winning a state lottery on a Pick Six ticket, versus the potential wins and much lower odds against, of winning a Pick Six ticket in casino Keno. Viewed only in this comparison, the answer is simple: the casino keno game offers far lower odds against a win and can produce winners of amounts proportionate to many lottery payoffs.

The state lotteries and casino keno games have one thing in common—making money for the operator. States like them because they raise millions of dollars annually for state-funded programs, and do so without the state legislature needing to increase taxes. Sound familiar? It should. That was the same reasoning made by that hapless Chinese emperor about 3,000 years or so ago. Today, state lotteries in the United States are very well regulated, and the chances of any such game being corrupted are very low. Likewise, Keno is also a game that makes money for the casinos, but not nearly as much as lotteries make for state governments. This is not only because the game offers lower odds against wins, but also because it is played mostly for low stakes, takes a long time to play—relative to the frequency of other casino game events. However, the payouts can also be quite large. The average casino keno game is played only about once each 10 minutes. While this is fast compared with the state lottery that plays only once in 3 days, or even daily, this is very slow in casino parlance. By comparing the speed of the keno game with other casino games, you will understand why. A blackjack game, for example, deals about 50 hands per hour. This means a decision about each 1.11 minutes. For this, the casino can expect about 1,200 decisions per each 24 hours. Assuming the average bet is $15 per hand—a very conservative estimate—this means each casino blackjack table will generate about $18,000 of action in each 24-hour period. Most casinos have an average of 20 blackjack tables, and so in general all of these tables together will make about $360,000 in gross action each 24 hours. If the casino's blackjack games average around 10 percent hold, this means a gross drop for the casino of $36,000 each 24 hours. Now compare this to Keno. Keno does about 6 games per hour. This is 144 games per 24 hours. The average keno bet is about $1.50. This makes the casino about $216 per 24 hours, per player. Assuming about 1,000 players per 24-hour period—a very generous figure—this will make the casino about $216,000 in gross action over 24 hours. This is significantly less than the blackjack tables, but not too bad considering there is only one keno game in most casinos, versus about 20 blackjack tables.

But what about the winners? These figures were for *gross* action, remember? Well, if the keno game holds an average of 25 percent, this would give the house a gross drop of about $54,000. This is statistically greater than the gross blackjack drop, and that's why casinos still offer this game: it is slow and labor-intensive, but, there are often many winners. What if this game hits a big winner, or several? Keno games are accounted for by shift, and I have often been in casinos when the keno shift supervisor hurriedly runs over to the counter and starts to add up the bets versus losses. Upon being asked what's happening, he replies "We've just been hit for $50,000." This happens a lot more often than you may think. This shift thus becomes "in the red," posting negative results for as long as it takes for it to recoup the wins. Many keno games have posted limits, such as "$100,000 maximum aggregate." This means that all winners combined for all wins during any one game can only accrue to that total amount. So, if you were the lucky player who hit for a $100,000 payoff, in this casino they would first deduct from this the smaller wins held by any other players and then pay you the difference, because this is the "aggregate limit." Don't worry too much, however, because if that happens to you, you are very lucky and should be glad for what you get. Most of the time the other winners will be small, so you would get very close to that big win total, even after the smaller winners' shares were deducted. Nevertheless, this is one of the important lessons to learn, and as we continue exploring Keno in more details later, we will discover that the selection of casinos with a high aggregate is part of the skill decision you can employ in Live Keno.

Although we could easily go on comparing the various keno pays and house holds to other games, such as slot machines, the point should be clear from the above blackjack example. Casinos mostly offer Keno not solely because it is a statistical moneymaker, but mostly because they have many customers who prefer to play more leisurely games. Many players don't enjoy the fast action of Blackjack, Craps, Roulette, or Slots. These players wish to extend their casino experience and expand their enjoyment. Many such players also have limited bankrolls, and one of the major attractions of Keno is that it can provide large wins for small investments. For these reasons, and many others, casinos have offered something that is possible only in Live Keno, and not in any lottery—this is called "way tickets." With these tickets, players can play more than just the standard number of "straight up" numbers. For example, instead of being limited merely to the Pick Six, as one ticket with only six numbers selected, these "way" tickets allow you to play many more numbers and group them together to make many more 6-spot combinations, as well as many other combinations. In fact, there are so many possibilities that these combinations often run into thousands of possible wagers.

This is designed to make the keno players play more money, because each of these tickets costs more to play, but you also get many more opportunities to win and many more such wins along the way. In fact, playing "way" tickets is the only method to play Live Keno, and the game should never be played otherwise. Furthermore, casinos often offer reduced rates for these tickets, meaning that you can play many such "way" ticket combinations for just a little more money. Wins become far more frequent, and large wins become even more accessible and possible. I have hit many such jackpots on many tickets, such as those I will show you in examples in later chapters. These "way" tickets also offer the possibility of doing something called "wheeling" your numbers. This is a principle used by many lottery players, but they must buy many different tickets to do this. In casino Keno, you can do all of this on the same ticket, and with much more consistency and many more chances at a very large win. Frequent wins on these way tickets also means that most of the time the tickets will not cost you the full price for the next game, even if you don't win a "big one." For example, your ticket may cost you $6.50 to play, but you win an average of $4.75 each game. So, each time you play that ticket for the next game—assuming you are playing a series of games in one session rather than just one ticket this day and another next week or some such isolated games—the next game this same ticket will "cost" you only $1.75, yet you are still playing all of the "ways" to make those winners. Many of these tickets soon become self-propagating, and many pay for themselves, and many more still produce enough "small" winners to keep you in the game for a long time. And, of course, the longer you play, the more chances you have for a good win.

These are the principles of playing Live Keno. Many of these are also applicable to Video Keno, though that game is actually quite different from Live Keno. The main point I'm wishing to make here is that Keno is most definitely not the "boring" game you may have heard about and certainly not nearly as much of a lousy "house" game as you may have read, or thought. There is a lot more to Keno than first meets the eye, and there are many means of making powerful profits.

In the chapters that follow I share with you decades of experience—my own and that of other keno players—and information I have obtained through play, investigation, thousands of hours in casino keno lounges, and endless conversations with keno professionals and casino employees.

If you want to spend little to win big, this is the perfect book for you.

Why This Book?

Keno can easily be classified as a casino subculture all its own. Keno players are usually a particular crowd, mostly made up of four distinct types of players. Group one are the elderly players, usually retired locals who now live close to their favorite casino. These people play every day, and mostly live on a fixed income, such as a pension. They aren't interested in the hype of the casino, but enjoy the ambiance and atmosphere. They want the slow game, the simple game, something they can play each day as a form of entertainment that won't cost them too much, but gives them a shot at a nice big win—"big," of course, being relative. To some such players, a win of $500 is "big," while to others nothing short of a million will do. Such individuality is what makes casino gambling so entertaining and enjoyable, while at the same time also so different and difficult for so many players.

The second group of players are the tourists. These people are on their gaming vacation, and include players who make frequent visits, perhaps as often as once a month. These casual players often play Keno while eating in restaurants, and take a shot here and there to see if they "catch something." I have done this kind of playing many times, and I can assure you it is a lot of fun, plus it also makes the time go faster as you are waiting for your food. It is also a nice sociable means of playing, and if you do get a winner, well, then, it makes the whole evening more exciting and enjoyable. These are casual players who occasionally wager a few dollars on a keno game.

The third group can be called "semiprofessional" keno players. These are mostly locals, who play not merely for the enjoyment but also for a supplementary profit. Keno can be a slow game, particularly in busy casinos and during busy times. Six games per hour is about the average, and it can get as slow as two games per hour. Players in this group usually tend to patronize "locals'" casinos, those off the Strip in Las Vegas, casinos where the keno games move faster and where the remainder of the facilities are geared more toward locals and less to the tourists. These players like to accumulate comps and often play for various additional rewards, such as Player's Club points, and other incentives. They may live on a fixed income, and may not have the necessary bankroll to play larger and more volatile casino games, but they have the skills, abilities, and knowledge to try their hand at some additional income. There are many more such players than you may think. They are smart, realizing that they can supplement their income by wagering small amounts wisely over longer periods, thereby preserving their bankrolls and enhancing their win opportunities. I have known many such players, many of whom used to play other casino games professionally or semiprofessionally. I know several players who are sixty-five and older, many in their seventies, who were very good poker, blackjack, or craps players, and horse and sports handicappers. Their skills in those other games have declined with age, and they are smart enough to recognize it. So, while they still enjoy the excitement of the casino, now they prefer to settle back and enjoy a slower pace of life, and a game that can be played for very little and yet offer many large win opportunities. These players are mostly semiprofessional, in that they use the game both as entertainment, and as a form of supplementary income. They are very careful players, and play only selected times, hours, and amounts of money.

The fourth and final group are the professionals, gamblers who have recognized the value of the keno "way" tickets, and often play many different casinos at the same time. Often they utilize the twenty-one-and-more consecutive game tickets, which are tickets that do not need to be collected after each game (more on this later). They play in casinos that offer large progressive jackpots, or whose pay tables for various keno pays are more liberal than other casinos. I will discuss this later, and you will be surprised at how different keno payoffs can be from casino to casino. Some casinos even have more than one game, sometimes called the Red and Green games, which can have vastly different payoffs. Although generally casino Keno is not among the most player-friendly games, odds-wise, it is possible to reduce the odds against you by selection and skills. You can select casinos that pay better for certain tickets and combinations. You can wheel your way tickets, and dramatically improve your odds—skills any serious gambler will employ in all casino gaming. In Craps, for example, wagering free odds behind your pass line bet can reduce the house advantage from about 1.4 percent on the line without odds, all the way to only 0.02 percent for the line bet with 100-times odds. Similarly, a keno player can look for an 8-spot progressive jackpot. Usually starting at $50,000, most such games will hold about 25 percent for the house at the beginning. After that game reaches $100,000, that house percentage drops to about 18 percent. After the game reaches around $180,000, the game offers an even 50-50 proposition. Thereafter, for every dollar over and above (all other pays being equal), the game begins to yield an actual player-positive expectation. Many professional players approach Blackjack this way and

even Video Poker, as I have described in my other books in
this series.

Many players in this group have come to realize that
Keno is not the "dog" of casino games that it is often made
out to be. Keno can actually yield a good game and can be
played profitably. Though it is true that Keno requires a lot
more patience than other games, and may take longer because of the slow speed of each event, the game won't cost
nearly as much as other casino games, since it requires a lower
bankroll and offers easier money discipline. These are important factors to consider. Even though Keno is statistically
a really "bad" game, with that average house edge of around
24 to 25 percent, the real-world truth is that the game is not
nearly so bad as this may first look. Those who devise these
statistics, and focus only on mathematical analysis as the
method of game selection, miss the point: The point in all
gambling is *not* to validate the statistics of even occurrence
theories, but to *win money*. The winning of money does not
automatically exclude the validation of the statistical theory, but those who honor only "mathematics" and "statistics" and "probability" believe that the winning of money is
automatically excluded any time the game does not conform to the statistical norm and form. This is too bad, because those who gamble purely and only in accordance
with validating the statistical theory are in for a long grind
that will be expensive and may result in financial ruin.
Such play can never succeed because the statistics are
based around infinite occurrences, while any gambler can
only play for a tiny fraction of the overall infinite events
that go into the calculation of such a theory. Even if we are
to take the extremely finite slice of the overall infinite probability theory and use just 10 million events, how many
casino players do you know can play this many events in a
lifetime? Let us imagine a player who can play 10 hours per

day, 7 days per week, every year. Let us further imagine that this player will be playing a player-positive video poker machine where each event takes 10 seconds. This gives our imaginary superhuman player 6 events per minute, for a total of 360 events per hour, which comes to 3,600 events for his 10-hour day. Multiply that by the whole year, and this comes to 1,314,000 events. In order to reach the 10 million statistical events, this player would have to play continuously in this manner for 7.61 years! What if he or she was a slower player? Or could only play 5 hours per day? Well then, it would take 15.22 years to validate these statistics. What if the player was playing Blackjack instead? In casino Blackjack, you get only about 50 hands per hour—if you're lucky. At that pace—based on the above example—this player would play 500 hands in a 10-hour day. This comes to only 182,500 events per year. Therefore, in order to validate the 10 million-event statistics, this player would have to play 10 hours per day, 365 days per year, for a total of 54.79 years. Beginning at the legal age of 21, he would turn 75 years and 8 months old before he would ever expect to validate the statistics that many gaming experts tell us we must follow if we expect to win. Got that?

What would this player achieve at the end of those 55 years? Well, in Blackjack, if he was very good, he could expect to validate the mathematical theory by gaining about 0.5 percent edge over the house—provided that he never made a mistake. Thus, if he was risking an average of $50 per hand—increasing and decreasing his wagers appropriately as the skills of the game dictate, but averaging about this much—he would risk $2,500 per hour, which comes to $25,000 per his 10-hour day, which comes to $9,125,000 for each year. Playing for 55 years in this manner, he would have risked $501,875,000, for the end-result statistical profit of about $2,509,375. This comes to an income of about $45,625 per year—assuming no other expenses and costs, of course.

So, if you are able to acquire all these required skills by age 21, and are actually able to find casinos over the next 55 years that will allow you to play that well, and you play exactly like this, and you play perfectly at all times and never once make a mistake, then you can expect to validate the statistics. Well, maybe. You see, the problem is that these are not the "real" statistics; they are only an assumed slice of the overall statistical picture. As I pointed out at the beginning, this situation is an example based on our arbitrary selection of a mere 10 million events, from an infinite pool. What if these 10 million events were not the "statistically average" sample? What if these 10 million events were, in reality, an anomaly—something different from what the actual figures should have been? Well, dear player, you would have spent 55 years trying to validate a theory that was faulty in the first place. And this, dear reader, is the fallacy of applied mathematics.

The video poker player in our example would have hoped for something around 0.17 percent in expected value (EV), and therefore his overall income would be even lower. The point I am making is that our purpose in gambling is not to make the stats work and validate the theory of the game, but to make the money work and make *profits* for us. Profits *today*, not fifty-five years from now. And even games whose "math" indicates that they are "lousy" can—and do— produce *financial winners*. This happens every day, in every casino. Every casino game pays winners, regardless of what the "stats" say about how "lousy" the game may be. Although I agree that mathematics and statistics, and probabilities, are extraordinarily useful in describing the games, their inherent number theories, and potential payback and hold percentages, I vehemently disagree with anyone who claims that no such "negative expectation" or "house" games should be considered as games to play. Just because a game may be statistically "lousy"—such as the average house edge of about 24 percent in Keno—doesn't mean the game won't pay. Even if the game holds 24 percent for the house, it pays out 76 percent. Employing some simple methods of play, even a keno game can reduce that house edge to percentages comparable to many popular casino games, and even liberal slot machines. So what if the game "holds" as much as 8 percent for the house with skilled play? Doesn't this also mean that the game pays back 92 percent? Hmmm? Well, it should, but those mathematical geniuses who scare the shingles off the roof of most casual players conveniently forget that *these games pay back much more than they hold.* Bottom line: Keno is not nearly as much of a "dog" as it is made out to be, and it can be played for profit.

The trick is to understand the truth of the game, and while this does not necessarily exclude the understanding and application of the statistical percentages or the mathematical theory, it does reflect the reality of the game. The reality of this game of Keno, and indeed of all casino games, is that they do pay, and often pay well, frequently, and for large amounts of money. Just because most experts shun the game of Keno because of the faulty reliance on statistics and percentages doesn't mean no one can win at it. Keno pays big winners many times each day. Why wouldn't you want to play a game where you can wager $1 and win $1 million? So what if the "math" says these are "long odds against" you? If that were true, why would anyone wager a dollar on a lottery ticket, where the odds against can be as much as 300,000,000-to-1?

The point is that making money is different from trying to validate a mathematical or statistical theory. Making money in the casino happens all the time, every day, every hour. Keno can—and does—produce many winners. So, here in this book, I want to show you how.

PART ONE

Casino Keno

The Language of Keno

Before we begin to discuss Keno, we need to know some of the special words and terms that apply to this game. Each gambling game has its own special language and terminology, and the world of gambling in general also contains specific uses of language and words that may not be what you think. I have even written a book on the subject: *Casino GambleTalk: The Language of Gambling and New Casino Games*. I refer you to that book for details about the general language of gambling, as well as more details about the language of Keno and Video Keno. Meanwhile—in this book—I'll list, and define, some of the most common terms and expressions that apply only to Keno and Video Keno.

AGGREGATE

This is the total accumulated payoff limit for any single keno game. It applies only to the live keno game, and it was imposed in the past upon the keno operators by the legislature and gaming regulations. It used to be set at a $25,000 limit, then it was increased to $50,000, and now the restrictions are all but gone; casinos can list whatever aggregate they want. Some casinos have a limit of $100,000, some less, and many will have more, up to $1 million and beyond. It all depends on the casino, and what kind of a keno game they wish to play, as well as their overall commitment to the game itself.

BIG BOARD

Live keno games are "broadcast" to other areas of the casino by the use of big boards with the keno numbers on them, just as they appear on the ticket. In each game, as each new number is being drawn, the corresponding number drawn lights up on the keno board. In days past this used to be called the "flashing board" (or flashboard), because the numbers drawn in each game were "flashed" on that board. I often call the live keno game the "Big Board Keno," and that's why—these keno boards are very large, so that they can be easily seen by players everywhere. Gambling changes dramatically with advances in technology, so the days of the big board are numbered (pun intended). TV sets have replaced the big board, and closed circuit television has replaced the broadcasting of the drawn numbers. The games are now also available to guests in their hotel rooms. By tuning in to this TV keno channel, you can play the games in your room, or buy your multirace tickets and then relax in your room— or perhaps your own room spa—and watch the games being drawn.

BIRD CAGE

This a round, wire-mesh-type cage that looks a lot like the older-style bird cages. It is used to roll the keno balls around and then pick them out one by one by rotating the cage backward. This is the same style mechanism often used in church bingo games, and works on the same principle. It is similar to the Bubble, or Blower, and is also sometimes referred to as a "tumbler."

BUBBLE OR BLOWER

I call it the "bubble," because it reminds me of the bubbles I used to blow as a small child, with soapy water and a stick with a circle on the end. I always remember that when I see a keno game that uses this Plexiglas bubble for the drawing of keno numbers. It is perhaps better described as a "blower," because that's what it does—it blows out the keno numbers through a tube, by forced air, and that's how the game picks the twenty numbers for each keno game. This is also similar to the bingo blowers and also to the method by which lotteries are generally drawn.

BRUSH

In the days before computers, keno games were marked in messy black ink, applied to the keno ticket by the keno writer using a painter's brush, hence the name. It is not used anymore (for which we are all grateful).

COMPUTER GAME

Not to be confused with Video Keno, this game works very much on the same principle. This is a "live" game—as opposed to a slot machine called Video Keno—that uses a computer system to draw out the game's twenty numbers, as opposed to either the Bird Cage or the Bubble. Games like this are used mostly by casinos that have a separate game for their keno runners. This is traditionally done in large casinos that cater to keno players in the restaurants and bars, and even at gaming tables. In these casinos such wide availability of the keno game would slow it down to a crawl, and the live players in the keno lounge wouldn't like it very much, not to mention the players in the restaurants and bars, all of whom would have to wait a long time between games. Keno is already a slow game—comparatively speaking, of course—and therefore casinos that are large, and have such runners in these often remote parts of the casino, usually have this second game. Such games are referred to as the Red and Green games, or some other color designation. This allows the runners, players, and keno writers to easily tell to which game the tickets belong, avoiding confusion. It also speeds up both games. This secondary game—the one used by the runners—is traditionally drawn by the computer, which makes it faster, requiring less equipment in the restaurant location of this game. This also allows for the *main* game to be played faster, because it doesn't have to wait for the keno runners to come back from all corners of the casino, then for the writers to write all of those tickets, then for the runners to take them back to the players again. Although this computer game is almost identical to the video keno games we will discuss in part two, it is very important that you do not confuse these two versions of keno games where the drawn numbers are generated by a computer. The game discussed here is a "live" game, and the method of playing it, and marking the tickets, mirrors exactly the game in the keno lounge, regardless of whether that game is, or is not, also drawn by a computer. The video keno games—discussed in part two of this book—are completely different. There you can only play in accordance with the available selections, as allowed for by the machine's keno program.

DRAW

In this event, twenty numbers are selected for any one game of Keno.

KENO MANAGER

The supervisor in charge of keno operations at that casino is the keno manager. Usually able to be found on day shift only, this person is the big boss of the keno department.

KENO SHIFT BOSS

This usually refers to the supervisor in charge of the specific shift, such as "swing" or "grave." The keno manager usually does this job on day shift, as well as being the head of the keno department. The keno shift boss is the top authority on each shift and works under the keno manager.

KENO RUNNER

In casinos that offer this service, these are the employees that "run" your ticket from various locations in the casino, saving you from going to the keno counter and doing it yourself. This service is normally found in the restaurants, bars, and lounges, and is helpful when you are having dinner and like to have something to do while you wait for your food to arrive. Most people don't realize that a keno runner can be dispatched to serve you anywhere in the casino, including at table games and slot machines. If you want to play Live Keno at the same time that you are playing, say, Blackjack, just ask the dealer to ask the pit boss to come over. Tell the pit boss you want to play Keno and request a keno runner. If this casino has keno runners (all major casino resorts do) the pit boss will simply call one and she will come and take care of your tickets for each and every game as long as you wish to play. This also applies to slots. If you want to play Live Keno at the same time as playing a slot machine, but don't want to leave to go to the keno counter and get your tickets, simply call the floorperson over and tell them to send the keno runner. The same situation will occur as that described above for the blackjack player: You can enjoy your keno game for as long as you wish to play, regardless of where you are in the casino, or what other game you may be playing. While keno runners are mostly female, several casinos have male keno runners as well.

KENO WRITER

This is the person who transfers your market ticket into the computer-generated version. In days past, this was the person wielding that messy brush full of ink. You could always tell who worked in Keno by the ink stains on their hands and cuffs. These days, it's all done with computers.

KING

In Keno this is the marking of a single spot, circled. The proper use of "kings" in your keno ticket will make your game a lot more profitable. We will discuss this in more detail later.

MULTI-RACE TICKET

A ticket bought for more than one game is called a "multi-race ticket." Many casinos will let you buy a ticket for any number of games, from 1 to 20, and give you 48 hours to collect. There are also other tickets that allow you to play from 21 to 1,000 games, and have up to a year to collect any winnings. This becomes very handy in case you have to leave in a hurry, or forget all about the ticket you bought. I remember one time when I was still living in Los Angeles and used to visit Las Vegas quite often. Well, it so happened that this time I had to rush back home, and forgot all about my keno ticket. Luckily it was a 21-gamer which meant I had up to a year to collect. About 3 months later I was going through my bags and found the ticket. I called the casino, they found the ticket in the computer, and smilingly informed me I had a $3,000 winner! Well, I didn't even need this much of an excuse to revisit my favorite city, so I promptly hopped on a plane and was there, cashing in my ticket—so quickly that the keno manager remembered my call. Many people forget their multi-race tickets, and that's why casinos can now allow you to have this much time to collect your wins. This wasn't always so. As recently as a few years ago, casinos couldn't give you the time because of gaming regulations. You had to collect all your winnings immediately after the drawing of the last game on your multi-race ticket. This resulted in many angry customers and several law suits. Eventually the casinos convinced the gaming regulators that this was a bad idea, and the regulations were relaxed so that casinos can now allow you 48 hours for any ticket up to 20 games, and a whole year for any tickets bought for 21 or more games, up to 1,000 consecutive games. Incidentally, the reason why this is still called a multi-race ticket dates back to when race horses were used instead of numbers—when California made Keno illegal—in the days of the San Francisco Barbary Coast.

PAY TABLE OR RATE BOOK OR PAYS BOOKLET

This is the brochure-style pamphlet presented by casinos wherein they print the various payoffs for keno tickets. This brochure is usually available at the keno lounge, and also at every keno runner station. They can also be found on tables in restaurants, on bar counters, and just about everywhere else in the casino where keno is played, or where keno runners usually go. These brochures are available in stands that also include several blank keno tickets and keno crayons, as well as other implements for the game. Often there will be several other booklets, or brochures, some of which may contain various special offers, such as special keno tickets that can be played either for lower amounts, or in specific combinations, or during special hours, and so on. These brochures will also often show various "ways" in which Keno can be played, particularly several sample way tickets. Be aware, however, that these brochures will traditionally not show you the best way to play these tickets. Later in this section, I will show you the best tickets to play, and explain why. Here, the first advice I would give you is not to play the ticket samples shown in these brochures unless you can compare them with the samples I will show later in this book. You can also adapt them to be able to be played in a better manner, once you have learned how.

STRAIGHT UP or STRAIGHT WAY or STRAIGHT TICKET

All mean the same, which is to mark any keno ticket with only single numbers, none of which are grouped in any manner. This is the same method as that used to mark tickets singly when playing any lottery. This is the opposite of "way tickets," where many numbers are grouped together. (See below, Way Ticket.)

SPLIT RATE

This applies to way tickets, and means that you have chosen to play certain ways at a reduced rate, and certain other ways at the full rate (or different rate). This is available in almost all casinos that play Keno, and on almost all keno tickets, as long as they are "way" tickets. Most casinos will allow you to reduce the amount of your per-way wager all the way down to 10 cents, and even 5 cents per way, the more ways you play. For example, many casinos will allow you to mark 100 ways or more for that low rate—either a nickel or a dime per way—while also allowing you to play other ways for different amounts, such as $1 per way for the selected ways. This becomes incredibly important when we start to talk about the many ways that way tickets can be played. More on this later.

TOKE or TIP

This means a gratuity—money you give to the keno writers, or runners, as a means of thanking them for service, or when you win. Many people who are not familiar with the gaming industry do not realize that virtually all people in the casinos work for minimum wage and rely almost entirely on tips to survive and make a living. In casino parlance, this "tipping" is called a "toke," but means the same thing. Remember, next time you get great service or win some money, be generous and give a toke to the nice people who work there.

WAY TICKET

This is the multinumbered ticket whereby you select several numbers and group them together by circling them. The Kings can be used on such tickets, as well as other groups, such as groups of two numbers, groups of three, groups of four, and even groups of five. The more groups you make, the more ways there will be for the various possible hits. These tickets are valuable as long as you use them wisely, because they will allow you to cut the house edge down to almost nothing, and on some rare occasions even allow you to play a player-positive expectation game, such as when progressives are factored into the mix. Playing way tickets is the *only* method of playing Live Keno, that game which I call "Big Board Keno." If you play this game without using way tickets, you are a tourist giving away your money. That's why this game has such a bad rap among many casino-wise players and among most gaming authors and experts. A straight up ticket can face a house edge of anywhere from around 24 percent to 48 percent. This is enormous! Casinos offer this labor-intensive and expensive-to-operate game because they can make such high profits. Players who don't know how to play the game well play these straight tickets, or play the house-shown way tickets, none of which do anything to lower the house edge or give the player any better odds. While way tickets can be used to the player's advantage, they must be used intelligently, and with skill, knowledge, understanding, and patience. I will discuss this in more detail in Chapter 4, "Best Tickets."

Well, there you have it. The language of Keno. It is simple to learn and will quickly become second nature to you, even if you have never played Keno before, or perhaps have never even been to a casino. Keno can be a great game to play, especially if all you are after is a fun experience, for little investment, and with big profit potential. Although Keno can be played in that manner, the main benefit of this game is in the big wins it can provide for the smart keno player. Playing Keno badly is easy—it is like playing Slots badly, which is also easy. All the game requires is that you pick some numbers, which the computer can do for you, and that you have the money to make the bet. Other than that, no other skill or knowledge is required. That's precisely how the vast majority of people play, which is why casinos can make such huge profits from Keno and Slots. It is silly play by silly people—silly because they did not take advantage of the information that is available to show them how to play these games better. It is not necessary that you try to become a professional gambler, or try to learn pages and pages of strategies. To succeed in playing relatively easy games like Keno and Slots just takes a few minutes of your time to learn the better methods and means.

Because Keno and Slots both require only that you drop in the money and then wait to see if you won something, both games are attractive to novice players and millions of casual casino visitors. The expression "it's only a few bucks" is often heard when these players approach the keno game or the slot machine. They drop the money, wait for the outcome, and if they don't win then and there, they shrug their shoulders and move on. Or, which is much more often the case, they reach for more money and try again. And again. And so it goes, more money and more games, and all of them played about as badly as is possible. This is why many casinos can actually offer games that are made to win for the players. These are called "positive-expectation games," and many video poker machines are precisely of this kind (see my video poker book for more details). Keno is perhaps the easiest and most classic example of how people can throw away their money, ignorant of even the most rudimentary means of improving their chances.

First of all, players should always play some kind of a way ticket in Live Keno, and never play a straight ticket unless it is part of the way ticket combination, such as when the jackpot pay way is played singly as a straight up ticket in addition to the way ticket. Second, just because a player is playing way tickets doesn't mean that he or she is playing the *correct* way tickets, or playing these tickets correctly. To play Keno better, or at least in the most lucrative manner, you need to educate yourself. That's why I'm sharing information that regular keno players have known for as long as Keno has been a legal casino game: play smart tickets intelligently.

How? Well, first you need to know "which." And, of course, before we get to that, we need to get a little more comfortable with the game itself. To start this process of discovery, the next thing we need to know are the odds. In the next chapter, we will find out exactly what does what and what are the percentages.

Keno by the Numbers

Keno is a game of numbers, and it is calculated by numbers, and everything to do with it is about the numbers, and the mathematics, probabilities, and odds. Although we already know that the average house hold for any live keno game is between 24 percent and 48 percent, depending on the game and payoffs, this doesn't mean that we can't win at the game, or that it never produces a winner. Winners are produced daily. Some wins are small, while others are large. Although it is always important to understand the percentages, odds, probabilities, and mathematics behind any casino game, it is likewise important not to overvalue that information. I have stated in many of my books that the role of the math is to *point the way*—it is a useful tool for explanations of the game. To consider only the mathematics in your choice of game, and in the manner in which you play that game, however, is foolhardy. Using only one guide to achieve your goal is akin to placing all your eggs in one basket. If you drop the basket, you break all your eggs.

Many books and articles are written by people so blinded

by the mathematics of gambling games that they fail to focus on the *purpose* behind all gambling games, which is *to win money*. While I agree that—mathematically speaking—knowing the odds of the game, or event, either against you, or for you, is absolutely helpful as part of your decision process and playing strategy, I vehemently disagree with anyone who claims that this is the only means by which to make such determinations. Instead of being the only guide, or the only basket, I suggest that it is only one of many baskets. Deciding which game we should be playing—or want to play—is the first of many such decisions and determinations. After that comes the part about how to play the game, when, where, what limits, with what objective, how long a session, what bankroll, and so on.

We play casino games for two reasons: to have fun and to win money. We do not play casino games in a desperate attempt to somehow validate the percentages, odds, probabilities, and mathematics of the theory. That's where many gaming analysts fall far short of the reality, because they are so locked up inside a box called "mathematics" that they forget to realize that this is limited to only the parameters and perspectives on which they—and others like them—have decided to agree. It means nothing, other than to help illustrate the perceptual event occurrence theory of applied events.

Okay, I'll get off my soapbox now. As this applies to Keno, I will let you know that the availability of the mathematical analysis of odds of occurrence is very helpful in the understanding of the game and how it should be played. If nothing more, this shows which number or numbers should be played, and which should not. For example, this understanding of the odds—and their respective financial payoffs—will clearly illustrate that playing from 1 to 4 numbers in Keno is never a good idea, and likewise playing 11 to 15 numbers is also foolish (unless these are part of way ticket combinations). This framework of understanding will show us that the majority of our action should be in the selection of 5 to 10 numbers. That's where the "meat" of the game is. Of course, there are further refinements within this as well, such as precisely *which* combinations of numbers we should play, and why. I will discuss this later in chapter 4, "Best Tickets." For now, refer to the chart on page 52 that shows all of the odds of occurrence for keno number events from 1 number through 15 numbers. When reading this chart, remember:

- A standard keno game draws 20 numbers from a field of 80.
- Players select any number of numbers allowed for by the house rules of any keno game from that field of 80.
- To win, the player's selected numbers must be identical to the required combination of the 20 numbers drawn in any one game.

The chart shows the odds *against*—this means that, for example, if you selected 5 numbers, your odds of hitting all 5 are 1,550:1 *against*, meaning you will hit a solid 5-spot about once each 1,550 games. All of the odds in the chart are listed in this manner. If you forget what this means, simply turn it around—a listing of odds as 7,753:1 simply reads as: The odds of this event are 7,753-to-1 against happening, but you can also understand this by turning it around, because this same listing also means: You will hit this combination of numbers in the game of Keno about 1 time in each 7,753 games. Listing the chart as odds against is simply a cleaner and more professional way of showing this information and also saves space. It is easy to read, and if you plan on playing casino games, or reading more books, you should always know what the odds against mean, and what the odds "to" are, and how to read and understand it.

One more thing I'd like to point out before we move on

to the chart: I have *intentionally omitted* the numerical *fractions*, and *rounded that off to the nearest whole higher digit.* For example, odds that may have been, say, 7,775.8436:1, are simply listed as 7,776:1, instead of extending them to four digits, or longer, or to any fraction.

Chart of Keno Odds

Based on a standard keno game of 80 numbers from which 20 numbers are drawn, and the players win or lose based on the number of numbers selected matching those 20 of 80 drawn.

NUMBERS SELECTED	HOW MANY MATCH	ODDS AGAINST
1	0	3:1
	1	4:1
2	0	2:1
	1	3:1
	2	17:1
3	0	2:1
	1	2:1
	2	7:1
	3	72:1
4	0	3:1
	1	2:1
	2	5:1
	3	23:1
	4	326:1
5	0	4:1
	1	3:1
	2	4:1
	3	12:1
	4	83:1
	5	1,551:1

NUMBERS SELECTED	HOW MANY MATCH	ODDS AGAINST
6	0	6:1
	1	4:1
	2	3:1
	3	8:1
	4	35:1
	5	323:1
	6	7,753:1
7	0	8:1
	1	3:1
	2	3:1
	3	6:1
	4	19:1
	5	116:1
	6	1,366:1
	7	40,979:1
8	0	11:1
	1	4:1
	2	3:1
	3	5:1
	4	12:1
	5	55:1
	6	423:1
	7	6,232:1
	8	230,115:1
9	0	16:1
	1	5:1
	2	3.2:1
	3	4:1
	4	9:1
	5	31:1
	6	175:1
	7	1,690:1
	8	30,682:1
	9	1,380,688:1

NUMBERS SELECTED	HOW MANY MATCH	ODDS AGAINST
10	0	22:1
	1	6:1
	2	3:1
	3	4:1
	4	7:1
	5	19:1
	6	87:1
	7	621:1
	8	7,385:1
	9	163,381:1
	10	8,911,711:1
11	0	31:1
	1	7:1
	2	4:1
	3	3:1
	4	6:1
	5	14:1
	6	50:1
	7	277:1
	8	2,431:1
	9	35244:1
	10	945,182:1
	11	62,381,978:1
12	0	43:1
	1	9:1
	2	4:1
	3	4:1
	4	5:1
	5	10:1
	6	31:1
	7	142:1
	8	981:1
	9	10,482:1
	10	184,230:1
	11	5,978,273:1
	12	478,261,833:1

NUMBERS SELECTED	HOW MANY MATCH	ODDS AGAINST
13	0	61:1
	1	11:1
	2	5:1
	3	4:1
	4	5:1
	5	8:1
	6	21:1
	7	81:1
	8	458:1
	9	3,848:1
	10	49,645:1
	11	1,060,033:1
	12	41,694,621:1
	13	4,065,225,582:1
14	0	87:1
	1	15:1
	2	6:1
	3	3:1
	4	4:1
	5	6:1
	6	15:1
	7	50:1
	8	239:1
	9	1,644:1
	10	16,740:1
	11	262,397:1
	12	6,764,019:1
	13	324,250,136:1
	14	38,910,016,282:1

NUMBERS SELECTED	HOW MANY MATCH	ODDS AGAINST
15	0	125:1
	1	19:1
	2	7:1
	3	4:1
	4	4:1
	5	6:1
	6	12:1
	7	34:1
	8	136:1
	9	789:1
	10	6,576:1
	11	81,021:1
	12	1,539,397:1
	13	48,362,732:1
	14	2,853,401,194:1
	15	428,010,179,099:1

Some of these numbers are mindboggling, and clearly approach lottery odds—in some cases even exceeding them. It is not my intention to bog you down in a numerical analysis of the game. I merely wanted to provide a clear chart that shows what these odds are, because as we start to delve more into the nuances of playing Keno to make profits it will become even more important to be able to refer to a chart like this. It is helpful to illustrate precisely why players who know how to exploit this game limit their play to certain number selections, and how these odds often compare very favorably with some other games—games that may often be perceived as "better" than Keno.

Some casinos have a brochure that shows how you can play 16 numbers, and even 20 numbers. These are not included in this chart, mostly because you should always avoid tickets with more than 10 numbers straight up (way tickets that have more numbers are not counted as "straight up" numbers, so they can have more numbers marked, but are limited to the more lucrative groups).

As far as the 20-spot ticket is concerned, it can be a good diversion every now and then, but the odds are astronomical. Most of the time, when you are playing Live Keno, you should keep your number selections within the 5-to-10 range. A little later we will refine that to specify exactly what I mean by the best number selections, and at that time you can easily refer back to this chart and look up the odds against. You should also know that by using way tickets smartly, you will be able to cut these long odds down to very manageable numbers. You will give yourself more chances to win by combining events in a method called "wheeling" and "grouping." In this way, multiple pays are possible, including much more frequent large pays, and all of these combinations directly affect the odds against you, often lowering them dramatically.

It would be inappropriate to try to make a chart of each and every way ticket combination. That would require pages and pages and would bog us down in mathematical analyses to a point of absurdity. The chart shown here is the perfect reference point to which you can always go at any time to check out what the odds against any number combination are, when considered as a straight up play. As you play the way tickets, the more chances you give yourself to hit the top pays, and all the smaller pays in between, the lower the *combined* odds against will be. Although each event is independent, and its individual odds do not change, you can often use combination bets and groups to make your *financial* odds better, even though the math may indicate that the event odds do not change. This is all part of exploiting short-term events and anomalies, and those are some of the key factors that you will be able to employ as you get better at the game of Keno.

The odds and paybacks on video keno machines are a little different. These games are mostly limited to straight up selections of only 1 through 10 numbers, and because these machines must conform to state-regulated slot machine payback percentages, the games can be played for considerably more events in terms of game frequency than Live Keno. All of these factors combine to make the video keno games just a little different from the live keno games, even though we can still use our chart for the straight up number selections of 1 through 10 as a guide. In part two I will discuss Video Keno in more detail. For now, use this chart as a means of understanding how hard it may be to get a pay for some of the keno tickets you may wish to play, as well as for comparing the various odds against, versus other games. For example, if you are interested in Video Poker—or perhaps are a video poker player—you may be interested to know that your odds of hitting a $1,000 Royal Flush (25-cent machines) are about 40,400:1 against. This is for an investment of $1.25 per hand (25-cent machines). On Keno, however, both for Live Keno and Video Keno, a wager of only $1—which is 25 cents less per event than Video Poker—a hit of 8 out of 10 will also pay $1,000, but the odds against are only 7,385:1. So, while in Video Poker your win of $1,000 on a quarter machine will happen only about once in each 40,400 hands played, in Keno your $1,000 win will happen about once in each 7,385 events, which is 33,015 events *more often* than in Video Poker. And all of this for 25 cents per event *less* investment! Next time someone yells at you and says you're a fool for even trying Keno, tell them this example. You can use this chart to compare other games and their payoff odds with Keno.

Now that we have learned the basic language of Keno and the various odds against any single straight up event happening, it is time to get to the basics of the game. These two opening chapters provide the crucial background required for understanding the basics of Keno and how to play it. I realize that some of this information was very detailed, but when it is viewed in combination with the following chapter, it provides a complete background of the game.

And so, after all that, we have arrived at the beginning.

Keno Basics

As stated previously, I have often referred to the live keno game as "Big Board Keno." This was because the keno flashboards were prominent in casinos, making it easy to identify the game. Recently casinos have changed dramatically. Although some casinos still use these boards to flash the numbers, in most modern casinos this is now accomplished by closed circuit television, often displayed on plasma- or wide-screen TVs. Nevertheless, I still want to differentiate between the keno games played "live," as in the keno lounge, and the video keno games found in modern video slot machines and video multi-game machines. To do this, I have decided to call this big board keno game "Lounge Keno" as a means of differentiating between the live keno and machine-based keno games. So, from now on, the live keno game is Lounge Keno, and the other games are Video Keno.

If you have never been to a casino, or perhaps never considered Keno, you may not know how to find the keno lounge. It isn't hard to find, though, because it is that area of the casino where there are no table games and no slot machines. Instead there are rows of comfortable lounge chairs, or, in some smaller casinos, chairs that look like school chairs, with a writing arm attached. In front of these chairs is a large counter, called the Keno Counter, behind which are the positions for the keno writers and the equipment to draw and call the games. Usually there is also a very large flashboard mounted on the back wall, directly behind the staff that runs the game. In many of the large casinos there are several of these flashboards, as well as some TVs. Even if you have never seen a casino keno lounge before, you will quickly recognize it by these features. If you're still not sure, ask the staff if this is the "main game," or the "satellite game." In larger casinos they may play two games, often called the Red and Green games. Most of the time one of these games is the main game, played for players in the keno lounge, while the other is the satellite game played mostly for the benefit of players served by keno runners. Although rare, some casinos have more than two games. In these casinos you may find two games played in the keno lounge, one after the other. This is done to speed up the game for everybody; each game is played alternatively, one after the other. This way, players can play tickets in both games, and each game will have half the counter to itself. You can find out if this is so in your casino very easily, because these games will have two sets of tumblers or blowers, and two sets of keno staff, even if they are in the same lounge and behind the same counter. The Stardust Hotel and Casino in Las Vegas is one where this kind of a keno game is played. In these casinos there may be a third game, played exclusively for the benefit of keno runners, and for players in restaurants, or other areas serviced by the keno runners. This game may be known as the "White Game," or some other color designation to indicate that there are more than one, or more than two, keno games being played, and to differentiate between tickets bought to avoid any confusion about potential winners.

Sometimes players in the restaurant, for example, may look at the wrong TV screen, or the wrong flashboard, and think they won on their ticket, only to discover that they were playing in the White game played only for keno runners, and not in the main game for which they saw those results by mistake. These players can get agitated and feel that they are being misled. However, the perception of being misled is only due to their own failure to ask about the keno games and to look at their ticket where it clearly says "White Game," or whatever the designation of the game may be. It is important for you to recognize and understand these points. If you play blindly, or without bothering to identify what you are playing, you may wrongly think you have won. If this happens, dear friend, the fault is entirely yours. And that is perhaps the most important lesson I can teach you in any book about gambling. Learn, observe, find out, understand, and act with *knowledge*. Otherwise you could easily waste your money, or become upset without cause, with only yourself to blame. It seems obvious to all of us when we are considering situations such as these, but you would be surprised how many times people risk their money, and then don't even have the slightest idea what it is that they bet on or what wins and what doesn't. Millions of people every year do just this, in casinos everywhere, and that's why casinos can rake in hundreds of billions of dollars each year. If you learn nothing else from this book, at least learn to take a few seconds and look at the keno brochure provided in every keno lounge and keno runner station, and find exactly which game you are going to be playing, and where the results are displayed. Then check the ticket you get for accuracy. At the very least this will help you avoid disappointment, and that's just as valuable as avoiding the wrong bets.

If you know how to play the state lottery, you already

know the basics of playing casino Lounge Keno. Like the lottery, Lounge Keno involves betting on a single number or a set of numbers that you can choose as you wish, in the hope that your number or numbers will be selected in a random drawing. There are, however, substantial differences from the lottery—not so much in the basic way the game is played, but rather in the variety of ways you can play. These options offer much more enjoyment, and often many more wins, than any lottery. On any keno game you can pick from one to twenty numbers. You do this by taking a blank keno ticket and—with the keno marker provided at any keno location—simply mark the numbers you wish to play. The keno ticket is about five inches square, and on the face of it is a printed grid of eighty numbers, divided into what is called the "top"—containing forty numbers, and the "bottom"—containing the other forty. You can mark these numbers by crosses, or circles, ticks, or in any manner, so long as you make it clear that you are marking a specific number. Once you have marked the ticket with the numbers you wish to play, you mark the amount you want to bet in the top right hand corner of the ticket (where it says "Amount"). Then, below on the right-hand side, you write the total number of numbers you picked.

Take the ticket to the keno writer, who sits behind the keno counter. Since most keno games are now computerized, the keno writer will generally take your marked ticket, place it over a computer display the size of which corresponds to the size of your keno ticket, press the numbers you picked, enter the amount you are betting, enter the number of games you wish to play, and then press a button marked "Video." The computer will then print out a computerized version of the ticket you marked, which, once you've paid the amount of your bet, the keno writer gives to you. This computerized printout corresponds directly to the ticket you had marked, but also includes other information such as game number, ticket code, writer's code, and date and time of purchase. This ticket can also include your account number, if you are a regular keno player and wish your action to be tracked for casino rating purposes. It can also list the number of consecutive games played if you play your numbers for more than one game. Since Keno is already a pretty slow game, compared with other games in the casino, the advantages of computerization are obvious. It is important that you hold on to your computerized ticket. You will need to produce it in order to collect any winnings to which you are entitled.

To claim your winnings, you must also remember to return to the keno counter at the completion of your game, and *before the start of the next game.* Many players often stray away, distracted, and forget to claim their winning tickets before the next game. Gaming regulations in some jurisdictions still stipulate that winnings must be collected on any ticket prior to the start of the next game. Thus, failure to do this forfeits any winnings. But Keno also allows for so-called multi-race tickets. With this option you can play whatever numbers you pick on the same ticket for up to 20 consecutive games. You must, however, play the *same* numbers for each game and, of course, the cost of your bet will increase proportionately to the number of games you play. With multi-race tickets you cannot claim winnings at the end of each game, but must wait until the final game in your series has been called. This can be a long wait, especially if you play up to 20 games in a row, which is the maximum number of consecutive races allowed on such tickets. Therefore, to give players the option of doing something else while playing Keno, and to combat player complaints from those unlucky lucky players who win but forget to claim their prizes in a timely fashion, a new multirace variation of Keno has been introduced at most casinos. This is the option that allows players to play from 21 to 1,000 con-

secutive games *without having to be present* and with up to
one year to collect winnings. A player can actually return
home, mail in the ticket a few weeks later, or even keep it
and come back within one year and collect any winnings. I
would also like to mention that many of the gaming regulations regarding time to collect on winning tickets have been
recently relaxed—particularly in Nevada—and now most
casinos will allow up to forty-eight hours to collect on *any*
winning ticket, regardless of whether you played a multi-
race ticket or just one game. However, if you fail to collect
your winnings within that forty-eight-hour period, you for-
feit any wins to which you may have been entitled. The option of 21 to 1,000 games eliminates that problem, because
now you have up to an entire year to collect.

In any keno game, whether Lounge Keno or Video Keno
you, as the player, are a passive participant. You have no
control over the outcome of the game—much like in Roulette
or many Reel Slots, for example. Once you mark your numbers and make the bet, the rest is up to "fate." If the numbers
drawn correspond to the numbers you picked, you win; if
they don't you lose. That's about as simple as it gets.

Depending on which casino you play in, Lounge Keno is
a "house" game that holds between 24 percent and 48 percent for the "house"—the casino owner. This makes it, overall, by far the worst-odds game available in casinos. Sound
depressing? Not necessarily. Your odds of winning a state
lottery, for example, can be around 160,000,000-to-1 against—
or more. A far greater swing against you than in most keno
games (some keno games, such as the Pick 15 for example,
can run into the billions to one against!). However, casino
Keno offers you many other playing options that lotteries
simply do not. For starters, you don't have to wait for a drawing once each week, or twice weekly, or even once each day.
Casino Keno averages about one game each five to ten minutes, which means that you can play many more games much

faster than in any lottery. The options for multirace tickets, as mentioned earlier, also give you the opportunity to play the game for many consecutive games, without having to sit there and wait for the outcome. In addition, Lounge Keno also offers an array of playing options such as way tickets, wherein you can mark several groups of numbers. Each group can be as little as one number, or as many as that casino will allow (ask the keno writer). In fact, many casinos will publish a range of sample way tickets in their keno brochure. Always check them out, then ask for further information from the keno writer. Do not always play precisely the kinds of tickets the casino publicizes. Often they show these tickets in combinations and for prices that are best for them, not for you.

The best strategy for any lounge keno play is to play way tickets, as opposed to just a series of individual numbers (such as lotteries allow). By grouping your numbers in a way ticket, you increase your odds of winning quite substantially, especially since any wins are multiplied and cross-applied cumulatively. Of course, the ticket will cost you more to play, but in many casinos you can play way tickets for as little as 10 cents per way, and sometimes even less than that. **A word of caution:** Always investigate the range of playing options and their respective payoffs in the casino where you happen to be. Not all casinos play the game the same way, or pay on winning tickets in the same amounts. If you want to play Keno to your best winning potential, check out the game's payoffs in as many casinos as you can before starting to play. Often you will find that one casino, for example, will pay $2,000 for a 6-spot (all 6 caught), while other casinos will only pay $1,480 for the same ticket. This is a swing of $520 and makes a lot of difference to your bankroll. Also watch for the frequency and amounts of smaller pays, as listed in the casino's keno brochure. For example, on a 6-spot ticket, see if the payoff is 1:1 (even money) for 3 out of 6, or if this payoff is even being offered. If not, don't play this ticket in that casino. The best combination possible is to find a casino that pays off on all smaller pays and pays a higher top prize jackpot. This will take some research, but it's well worth the effort. Strategy-wise, way tickets in combinations of 10 groups of "twos," or 10 or 20 or 24 groups of "threes" are your best bets. But many other combinations are possible, including several versions with "king" tickets (for examples refer to the chapter on Best Tickets).

SAMPLE TICKETS

At this point I would like to introduce you to some *sample* tickets, in order to show you how the tickets look and how to mark them. Included are samples of various tickets, although these may not necessarily be among the best tickets I have selected for actual play. I want first to show you just how large a variety there can be in the kinds of tickets you can select. Later, in Chapter 4, I will focus more directly on the best kinds of tickets for your play. After that, you can decide for yourself how to further enhance your keno play, based on your skills, abilities, and playing experience.

Figure 1 is an example of the kind of blank keno ticket you will find for all lounge keno and runner keno games.

The information the tickets contain are prompts to direct you to the appropriate areas where you should mark what you actually want. First, however, you need to mark your numbers. To make this initial sample as easy as possible, I will first show you a 6-spot straight up ticket. This is the ticket played most often by everyone who plays Keno. While it is generally a good ticket to play, there are better methods of marking this ticket. (We will save that for later, in Chapter

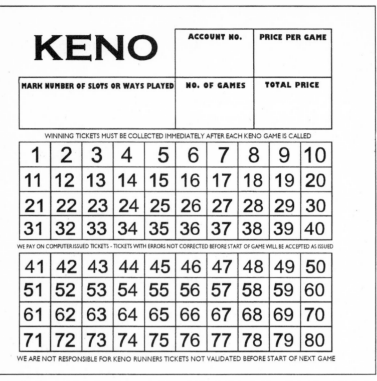

Figure 1. A sample of a "Lounge Keno" blank ticket. Use this blank ticket to mark your numbers.

4, "Best Tickets.") For now, please look at Figure 2. This is how you mark a blank keno ticket if you wish to play six numbers, called a straight up 6-spot.

You will notice that there are several items on this ticket, all of which you should know how to mark. However, don't be too concerned; the keno writers will help you out. Nevertheless, for future reference, you should learn how to do all of this because you will need those skills when marking more complicated tickets, such as way tickets. When I show you some of the many ways that a way ticket can generate, you will need to know how to mark all the rest of this infor-

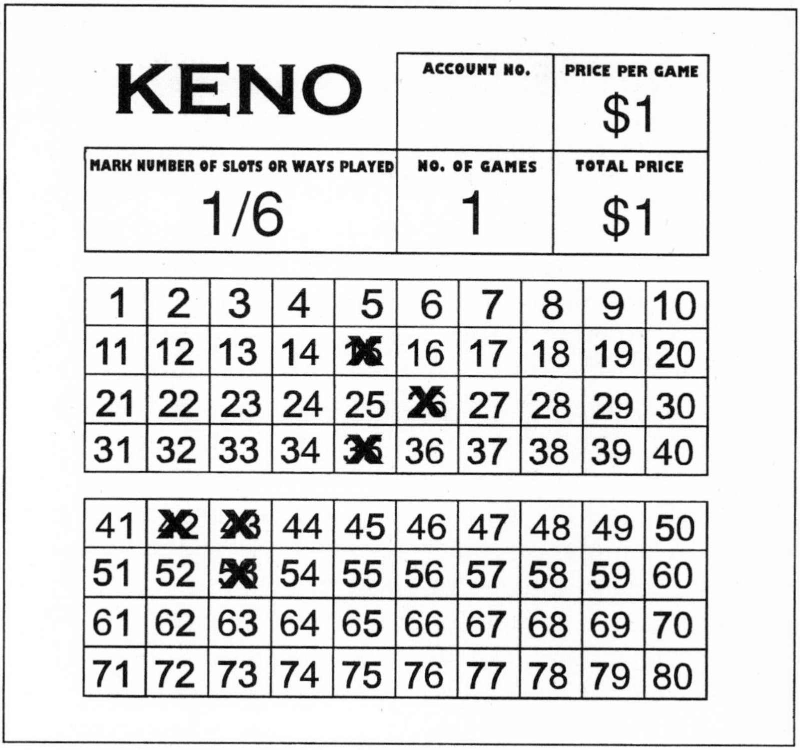
KENO

ACCOUNT NO.	PRICE PER GAME
	$1

MARK NUMBER OF SLOTS OR WAYS PLAYED	NO. OF GAMES	TOTAL PRICE
1/6	1	$1

1	2	3	4	5	6	7	8	9	10
11	12	13	14	X15	16	17	18	19	20
21	22	23	24	25	X26	27	28	29	30
31	32	33	34	X35	36	37	38	39	40
41	X42	X43	44	45	46	47	48	49	50
51	52	X53	54	55	56	57	58	59	60
61	62	63	64	65	66	67	68	69	70
71	72	73	74	75	76	77	78	79	80

Figure 2. An example of the straight up 6-spot Lounge Keno ticket.

mation on the blank keno ticket in order to get the kind of pays to which you are entitled, and to tell the keno writer precisely which of the many ways available you actually want to play, and for how much. It can get a little tricky. The keno writers will generally be able to help you out, but be aware that many of them know very little about the game and rely on the computer station to tell them what they need to know—provided, of course, they know how to ask the computer the right question. Therefore, knowing how to mark your tickets correctly will make your gaming life easier and assure you of getting what you paid for.

The first thing you will notice on this sample 6-spot ticket are the six crosses over the numbers in the main eighty-number grid of the ticket. This is how you mark your numbers, and this tells the keno writer that these are the numbers you selected. Using crosses is the best way to do this because it helps to differentiate between some of the other tickets, wherein circled numbers and groups are used. Many people mark tickets with ink blobs, dots, or other means, which can lead to confusion. Therefore, to make it simple and easy and fast, use crosses to mark the selected numbers on your ticket, as shown in Figure 2. The second thing you will notice is the marking of 1/6, in the area on the ticket indicated with the heading: "Mark number of spots or ways played." This indicates to the keno writer that you have selected one 6-spot. This information is always written in this area, or marked to the right-hand side of the ticket in case the number of ways played are more than the space allows. Most of the time, you will need this space only to indicate the number of numbers, or ways, you wish to play. The third thing you will notice is the smaller box with the heading: "No. of Games." This is where you would mark how many games you wish to play. In this example (Figure 2) we are playing one game only, so the number "1" is written there. The fourth item to complete is in the similarly sized box diagonally toward the top-right corner of the ticket, with the heading: "Price per Game." Here, you will write how much you want to bet on this ticket, for this game, or for each game played if you are playing more than one. In this example, we are playing $1 per ticket, and one game only. The fifth item to complete is directly below that box, in the area with the heading: "Total Price." Here you will write the total price of the ticket. Since we are playing only $1 per game, and only one game, this total price will, therefore, be $1. However, if you were to play this ticket for, say, five games, then this area would indicate the $5 amount of the total price of the ticket for all of the five games played. And so on for as many games as you wish to play, and for whatever the amount per game may be. The last item to look at is the box with the heading: "Account No." If you are a frequent keno player, and wish to have your action tracked for the purposes of earning free stuff—comps, rooms, food, invitations to special events, and so on—ask the keno writer for an account number, and he will create one for you. Usually, such an account number is the last four digits of your social security number, your telephone number, or any other numbers you can easily remember. Once you have this account number set up—which only takes a minute or two at the keno counter—each time you play Keno in that casino you will write your account number in this same place on the card. This will indicate to the keno writers that you are a tracked player. All your action will be listed and accumulated, and you will thereafter be able to receive whatever comps or offers you may have earned, or have become entitled to obtain. And now you know how to mark a keno ticket for any lounge keno game.

This type of 6-spot ticket is popular for many reasons, perhaps the most important of which is the fact that it pays quite well for even small hits. In fact there are only three hits—or non-hits—that won't give you a pay, and four hits that do. To give you an even better idea about this kind of ticket—now that we have learned how to mark it—I will soon show you a sample payoff schedule for a 6-spot that I have played myself. This payoff structure comes from the main game played at Caesars Palace in Las Vegas. Although I show it here as a $1 wager, the actual ticket I played was for a $2 wager. Incidentally, that is another advantage of Keno: this game allows you to select not only the numbers you wish to play, and the ways in which you wish to play them, but also the amounts you wish to wager. In most casinos, the minimum full-value ticket is at the $1 per way rate; however, you can play it at higher rates as well. If you wish to play the 6-spot ticket—as in this example with the pay-offs I will shortly show—you can either play it for that $1, or for $2, or for $3, or for as much as the casino will allow. For each additional dollar played, the payoffs are increased proportionately, and often even rise to considerably higher amounts the more you wager. At the most basic level, such increases are akin to the doubler slot machines. In those situations, where some higher wagers pay even more than a mere proportionate double of the pay, these tickets are almost like the buy-a-pay slots I describe and discuss in detail in my *Powerful Profits from Slots* book. The converse is also true, particularly when you play way ticket combinations, where you can play for reduced rates as I have already mentioned. I say this again because it is important to understand that in Keno the $1 per way rate is the standard by which all other pays are measured.

All pays, and keno odds, are based around that $1 pay table. It is therefore important for you to check the $1 pay table on any keno game (which you can do by looking at the rate brochure provided in all keno lounges and runner stations) and then compare it with any reduced rates that the casino may offer. For example, if the casino offers reduced rates to 25 cents per way for way ticket combinations, or even reduced-rate straight up tickets, you should make sure that the payoffs so listed are correctly prorated from the $1 pay rate. If the reduced rate ticket is offered at the 25-cent per way rate, then the payoffs should be one-fourth of the $1 pay rate. If the casino offers rates of 40 cents per way, then the rates should show a pay table at exactly 60 percent less of the $1 rate, and so on. Some casinos offer these reduced rates, but also reduce the pay table a lot lower than the comparable $1 rate, which has the direct effect of increasing the house edge on these tickets. This is definitely not good. In such cases you should avoid playing these reduced rates in that casino, and perhaps avoid playing anything there as well. Similarly, some casinos' pay tables may not have been well thought out, and instead of showing pay rate parity, they actually show a *better* pay rate for the lower-priced per way ticket rates. For example, a casino may show a pay rate of 10 cents per way for tickets with 100 or more ways, but instead of showing the pay rate ratio as one-tenth of the $1 rate, the payoff scale may be one-fourth instead. This adds a considerably higher value to such tickets.

Most of the time, however, if you find such a disparity among posted rates, it will be on the various different pay table rate charts for special kinds of reduced rate tickets. For example, many casinos—particularly in downtown Las Vegas—offer 80-cent rates, 50-cent rates, 40-cent rates, and even 30-cent rates. These reduced rates have their own chart inside the casino's keno rate brochure. These situations allow you to easily find out if the casino correctly prepared its brochures, or if they have in fact made a mistake in calculating some of these rates. Often you will find that although the standard may be the $1 rate, when the casino was preparing the 40-cent rate it didn't do exactly a 60 percent reduction off the $1 rate, but instead did something fractionally different. If the error is in a higher payoff, then you are sitting much prettier on the reduced rate tickets than you would on the standard $1 rate. If the rates are lower than the correctly prorated $1 rate, then you are better off at the higher rate, or perhaps should find another casino where the error is in your favor. You may have to investigate many such rates, because they may not be the same for all the various tickets available in Keno. One casino may have a reduced rate player-positive error on, say, 7-spot and 8-spot tickets, while having a player-negative error on the other rates. So, here you would exploit this for only the 7- and 8-spots. Another casino may have a reduced rate error in the player's favor on 5- and 6-spot tickets, so there you would concentrate on these tickets, and so on.

I am saying this now because I want you to become aware, here at the outset, that there are many skills to Keno other than just blindly betting numbers as one does in a lottery. All of these factors contribute directly to your ability to make powerful profits from casino Keno. Sometimes the casinos make these errors unconsciously, and other times consciously. A casino may want to give a better reduced rate payoff on some tickets and make it up with the converse negative reduction on others. Most of the time, however, this situation happens by accident, such as when the person designated to make up these rates is trying to calculate exactly 60 percent less from the $1 rate. Sometimes the payoffs on the chart would mean fractions, such as a pay of $8.72 for a reduced-rate ticket. Well, casinos don't want to bother with pennies because the costs of administering these tiny pays would far outweigh any benefit gained by correctly fractionalizing the rates. So, in this case they may list the pay as $8.75, which will allow them to pay you in 8 dollars plus 3 quarters. Easier to manage. However, it also gives you an extra 3-cent profit, which substantially increases your win expectations, even though this is a tiny amount when viewed singly.

If you are a smart keno player, you will be playing way tickets, and so this one payoff can easily be multiplied many times on the ticket. Let us assume, for the sake of this example, that you are playing ten ways, in which such a payoff figures. So, you are getting 30 cents more than the parity with the $1 rate would indicate. Often this variance can be much more significant, so always take a close look at all the various rates and do some calculating before you play. You could increase your wins and reduce the house edge against you considerably, just by taking a few minutes to exercise the gray matter between your ears before starting to exercise the green stuff in your wallet or purse.

The chart opposite shows the sample 6-spot payoff.

6-Spot Sample Pay Rate for $1 per Way Rate

HITS	OUT OF	$$$ WINNINGS
0	6	0
1	6	0
2	6	0
3	6	1
4	6	3
5	6	88 *
6	6	1,500 **

* In some casinos, the 5-out-of-6 hit will pay $90, or $80, or $75.
**In some casinos, the 6-out-of-6 solid hit will pay $1,480, or $1,450, to keep the win under the $1,500 taxable limit. In others, there will be a bonus associated with this win, and the win may pay $2,000 or more. In these casinos, such higher wins for the solid hit are usually offset by the fact that these casinos may only start their pays from hits of 4 out of 6 instead of 3 out of 6, and only pay $75, or $65 or even only $60 for a hit of 5 out of 6—stay away from these games and casinos.

WAY TICKETS

Now I want to show you some samples of way tickets, and how to mark them. First, take a look at Figure 3. This shows you the very same 6-spot ticket we used as an example in Figure 2, on page 69, but here we have used the variance called "way ticket," to play more than just the single 6-spot.

As you can see, we have divided this ticket into two groups of three, and instead of marking the ticket as 1/6—indicating that we wish to play merely one 6-spot straight up—we are marking this same ticket as 2/3 and 1/6. This means that we are now playing two 3-spots in addition to the one 6-spot. So, now if we hit a 3 out of 6, and that 3-spot is inside one of our circled areas designating it as out 3-spot, we will get paid not only for the rate of 3 out of 6, but we will also be paid for a solid hit of a 3-spot in addition to it. The normal rate for a 3-out-of-3 hit is about $45 in most casinos, so now instead of being paid only the paltry $1 for the 3-out-of-6 hit, you will be paid $45 for the solid 3 hit,

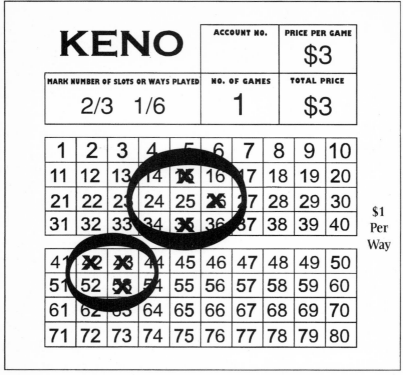

Figure 3. An example of a keno "way" ticket, played as 2/3 and 1/6.

plus that $1 for the 3-out-of-6 hit, for a total of $46. Not too bad, eh? That's why way tickets are so important if you wish to play Keno for profit, and not just for fun. All those millions of players who don't know this will have been tickled pink by hitting that 3 out of 6 for the $1 money-back pay. You, however, are tickled green because that's what you are getting—lots of greenbacks to fill your wallet—while all the other players are digging for more cash from theirs. Plus, of course, you also get smaller pays, and so on, all of which you will soon learn and be able to find out from learning Keno here, and then learning more from the rate

pay tables in the casinos. Naturally, way tickets will cost
you more to play, because you are playing more ways. As you
can see from the example in Figure 3, this is a three-way rate,
with 2/3s and 1/6, adding up to a total of three ways. So, for
a $1-per-way rate, this ticket will now cost you $3 total to
play, as opposed to only $1 for the straight up 6-spot. How-
ever, the advantage far outweighs the extra costs. On this
way ticket, as you have just read, you can get a hit of $45 for
a 3 out of 6 if that 3-spot is one of the groups of 3 you have
marked, considerably more than you would have received
otherwise. Plus, of course, you also have to count all those
times you get 2-out-of-3 hits, which may also combine with 3-
out-of-6 hits, and even 4-out-of-6 hits, all of which are pays
that cumulate and add together to increase all your wins.
This is the only way to protect your investment and make
your keno game pay for itself as you patiently await the really big hit. And that's one of the biggest secrets of successful keno play—playing way tickets intelligently so that you
will play many games that pay for themselves, plus get lots
of little extra hits for additional profits along the way. This
not only increases your longevity in the game, but also pro-
tects your bankroll and requires you to have a much smaller
bankroll with which to begin. This method of play also
eventually allows you to play for higher stakes, with tickets
containing many more ways, because most of the time the
tickets will not only pay for themselves, but will also make
profits to offset any smaller losses from games in which the
tickets do not cover their expenditure. Soon you will be
able to play tickets that may cost $100 per game, which is
the amount you will have to invest on the very first ticket
you play, but afterward will make sufficient hits not only to
pay for itself for additional games, but also to make small
profits as you go. At the very worst, these tickets may only
require you to make a small outlay of capital for additional
games, even if it doesn't make its own cost back each time.

For example, on some games you may get winners of $94.75 for a ticket that cost you $100 to start with. So, although you suffered a loss this game, the next game will cost you only $5.25 to play. In effect, this allows you to play a $100 ticket for only $5.25. And so on. What if in the very next game your ticket wins $107.50? Well, now you have made $7.50 over two tickets, covered the previous game's $5.25 cost, and still have $2.25 left over, and your ticket paid for the next game. Situations like these are many, and as you gain more and more experience in Keno you will realize the enormous importance of the correct use of way tickets, and how they can be exploited to make you able to play very high-cost tickets for very low costs and with very large win potential.

Okay, now I would like to show you a king ticket. Figure 4a is an example of an 8-spot ticket, called the King-8 ticket. For those of you familiar with a Motel chain called the King-8, you will also understand why this ticket is humorously referred to as the "motel ticket."

A king ticket is identified by the use of single selected numbers, each individually circled to identify each number as a "group of one." This is similar to the ticket we showed in Figure 3, wherein the two groups of three were each circled as a "group of three." Here, the king ticket is identified easily by the simple fact that each number is circled individually as a group of one. Using kings as part of way tickets is crucial to your financial success in Keno, and learning to use them wisely is part of the skills in profitable keno play. Many people will smirk at you for even thinking of Keno because they are unable to grasp that even passive gambling games require skills. The use of kings in your tickets is one of these skills, and it is therefore necessary to understand what they are and how they can be of direct beneficial effect on your financial profitability.

The sample King-8 ticket shown in Figure 4a is the clas-

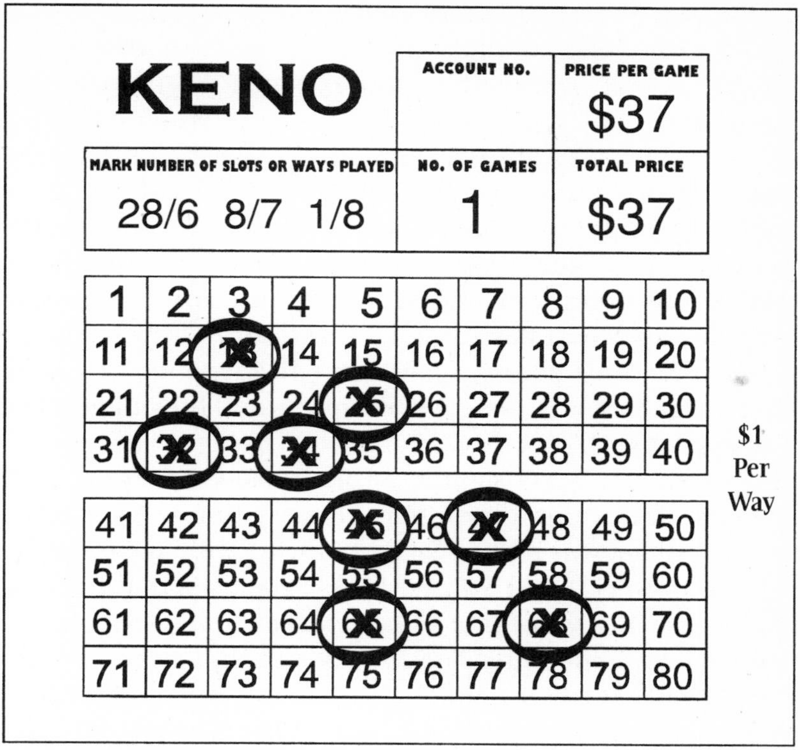

Figure 4a. The classic casino King-8 ticket.

sic of all king tickets. It is not only very popular, but also often showed as an example of a king way ticket in the pay-off brochures provided by the casinos. The reason casinos don't mind showing this ticket is because there are many different ways to play games with it, and most people won't select the right ones; therefore, they overbet the ticket. Also, many casinos will require that this ticket is played at the $1 rate only, thereby not allowing the lower rates on the higher number combinations. It all depends, naturally, on the casino, and to be fair this is not always so. Many casinos will show this ticket and provide only the $1 rate as an example, but if you read the fine print elsewhere in the brochure you may find a line of text that says something like this: "All way tickets of 100 ways or more can be played for reduced rates. Ask our friendly keno staff for more details." So, even though these casinos do not actually list the rate reductions, they do list the fact that they are offered. Be observant, read the fine print, and understand what it means. Then all you have to do is simply go to the keno counter and ask the keno writer, or keno supervisor, for the reduced rates information. Many times you will find that this casino may also offer the reduced rates for tickets with only fifty ways, for perhaps 25 cents per way, and this will then give you more knowledge in how to select your tickets and how to play the ways you select.

The King-8 ticket sample in Figure 4a is an example of an actual ticket that I have played many times. As you can see, this ticket was played for $1 per way, and I have chosen to play 28/6, 8/7, and 1/8. What this means is that from all of the possible ways this ticket makes, I have selected to play 28 way 6-spot, plus an 8 way 7-spot, and, of course, the 1 way 8. The total cost of this ticket is $37, when played exactly as marked. However, this ticket also offers many other possibilities. For example, there is a whole slew of possible 1-spot, 2-spot, 3-spot, and 4-spot combinations. To play all of these would be foolish, not smart. The advantage of way tickets is that you can select your numbers in a manner that allows you to then choose which of the many ways you wish to play and for how much. You do not always have to play each way for the same amount, which is called the split-rate way ticket. Similarly, you do not have to play all of the ways that are available on a ticket such as this sample King-8. To do so would be to waste a huge amount of money for a very small return because all of the hits of less than a 5-spot would cost too much to play, relative to the wins you could achieve. Even playing all the 5-spots becomes costly, but of all of the many other ways that this ticket allows, only the 5-spots would be a viable addition. Most of the time players who play this ticket do so just as I have, but selecting only the 6-, 7-, and 8-spots as part of this way ticket combination. This gives you the biggest bang for the buck, without starting to cost you a lot of money. However, the addition of the 5-spots can be a good idea, especially if you then play some of the ways at a reduced rate, and then play the 8 as a $1 rate way. This turns the ticket into a split-rate ticket.

In addition to the ways already listed on this King-8 ticket, it also produces 56/5, which is a 56 way 5-spot. If we were to play all of these ways together, this would be quite costly. To find out just how costly, simply add the ways together: 56 + 28 + 8 + 1 = 100. This would be $100 at the $1 rate. However, this also now gives you the 100 ways, which most casinos allow to be played at reduced rates. So, if you so chose, you could play this ticket at the 10-cent rate, and the whole thing would cost you only $10. However, this is not smart, because you reduce your wins to a mere pittance. What you want to do is make this into a split-rate ticket, while preserving as much of your win value as possible. To find out the best choice for each rate, look at the casino's pay rate brochure. Here we are interested only in the $1 rates for the 5-spots, 6-spots, 7-spots, and 8-spots. This will give us an idea of the casino's standard for these rates. The following sample pay table for these pays comes from a "generic" casino (by which I mean that this is not from any specific casino but is only an example I made up based on some rates from various keno pay tables around Las Vegas). Most of these sample rates are very close to what you will actually find in the real casinos, but I didn't wish to single out any one casino for this example, so I made the chart on the next page as a composite from several.

MARK 5 SPOTS		PAYS
Catch	0	$0
Catch	1	$0
Catch	2	$0
Catch	3	$1
Catch	4	$25
Catch	5	$600

MARK 6 SPOTS		PAYS
Catch	0	$0
Catch	1	$0
Catch	2	$0
Catch	3	$1
Catch	4	$3
Catch	5	$88
Catch	6	$1,480

MARK 7 SPOTS		PAYS
Catch	0	$0
Catch	1	$0
Catch	2	$0
Catch	3	$0
Catch	4	$1
Catch	5	$25
Catch	6	$400
Catch	7	$7,000

MARK 8 SPOTS		PAYS
Catch	0	$0
Catch	1	$0
Catch	2	$0
Catch	3	$0
Catch	4	$1*
Catch	5	$4
Catch	6	$86
Catch	7	$1,480
Catch	8	$25,000**

* Some casinos begin pays only at the 5-out-of-8 level, substantially increasing the house edge on this ticket. In these casinos, it is important to compare the other pays to rates in casinos where the payoff begins with 4 out of 8. Most of the time casinos that begin paying on from 5 out of 8 and up do so because their higher value jackpots are greater, or perhaps even progressives. You must learn what these are and how these compare with other casinos in order to make your playing decisions.

**Many casinos pay $50,000 for this hit, or even more. Seek out these casinos; however, be careful to check their actual pay rates—often the smaller pays will be substantially reduced to compensate for the higher top jackpot. Your dedicated research into pay table brochures from as many casinos as you can get is essential to being able to select the right game, right ticket, and right casino for the most profitable play.

As I've said, these are only generic samples. Many casinos will have pay tables similar to these, while others will have ones quite a bit different. There is no "standard" in pay tables; each casino is free to make up whatever pay scale it desires. That's why keno games vary so much in terms of house hold percentages, as well as game, play, and payoff options.

Continuing with the example of the King-8 ticket, if we

were to add the 5-spots to the 6-, 7-, and 8-spots we first listed (as shown in Figure 4a) we would now also be in the running for the 56 way 5-spots as well. This would add considerable "meat" to the cash value of our ticket. Hitting five of these numbers is not as hard as it may appear, and if you look at the odds chart in the previous chapter you will see that the odds of hitting pays on 5s are quite reasonable, including the smaller pays as well. So, perhaps we could consider that we will play this ticket for 50 cents per way for the 5s, 6s, and 7s, and then play the $1 rate for the one 8-spot. This is a pretty smart way of playing, because we preserve most of the value for our smaller pays, and at the same time preserve the full value of the 8-spot in case we are lucky enough to hit all eight numbers on this King-8 ticket. Although the odds of hitting all eight numbers are quite long, the purpose behind selecting eight numbers as kings—in this case— is to also allow for the many other ways that can be hit on this ticket to provide us with many more pays—and many more value pays—than would have been the case if we simply played eight numbers straight up, as most people do. One of the main reasons why keno games can generally average such a huge house hold percentage is precisely because people only play straight tickets instead of way tickets. Furthermore, even those who get the idea of playing way tickets mostly play the "house samples," not the tickets that will actually make them money. Even if they happen to luck across a "house ticket," such as this King-8, they may not recognize that they can play several different ways at different rates and thus reduce the cost while preserving the win value. Then, if they do get the idea of the reduced rate ticket, they will reduce the rates on *all* the ways, and not just on *some*, thereby defeating the purpose behind the rate reductions and missing the opportunity of playing the split-rate ticket. Finally, they may not even grasp the significance of using kings as part of *other* way ticket combinations, and this then further adds to the house take and lowers their win value.

In our example, the original ticket (as seen in Figure 4a) cost $37 for a $1 rate per way. Adding the 56 way 5-spot would make this ticket cost $100 at that same rate. However, if we were to reduce all the ways to a 50-cent rate, and only play the one 8-spot at the full $1 rate, we would now play the 56/5, and the 28/6 and the 8/7 for a total of only $46. Then, we add the 1/8 for $1, and so the entire ticket costs us $47. This is only $10 more than the $37 ticket we have first shown in Figure 4a, but we have also *added 56 more ways to get a nice win*! This is the preferred manner of playing this ticket, when adding the 5-spots to your win-value expectation.

Figure 4b shows a sample ticket using this alternative play.

We can refine this even further, because the intent here is to make the ticket pay for itself as much as possible, make many more smaller wins that happen with far greater frequency than the bigger wins, and accumulate money to keep playing even when we hit several games from which the ticket doesn't hit enough to pay for itself in the next game. This is why we added the 5-spots, and also why we did *not* add the 2s, 3s, and 4s. Adding the 2s, 3s, and 4s would waste our money because the cost would be much higher, cumulatively, than we could ever hope to recoup with even a small win, while adding the 5-spots *preserves* our win value, even on hits of merely a few numbers. On such tickets, hits of four and five numbers happen very frequently. Any hit of more numbers will give us a multi-way pay of all the 4 out of 5s, all the 4 out of 6s, and the 4 out of 7s, and if this casino also pays for hits of 4 out of 8, that hit as well. Any hit of five numbers will give us a solid 5-spot hit, and even at the reduced 50-cent rate this would be about $300, plus all of the hits of 5 out of 6s, 5 out of 7s, and

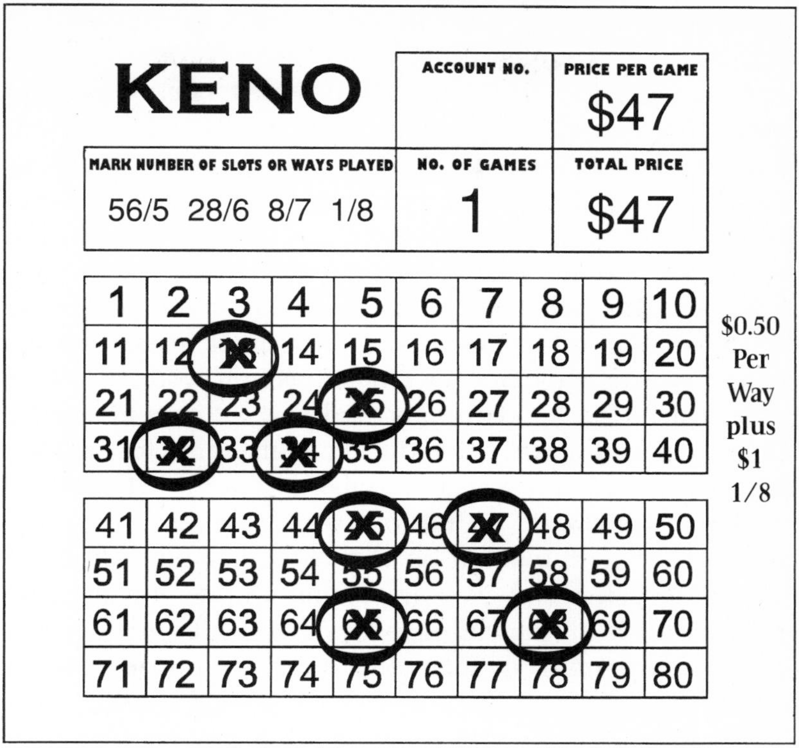

KENO

ACCOUNT NO.	PRICE PER GAME
	$47

MARK NUMBER OF SLOTS OR WAYS PLAYED	NO. OF GAMES	TOTAL PRICE
56/5 28/6 8/7 1/8	1	$47

1	2	3	4	5	6	7	8	9	10
11	12	13	14	15	16	17	18	19	20
21	22	23	24	25	26	27	28	29	30
31	32	33	34	35	36	37	38	39	40
41	42	43	44	45	46	47	48	49	50
51	52	53	54	55	56	57	58	59	60
61	62	63	64	65	66	67	68	69	70
71	72	73	74	75	76	77	78	79	80

$0.50 Per Way plus $1 1/8

Figure 4b. A King-8 ticket with the 56/5s added.

5 out of 8s. Of course, any hit of six numbers will give us several 5-spots, the solid 6-spot, plus the 6 out of 7s and 6 out of 8s. And so on. Get the idea?

To refine the method of playing this King-8 ticket even further, we may wish to reduce the rate on the 56/5 and 28/6 to 25 cents per way, and add more value to the top pays by playing the 8/7 and the 1/8 at the $1 rate. This is what is called making the ticket "top heavy," meaning you are forgoing the larger pays on the *more* frequent hits in order to gain the very large jackpot pays on the *less* frequent top hits. Though this particular manner of playing isn't actually a good one, it is a useful example to show you just how flexible way tickets and split rates actually are. Depending on the size of your bankroll, you could play the 56/5 and 28/6 at the 50-cent rate, and the 8/7 and 1/8 and the $1 rate, or perhaps even higher. It's all up to you. Even if you play other kinds of way tickets, wherein the groups aren't as easily identified as single kings but where you may have combinations of groups of two, groups of three and some kings, you can still easily calculate the costs by simply looking at the number of ways such a ticket can make. Although you could calculate all of this for yourself, there's a much easier way of doing this: simply mark your ticket as you wish, and then present it to the keno counter and say: "Please give me a printout of all the ways this ticket can make." This will tell the keno writer that you don't wish to play this ticket just yet, but merely want to find out what ways it makes. The keno writer will then press a button marked "off line," input your ticket, and give you a computerized ticket printout that shows all the various ways that can be achieved by the ticket you marked. Take all the time you need to study it, and select the ways you wish to play, and at what rates. After you have made your selections, simply mark another ticket wherein you indicate what ways you are playing— just as I have shown in the samples—then mark the amounts per way you are playing, if you wish to play split rates, and hand the ticket to the keno writer. The writer will then input this as a "live" ticket, tell you the total amount to pay, and you're set. It's that easy to learn to play way-ticket keno. Of course, knowing *which* tickets are better, and at what rates they should be played for best value, is another thing altogether. I will show you more of these value way-ticket samples in Chapter 4, "Best Tickets."

Figure 5 shows another example of a way ticket; this one is intended to show you a sample of precisely how many "way" possibilities there are when you mark several groups on a ticket, along with kings.

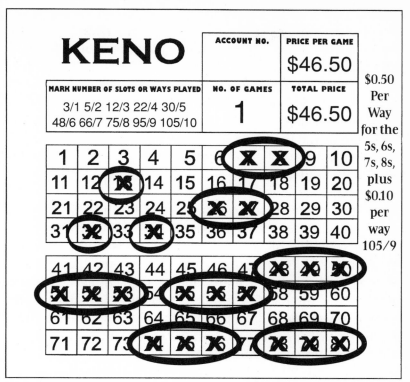

Figure 5. An example of the many possible multi-way tickets in Lounge Keno. This one shows the groups making the following combinations: 3/1, 5/2, 12/3, 22/4, 30/5, 48/6, 66/7, 75/8, 95/9, and 105/10s.

Here we have a very complicated looking ticket. It is a perfect example of how a way ticket can be made, using many different groups as well as kings. Here we have 3 kings, plus two groups of 2s, plus five groups of 3s. Together, this ticket makes for the following possible combinations: 3/1 + 5/2 + 12/3 + 22/4 + 30/5 + 48/6 + 66/7 + 75/8 + 95/9 + 105/10—a lot of ways! In addition, this ticket provides for a multitude of 11s, 12s, 13s, 14s, 15s, and 20s. None of these should ever be considered in play for any way ticket, or in fact for *any* ticket. Among the ways we should consider on a ticket such as this sample would be only the 5s, 6s, 7s, 8s, 9s, and—possibly—the 10s, although this is perhaps stretching it a little too far. Depending on your bankroll, you have a multitude of choices in how to play this ticket and how much it will cost you. Assuming you are not a multimillionaire, the best choice would probably be to play the 30/5s at the 50-cent rate; the 48/6s, the 66/7s, and the 75/8s at the 25-cent rate; and the 95/9s at the 10-cent rate. You have plenty of ways on this ticket to qualify for all of these reduced rates. This kind of a ticket would be called the "multi-split-rate way ticket," because you are using more than one rate on various ways. Based on this example, the 30/5s would cost $15; the 48/6s, 66/7s, and the 75/8s together would make 189 ways—a total of $47.25; and the 95/9s would cost $9.50. This comes to $71.75. Although this may seem like a lot, remember that you have many, many ways to get a winner, and therefore almost all the tickets you will play after the initial investment will cost less than this. Many times you will actually make more money than the cost of this ticket, which will allow you to accumulate cash for those games in which you *don't* hit enough to pay for this ticket. You can actually manipulate the cost of this ticket as you go along. For example, if you see that you are hitting a lot of 5s, consider increasing the 5s and 6s in value, from the initial 25-cent rate to a 40 or 50-cent rate, or whatever rate you wish. To do this, simply inform the keno writer when you are presenting the ticket for additional games: "Play this again, but play the 5s and 6s for 50 cents per way instead." You can continually change the value of the ticket as you see your games, hits, and wins.

Such a method of play applies to any way ticket you may choose to play, regardless of whether it is one of the samples shown in this book, or a ticket you have made up yourself. Part of the skills in Keno—and also part of the fun of the game—is to experiment with various way tickets and find combinations that you may discover as being real winners more often, even more so than any examples I can show you, or such as you may find elsewhere. My main purpose here is to show you *how* to play keno, how to mark the tickets, how to mark and make up way tickets, how to bet them, how to play multi-way tickets at reduced rates and split rates, and how to become comfortable with the game based on your abilities and bankroll. In addition, I want to show you the *better* tickets—those that I consider the *best* tickets—to provide you with reasons why I think so, and then empower you with the knowledge, skills, and confidence to take this further and develop your own keno game based on and around these principles. After that, it becomes easy. You will be able to make the game pay *you,* and exploit it for the good pays it can and does provide.

Every day casinos everywhere pay big winners in Keno, and tens of thousands of smaller winners. Taking your share is not that hard—all it will require is a little thought, some experience, the knowledge you find here, and your abilities to adapt this knowledge to your particular circumstances, goals, objectives, and bankroll. It is for these reasons that Keno is not merely the "dog" of the casino games, but a game in which really big and powerful profits are very achievable and much more easily hit than in many other games—games that may require a whole lot more effort and money.

Best Tickets

In gambling there is no such thing as "the single best way to play." Everything in gambling relies on something else, mostly information as it happens. In Blackjack, for instance, in order to count cards, first some cards have to be dealt out. As more cards are dealt, more information becomes available. It is almost the same situation in live Poker. Dice players, roulette players, slot players, in fact all gamblers are constantly adjusting their perspective on the game they are playing—and the strategy they are using—as the game continues, and as they continue to play. Winning at any casino game also requires many disciplines and skills; none of them alone will be "the" deciding factor. So it is in Keno, because in this game there is no such thing as "the best ticket." There are *many* tickets that *together* can be called "best tickets," but only if understood as *examples* of the *many dozens more possible combinations* that these tickets—and others like them as their derivatives—can produce. For this reason, "best tickets" may be a misnomer because there are many more than just the ones I show in this chapter or in this book. This makes a selection of the "best" tickets very difficult.

To understand what criteria are most useful in the selection of a "best" ticket, consider what the goals and objectives may be for different players. Some players wish to play Keno as inexpensively as possible for as long as possible, to pass the time and have fun. These players are less concerned with the winning of money, particularly large sums of money, than they are in the longevity of their limited bankroll. They are mostly frequent players, even daily players, and they have lots of time and wish to enjoy themselves without too much expense and with a shot at some nice wins. For these people the "best" tickets may be those that don't cost a whole lot, but still give them a chance at a few hundred dollars in wins. Other players may be vastly different. These could be casual visitors, who play Keno only three or four times a year on their casino trips. They may have large bankrolls, or perhaps simply larger bankrolls than the daily players, because these casual players play infrequently and can afford to save up large stakes. They are usually more aggressive, wagering bigger amounts for shorter periods of time because that's all the time they have in their trip and they wish to pack as much action into it as possible, with the highest win expectation possible. To them a "best" ticket may be a multi-way many-number ticket with a high per-game cost, and a win potential in the hundreds of thousands, even millions of dollars. Though the small-stakes daily player may be satisfied with a ticket that costs $1.50 and can win them $600, these more aggressive players wouldn't even consider this as "action." To them, "best" tickets probably cost $50 or $100 per game, and the wins they shoot for are huge.

Then there are the semiprofessional players who know a lot more about Keno than either of these other groups. These semiprofessionals play vastly different from any other. They look for weaknesses in the casino's pay tables and for ways and means to maximize wins at the lowest possible cost, although "lowest cost" may mean a lot more per game investment than it would ever mean to the casual daily player. These semiprofessionals may be daily players, casual players, or even professional players at other casino games, but they have recognized the value of intelligent keno play. To them, a "best" ticket could be one of several that they use at different times, for different games and, perhaps, at different casinos.

I mention these situations as examples because it is important to understand just how different people are, and can be, when considering what counts as a "best" ticket for them. For these reasons I have mostly used the $1 per way example on my sample tickets, and fewer split-rate examples. The tickets I have selected for this chapter represent a cross-section of the above types of players. Some of these tickets are perfect for daily play at low stakes, especially when fractionalized into either split rates or by being played for reduced rates at various casinos, depending on what such casinos may be offering on their rate cards. Some can be played for greater stakes and greater costs, but with huge win potential. And some can be adapted to meet the requirements of both frugal daily play as well as aggressive wagering for huge wins. It depends—mostly—on you. Only you can decide what you wish to play, how, and how aggressively based on your bankroll, your knowledge, your abilities, your skills, your available time, your goals, and your win objectives. The tickets I have selected as "best" are those that can easily meet all of these criteria and can be adapted by each player for their individual purposes. Each of these tickets can be played frugally, daily, for little stakes and good wins, played aggressively for much larger stakes and really huge wins, or as a balanced approach for the more knowledgeable player who can decide how, why, where, and to what end to play a variety of tickets to suit the situation. I cannot teach you *all* of the required skills as a keno player—I can, however, teach you what you need to know in order to *become* a skilled keno player. By being able to acquire this knowledge and information, as shown in the preceding chapters, and applying it to the sample keno tickets I have chosen, you will be able to exploit Keno for great wins at low costs, and as a result be far, far ahead of people who either play Keno badly, or simply don't know how good a game it can be.

Many people dismiss Keno as a terrible game. Many more self-described casino experts (mostly casino players who think they are experts) dogmatically regurgitate some basic math they once overheard, or learned, and now parrot as if it were Scripture. They smirk at those "poor deluded slobs" in the keno lounge, all the while losing thousands of dollars on their "good" games in order to win a few bucks, while the keno players wager merely a few bucks to win thousands. If you're looking for gambling value, then Keno is it. Where else can you wager, say $9, and win $25,000? Not many casino games will give you that chance. Unfortunately, many potential players will either listen to the blowhards who claim Keno is "just the worst house game there is," play only the way the casinos show in the brochures and rate cards, or—worse still—play ignorantly and badly. All of this can be overcome with simple knowledge and learning to play some of the "best" tickets that I have selected. All of these tickets can be played in a multitude of other ways as well as those shown, and in many more configurations. I chose these samples to provide a strong base upon which to lay the foundation of your Keno playing skills.

6-SPOT TICKET AS 2/3, 1/4, 1/5, AND 1/6

Figure 6 shows an example of this 6-spot ticket. The main advantage of this ticket is that it gives you two groups for smaller pays, and two groups for bigger pays. As shown, this ticket costs $5 to play, but offers you the two 3s and one 4 as smaller hits that keep you playing and provide you with enough wins along the way for you to keep at it without too much expense.

Each hit on the 3-spot gives you about $45, and even a

Figure 6. A 6-spot played as 2/3, 1/4, 1/5, and 1/6.

hit of 2 out of 3 gives you $1. If you hit the 4-spot, you will get $150; hits of 3 out of 4 will pay you about $4, and 2 out of 4 will pay you $1. Plus, of course, all of the other pays for the hits of these many numbers out of the 5s and 6s. The 5s and 6s give you the two chances at some big money, with the solid 5s paying about $600 to $800, while the solid 6s pay about $1,480 to $2,000, and more in some casinos. These hits aren't very frequent, as you have seen from the odds chart shown earlier, but they do happen, and the point and purpose of this ticket—as indeed this is so with all of the ticket examples in this chapter—is to provide you with at least some pays to keep you going while you wait for the bigger hits. Naturally, even some of the smaller hits can accumulate and provide you with a nice profit. What if you play this ticket for a few hours, and at the end have not hit any of the bigger pays, but have accumulated a $135 profit? Not bad for a half-day's work!

As I mentioned earlier, all of these tickets can be played for split rates to reduce the cost. For example, you could play this ticket at the 50-cent rate for the 3s and 4s, and the $1 rate for the 5s and 6s. That way, this ticket will cost you only $3.50. This also means that you will halve your pays for the 3s and 4s. It's up to you, depending on how you wish to play, what your objective may be, what your bankroll may be, and how you want to choose your wins. Conversely, you can play this ticket at the $2 rate, which means it will cost you $10 per game, but also double all pays. See how it works? The beauty of Lounge Keno is that it is so adaptable—everyone can find a method and means to play at whatever level is best and most comfortable for them. All you have to do is learn the tickets, how to play them, and then make it work for you based on your own circumstances. No other casino game is that flexible or player-friendly.

6-SPOT TICKET AS 3/4, 2/5, AND 1/6

Figure 7 gives an example of this 6-spot ticket. As you can see, this is the same 6-spot ticket as we have been using for an example, but this one shows the better use of the way ticket options. Here, instead of playing for the 3s as in the example in Figure 6, we have instead shifted the focus on the 4s and the 5s, in addition to the single 6, of course.

This ticket is a perfect example of the smart use of kings in a way ticket. In the previous example, we used a 2-spot, a 3-spot, and a king to make that ticket. Here we are using two groups of 2-spots and 2 kings. This gives us far more flexi-

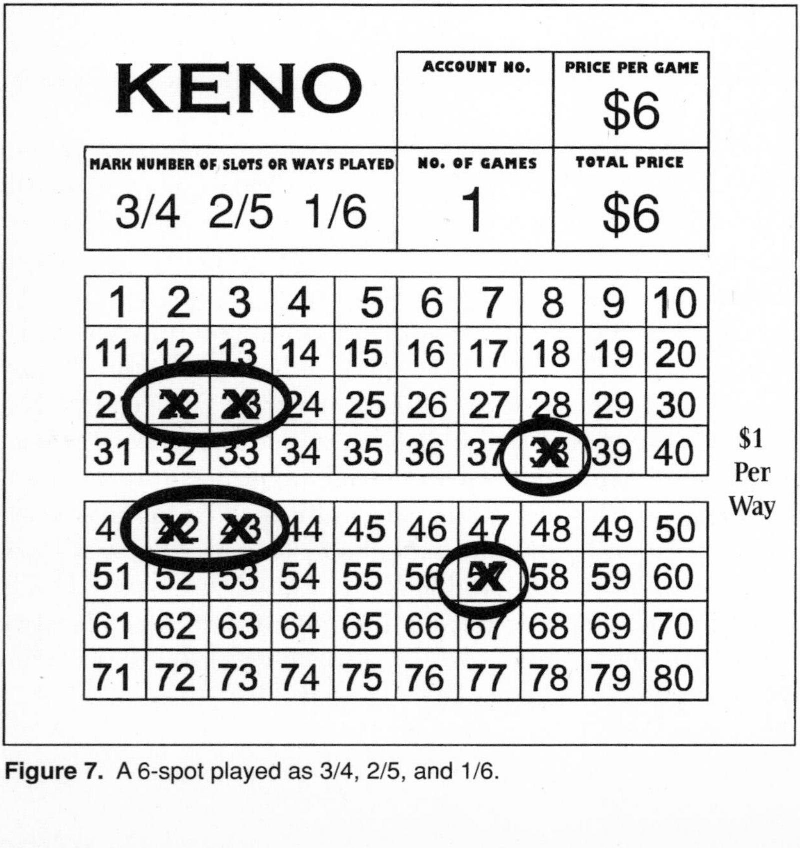

Figure 7. A 6-spot played as 3/4, 2/5, and 1/6.

bility and bigger hits more frequently. Although we could also easily play the 4/3s on this ticket, that would cost too much relative to the win potential. It is better—in this case—to shift the value of this ticket to the more 4s and the two 5s. On this ticket we will hit better value wins more often, because groups of 2s and 1s (kings) are hit more easily than groups of 3s (later we will see how groups of 3s are better in other kinds of tickets). At a cost of $6, at $1 per way, this is only $1 more expensive than the previous ticket, but gives us more 4s and one more 5, and provides us with better hit-value frequency. As with all these tickets, this one can be played for the reduced rates, but that would be inadvisable. You could reduce your costs by playing the 3/4s at the 50-cent rate, for example (making this ticket cost $4.50 instead of $6), but the mere $1.50 you save would have a much greater negative impact on your more frequent hits, which will be the 2s and 3s out of 4s. In all cases, these tickets should be played as much as possible to preserve the win value of the *most frequent* hits, as well as the win value of the *biggest* hits. This is, therefore, a more aggressive ticket when compared with the previous example and other 6-spot tickets.

6-SPOT TICKET AS 3/2, 3/4, AND 1/6

Seen in Figure 8 (page 98), this is an example of a way ticket that drops the kings, and thereby drops the pay for the 5s, and instead focuses on three groups of 2s to exploit the more frequent hits of 2s and 4s.

In this case we are playing three 2s and three 4s in addition to the single 6-spot. Again, this is being more aggressive, and as a result this ticket costs $7 to play at the $1 per way rate. Each 2-spot that hits will pay about $13 to $15, in addition to the pays of 2 out of 4. Hits of 3 out of 4 will pay

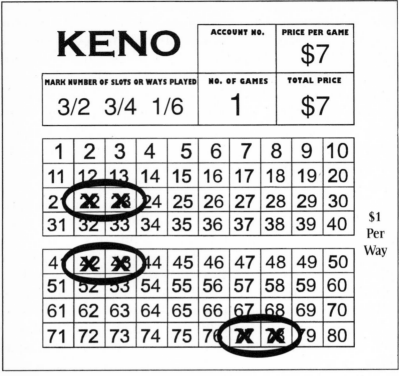

Figure 8. A 6-spot played as 3/2, 3/4, and 1/6.

about $3, and the solid 4s will pay about $150. This ticket should not be played for reduced rates, because the greatest win-value here is in the hits of the 2s and 4s. Playing them at reduced rates would reduce the "meat" of the ticket. Similarly, reducing the 6-spot would reduce the win value of that hit—for a mere savings of 50 cents. It simply isn't worth it if you play this ticket for rates lower than $1; however, it is possible. If you do, then I would recommend that you simply play all of these ways at whatever the reduced rate may be. For example, you may wish to play this ticket at the popular 40-cent rate, and this would then reduce the cost of all these ways on this ticket to only $2.80. Of course, this also means your wins will be 60 percent less in total value. Again, it's all relative to you and your bankroll and goals. If you do wish to save money, I would suggest you play one of the earlier samples; if you still wish to play this ticket for a reduced rate, then play all the ways at no less than 50 cents per way. That would make this ticket into a half-rate ticket, for a cost of $3.50 per game. If this sounds more manageable to you, then this ticket can still be played with a reasonable profit expectation, even at these rates.

6-SPOT TICKET AS 1/4, 2/5, AND 1/6

I call this ticket "frugally aggressive," because it is one of those rare tickets in which it is possible to take a long shot at the 4-spot as a group of four and include two kings. Figure 9 (on the next page) gives an example.

Having only one 4, and playing it as a group of four numbers, means we will not hit nearly as many 4s as we do on some of the other tickets. Being in a single group of four also means that the 4-spot will hit less often. However, this ticket is designed to provide more frequent *bigger* hits, because when the 4-spot *does* hit, it is far more likely also to be combined with at least one of the other kings, making a solid 5-spot. Now we are in the money big time (relatively speaking). This ticket costs only $4 when played at the $1 per way rate, although it can also be played at the half rate reasonably well. It should not, however, be played for any less than the half rate, which is $2 per game, because any less than that will invalidate the purpose behind playing it. This is a very aggressive ticket, primarily designed to hit the 5s.

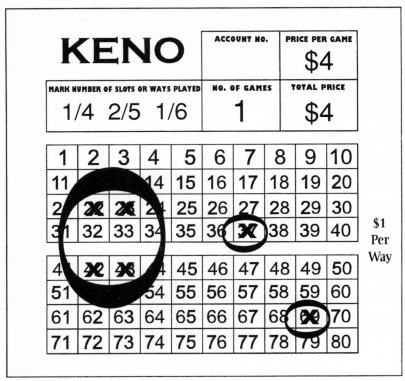

Figure 9. A 6-spot played as 1/4, 2/5, and 1/6.

8-SPOT TICKET AS 2/4, 2/5, 2/6, 2/7, AND 1/8

Now we are getting into the realm of the really "meaty" tickets, the kind that can give you huge wins. The costs of these tickets will rise, but the win value can be staggering. The first of my 8-spot ticket examples can be seen in Figure 10.

As you can see, this is an extension of the 6-spot ticket shown in Figure 9. On that ticket we played one group of 4 and two kings. Here we are playing that group of 4 and the two kings as well, but also adding one group of 2 to make eight numbers in all. This ticket is also a terrific example of how to use kings in a smart way and create a ticket with

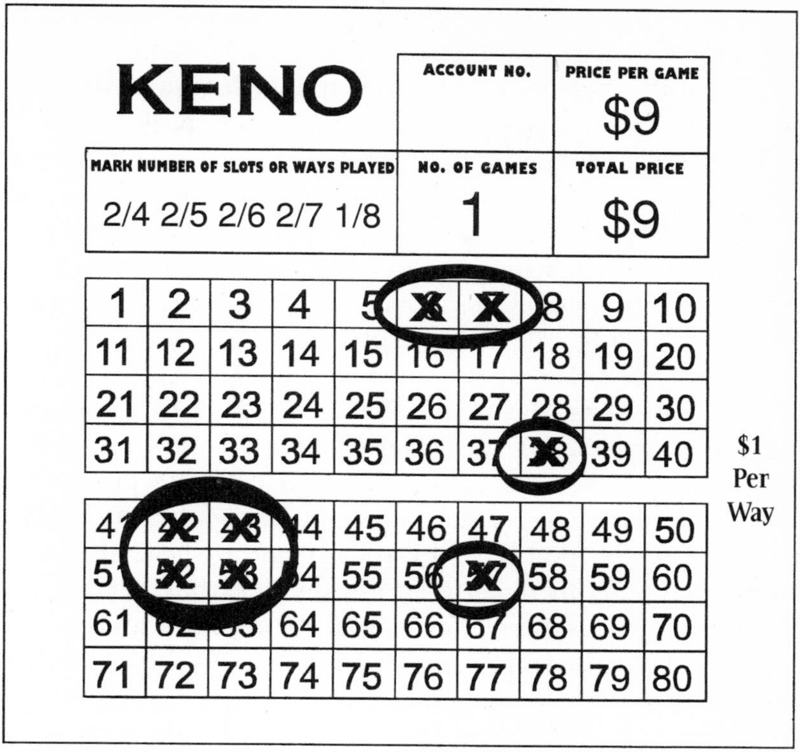

Figure 10. An 8-spot played as 2/4, 2/5, 2/6, 2/7, and 1/8.

many small wins frequently, and huge win value. On this ticket, as we have it marked, there are two 4s, with two 5s, two 6s, two 7s, and one 8. Out of just eight numbers we have made nine ways, and made these in a pattern that allows for terrific small wins, preserving the major "meat" of the higher-paying hits. On any hit of a solid 4-spot, all we need are either the group 4 or the group 2 plus both kings, and we have the average $150 windfall for either solid 4-spot hit. At the same time, we may hit one of the two kings with the group 4, and this gives a 5-spot, for the average win of about $600 to $800. We can also hit a solid 6-spot, and even several 6-out-of-7 spots, plus two solid 7-spots and, of course, the solid 8-spot. Hitting just 6 out of 7 can give us about $400 for that hit, even if we make it in a way that doesn't result in a solid 6-spot. Any solid 6-spot will give us that win as we have seen earlier, and if we are lucky to hit a solid 7-spot we can expect about $7,000. Naturally, the solid 8-spot is the big win, and here we can expect about an average pay of $25,000 to $50,000. Sometimes, we could choose to play the 1/8 for $2, because in some casinos the two-dollar 8-spot is part of a progressive, with jackpots many times starting at $200,000 and growing from there.

Although in this case we have a shot at that big win with that solid 8-spot, the value in this ticket is in the higher pays for the smaller hits. These happen more frequently, and on this ticket even more so because we are preserving the value of the small hits such as on the 4s. We could also play the 3s, but that would be costly and instead of adding to the value of our ticket it would detract from it. The trick in selecting the correct ticket is to figure out which of the smaller pays are worth the investment and which would cost more than they are worth. That all depends on how you configure your ticket and your actual goal. In this case the cost of the ticket is a mere $9, or $10 if you choose to play $2 on the 8-spot, and even the smallest solid 4 hit can pay us $150, or more (depending on the pay rates at the casino where you are playing). Although many people will play an 8-spot ticket, most will mark it as merely a straight 8 and cost themselves a lot of pays. Playing the 8-spot ticket in this manner allows you to gain frequent smaller wins that fuel your bankroll, not deplete it. At the very worst, most of the time the ticket will either pay for itself or will not cost you the full amount for the next game because of those smaller wins. Even just a few numbers will mean some may win, so the ticket costs less for the next game while still preserving the full value of the play.

8-SPOT TICKET AS 2/4, 3/5, 2/6, 1/7, AND 1/8

This is another version of the $9 keno 8-spot ticket, very similar to the one we have just discussed. Figure 11 shows an example.

Did you notice the difference between this one and the ticket shown in Figure 10? Look closely at the way the ticket is made. Instead of one group of 4 and one group of 2 and two kings, here we have marked two groups of 2s, one group of 3, and only one king. Notice how we marked the ways

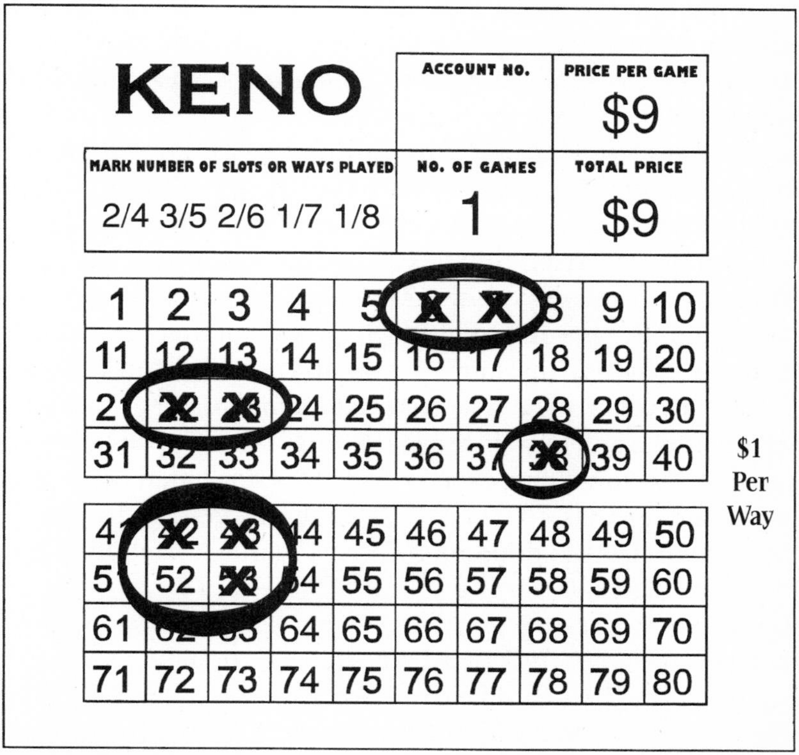

Figure 11. An 8-spot played as 2/4, 3/5, 2/6, 1/7, and 1/8.

played. See where the difference lies? If you look closely, you will see that on this ticket we have *increased* the number of ways the 5s can hit from 2 to 3, and *decreased* the number of ways that a 7 can hit from 2 to 1. That's what happens when you take away that one king and move it instead to join with one of the groups of 2 and now mark it instead as a group of 3. Although you still have eight numbers total, and can in fact have the very same numbers you may have previously selected, in this case you are taking a greater shot at a lower odds-against pay, and reducing one of the higher odds-against hits to account for the change. A ticket like this is worth the play if you are focusing more on the intermediate goals, such as hitting the pays for the 4s and 5s. The 6s will take care of themselves, as they remain untouched by this redefinition of the earlier 8-spot ticket, but here we have decided to make the 5s our "meat." By creating the groups of 3, anytime that is hit we have a greater chance of combining that with one of the other groups of 2s, and that will give us the solid 5-spot hit. We can also hit this the third way on this ticket, by hitting both groups of 2s along with the single king. That's the additional way that we added to this version of the 8-spot ticket, to give us more of those smaller hits more frequently, and all the "out of" pays in between, of course. Naturally, something has to give—unless we want to pay more. In this case, to preserve the cost and value of the ticket, we simply eliminated one of the 7s, reducing these from two 7s to 1. By giving up one of those options, we added more "meat" value to smaller wins.

8-SPOT TICKET AS 2/5, 1/6, 2/7, AND 1/8

This version of the 8-spot ticket is more aggressive, a little harder to hit, but for less money. Rather than playing these tickets for reduced rates, or split rates, if you want to make the ticket less costly, this version will do nicely. (Seen in Figure 12, below.)

As you can see, the price on this ticket is only $6 at the $1 per way rate, because here we have eliminated several of the "ways" we played on the tickets we have just discussed. Here we have marked two groups of 3s and two kings. By making these groups as groups of 3s, instead of groups of 2s as in the earlier examples, this ticket becomes a little harder to hit. Nevertheless, by making it into a ticket that hits two 5s, one 6, two 7s, and one 8, we have still preserved much of the value while reducing the per-game cost by $2. Here,

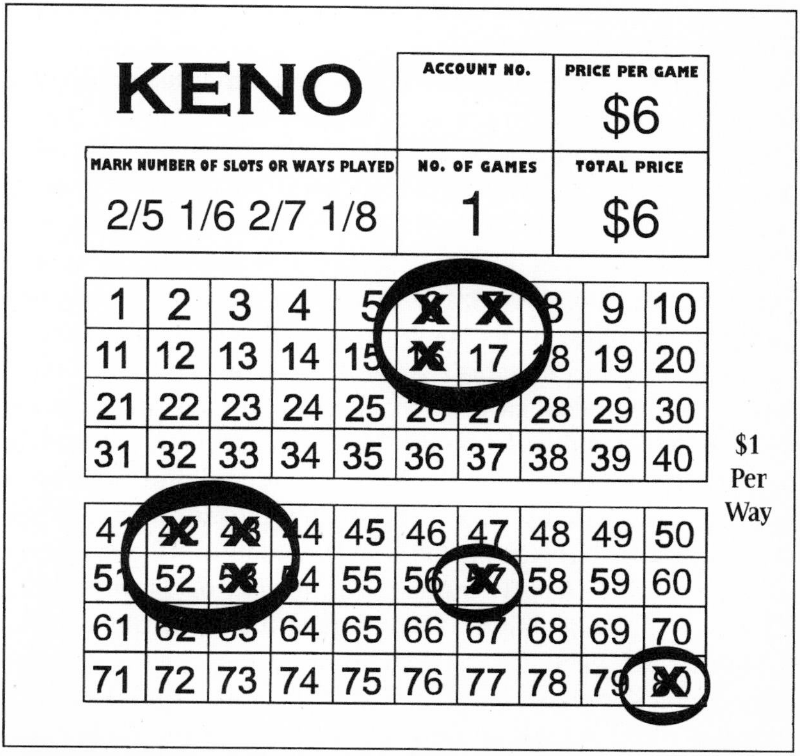

Figure 12. An 8-spot played as 2/5, 1/6, 2/7, and 1/8.

the reduction is in eliminating the 4s and reducing the 6s to one 6-spot, as opposed to two 6s in the earlier examples. We could easily play the four 4s that this ticket allows, but this would add $4 to the cost of the ticket and make it a $10-per-game cost, and this would invalidate the reason why we marked it in precisely this way. Marking the 8-spot like this is done for only one reason: to reduce its cost while still preserving most of the small and high win value, without going to a split-rate or reduced-rate ticket. Many players may feel more comfortable with this version of the 8-spot because the $2 per game saved easily means that you don't have to win that $2 more per game to keep pace with the ticket's costs. Over time, savings like this can add up and that's why frequent players often choose to mark this 8-spot in this manner.

Another reason has more to do with the observation of the game. As you sit in the keno lounge and watch the games, you may be noticing certain patterns of numbers. Although mathematically each number has no memory and no specific "intent" to group with any other in any specific manner, nevertheless the fact remains that it is possible to observe and identify patterns. We can identify patterns in numerals, and particularly patterns as they apply to keno games. Pattern recognition—and the ability to act on it—are profitable skills in keno play, because they may allow you to properly exploit short-term trends in certain pattern groups. As we will learn in the section on Video Keno, playing patterns in Keno is far more profitable than simply playing numbers. In this case, you may have observed that the keno numbers you are watching are currently running in groups of 3s, in similar shapes to those I have selected for this example. In fact these are the very groups that happen extraordinarily frequently in Keno, so much so that almost all regular players will have at least some tickets with such groupings, especially if they are playing several way tickets at the same time, as indeed they should (and so should you, as we will find out in the discussion on strategy). Being able to modify your ticket is one of the skills you will acquire as you become more comfortable with the game. Most players may not wish to change the ticket they started with—largely due to superstition—but if they see groupings of numbers in certain patterns they will often add another ticket marked in those ways. In this manner you could actually play all of the 8-spot tickets I have shown in my examples at the same time, although I would advise against it. It is best to choose one, then add another to it if you recognize a pattern, and perhaps modify the second ticket to this one, as shown in Figure 12.

Adaptability is one of the advantages that you have as a keno player, because you can easily modify your approach to the game as you see it unfold. This is similar to the tracking skills used by blackjack players, poker players, and even craps and roulette players. Baccarat players will, of course, swear by it, because their game is all about such trends in groups (more accurately referred to as "clumps" in the baccarat shoe).

8-SPOT TICKET AS 6/4, 6/5, 4/6, 2/7, AND 1/8

This is perhaps the best ticket to play when you are playing an 8-spot, other than maybe the King-8 ticket discussed earlier. It is also very aggressive, and can become expensive, especially at the $1 per way rate per game. You can see it on the next page in Figure 13.

On this ticket, instead of playing a group of 4 and a group of 2 and a king, or two groups of 3s and two kings, or any of the other examples above, we are making a power-play ticket by selecting three groups of 2s and two kings. Only the King-8 ticket is more powerful, and, of course, also

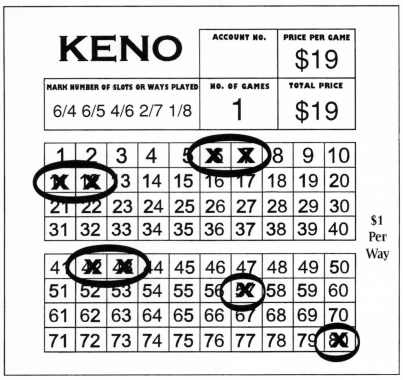

Figure 13. An 8-spot played as 6/4, 6/5, 4/6, 2/7, and 1/8.

more expensive. This ticket gives us six 4s, six 5s, four 6s, and two 7s in addition to the single 8. Basically, this is the next best thing to the King-8 ticket, but better in many respects. The King-8 ticket is usually offered by the casinos because of the many ways it makes, and the resultant extra costs it incurs for players. It becomes a house ticket simply due to the long odds of hitting worthwhile pays. Many of the smaller pays the King-8 ticket hits aren't enough to compensate for the extra cost of playing all those many ways that we should play in order to add "meat" to the ticket. Its expense becomes prohibitive, thereby forcing us to play at reduced rates, or split rates, which erodes the profitability and viability of the ticket. Of course if you are rich, and don't care about spending a few thousand dollars a session, then the King-8 ticket could be the one for you. However, most of the time playing this version of the ticket is instead a much better option.

Groups of 2s hit extraordinarily often in Keno, especially as here marked (not necessarily the numbers themselves, just the side-by-side grouping example—vertical groupings are also good, especially when you use this ticket in the form of the entire column and then match it up with other such tickets for the other rows as well—if you can afford such action). By marking the three groups of 2s with the two kings, this turns what could otherwise be a high-cost house ticket into a powerfully profitable ticket. We eliminate many of the ways that the King-8 provides, but we also add "workability" to the ticket, allowing us to play for the 4s and 5s with greater comfort and much lower cost than would ever be possible on the King-8. We can now afford to go for the more frequently occurring 4s and 5s, while still preserving the "meat" win value of the ticket in the higher 6 and 7 hits, as well as the 1/8. Even though this ticket still costs $19 at the $1 per way rate, it is far more manageable than the $47 the King-8 would cost us—and that's without the 4s. Allowing ourselves the hits of the 4s on this version of the ticket provides us with the increased frequency of hits. This increased frequency of win-value hits—as opposed to merely hits—gives us the power of profitability in this ticket. Although we would have to hit one of the 5s on the King-8 in order to make enough money to warrant extended play on such a ticket, here all we need is a few hits of 4s, and even several "something out of 4s," along with the "out of" the other possible number combinations in order to preserve the win value of the ticket. This allows longevity of play, more frequent profits along the way, and, at the very worst, much lower replay costs.

Most people don't understand the value of the reduced replay cost of a keno ticket, or the value of accumulated smaller wins that happen more frequently because we have made our ticket in a manner that will allow this to happen. Casual keno players merely take a flyer at something big and in the process lose their money and their interest in the game. This is giving money away. With a little education and some "smarts" in the method of number combinations, using these groups of 2s and the kings wisely produces a powerful ticket that sustains play for many sessions, provides many smaller wins along the way and growth capital accumulation, and preserves reduced replay costs and the best win value for the higher-paying hits. Other than playing more groups, this is about as good as an 8-spot ticket gets, and it is, therefore, my most recommended ticket.

For those of you who may be wary of the $19 per-game cost, I remind you that you can play this at reduced rates as a split-rate ticket and not lose too much from the ticket's overall profitability. For example, you can play the 4s, 5s, and 6s at the 50-cent rate—keeping the 7s and the 8 at the $1 rate—reducing the overall cost of this powerful ticket to merely $11 per game. It is well worth this cost. Naturally, this can be reduced even further, such as by playing some of the ways at the 25-cent rates, some at the 40-cent rates, or some at the 50-cent rates, and so on—all of which are available to you and up to you to select and decide. If you're not sure how to do this, simply mark the ticket as shown in this example and then take it to the keno counter and ask the keno writer to help you mark the ways played for whatever amounts you wish to allocate to each way, at whatever reduced rates you choose. That way you will make what is called a multi-rate split-rate ticket, and it will still work just as well.

9-SPOT TICKET AS 2/4, 2/5, 3/6, 1/7, 1/8, AND 1/9

Perhaps one of the best overall value tickets, with the "biggest bang for the buck" potential, is this 9-spot keno way ticket. Played as two groups of 3s, one group of 2, and one king, this is another classic example of how the smart use of kings and groups can turn an otherwise lousy ticket into a profitable one. You can see this ticket in Figure 14.

Similarly to the very powerful 8-spot ticket we just discussed, this is also a powerful way to play a 9-spot ticket. The "meat" of this ticket is in the 4s, 5s, and 6s. That's why

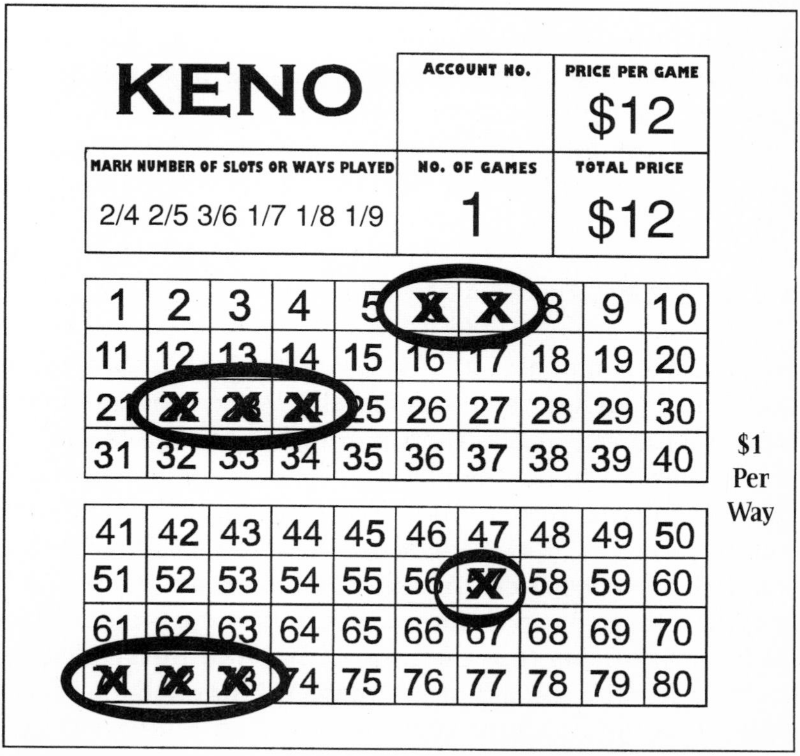

Figure 14. A 9-spot played as 2/4, 2/5, 3/6, 1/7, 1/8, and 1/9.

we are playing this ticket this way: we have two shots at each of the 4s, 5s, and 6s. We leave the 7-, 8-, and 9-spots as singles because they are the hardest to hit, but we also preserve the value of those hits by not overbetting them in too many ways, by allowing for the more frequent hits of the smaller groups, and by the "out of" hits factor that will happen on this ticket as we start hitting nonsolid combinations of 5s and 6s and 7s out of 8 and 9. At a cost of $12, it is a very inexpensive ticket, considering the many ways it makes possible. As with all of the tickets sampled in this chapter, this one is designed to make the smaller wins happen more frequently, thereby preserving the ticket's profitability and reducing its replay costs. If $12 per game is too costly for you, play this at the reduced rate of no less than 50 cents per way for the 4s, 5s, and 6s, and leave the 7, 8, and 9 at the $1 per way rate. Playing this way, this ticket will cost $6.50 per game and still preserve the major win value for the large hits, allowing for the "pay for itself along the way" objective.

10-SPOT TICKET AS 3/4, 3/6, 3/7, 1/9, AND 1/10

Finally, a 10-spot ticket. Playing 10-spots is my favorite method of playing Keno (particularly Video Keno, as I will show you later). In Lounge Keno, playing 10-spots can get tricky, because of the long odds of gaining some reasonable wins. Using this ticket will help make it easier to win. (See Figure 15.)

Here we see the classic use of three groups of 3s along with one king. By so doing we not only reduce the overall costs of the ticket, but manage to preserve the maximum yield win value on all ways played. Although there are many ways in which such a 10-spot ticket can be marked, this version is the most powerful for many reasons already

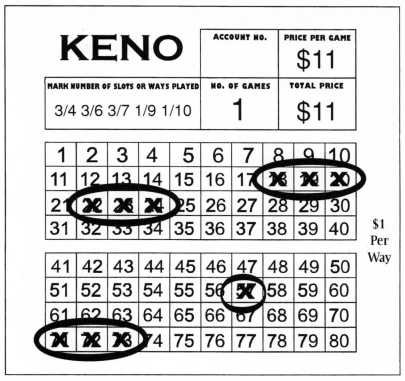

Figure 15. A 10-spot played as 3/4, 3/6, 3/7, 1/9, and 1/10.

stated. This ticket gives us three 4s, three 6s, and three 7s, along with the one 9 and one 10-spot. Much of the "meat" in this ticket is in the hits of the 4s and 6s, with some of the "maintenance" replay value also coming from the "out of" hits on the 7s, and the 9 and 10. Notice that we have left out all 5s and 8s, since none of those are possible with this particular combination of number groups. This is intentional, because we want to get as much payback as we can, without overplaying too many ways and reducing the win-value potential of the ticket.

As with all these tickets, you can also play this at the reduced rates for the 4s, 6s, and 7s, but should not play for less than 50 cents per way, and always leave the 9 and 10 at the $1 per way rate. This is because many casinos have jackpot pays for solid 9s and 10s, for a $1 per way rate, often with wins of up to $1 million for such hits. Playing the 4s, 6s, and 7s at the 50-cent rate, this ticket will cost only $6.50, and is perhaps among the best ways to play any 10-spot ticket when playing Lounge Keno.

Well, that's it for my choice of best tickets. In every casino, and in every keno game, you will find many other samples. As I mentioned earlier, there are even more ways than these to make many of these tickets, and many more possible combinations. Take another look at the multi-way ticket in Figure 5, on page 87, to remind yourself of just how many ways are possible the more groups you play. In the end, you will have to decide for yourself how you wish to exploit this knowledge, these samples, and the skills you will acquire as you learn and experience more during play. Remember that one of the advantages of live Lounge Keno is its flexibility—you have all the tools at your disposal to make fine tuning adjustments as you play. Once you get the hang of it, you will be able to select tickets with even more "meat" and win value than these. And that's great!

Nevada Numbers

The previous chapter showed you some of the best keno tickets you can play in the regular live keno game you can find in most casinos. One of those tickets deserves a chapter of its own, because it's about as good as a keno game can get. This is the Nevada Numbers ticket. It is a progressive Pick-5 game in which you play a keno 5-spot ticket straight up, just as you would any other keno ticket. The big difference here is the award. With this Nevada Numbers ticket, you can win a progressive jackpot that *starts* at $5 million! Not only is this a 5-spot that has a pretty good chance of hitting, but also pays something for *any* hit. Even a hit of merely one number pays $1. The ticket costs $2 to play, so if you hit only one number you will be paid back half your bet. How many lotteries around the country do you know that pay you something on hitting just one number? Unless it's the mega-number, or powerball number, you get nothing. Even in regular Keno you don't get paid for a 1-out-of-5 hit. But when you play Nevada Numbers, you do.

This means that you can lose on your ticket only when you don't hit *any* numbers.

Nevada Numbers is played in more than forty casinos throughout Nevada. Soon you may be able to play this game in other states as well, but for now, this game is only available in those selected casinos throughout Nevada. I will give you the list of those casinos a little later on in this chapter. Although this game is very similar to a lottery, it is important to stress that Nevada Numbers is a *keno* game, and *not* a lottery. Lotteries are illegal in the state of Nevada, so we must be careful to remember that Nevada Numbers plays like a *keno* progressive, and not a lottery. This is to comply with state law, and with the Nevada Gaming Control Board. This game may look, to you, the player, like some form of a lottery, and that's okay. As casino customers and players of keno games, it doesn't matter if you think of Keno as a form of gaming that is *similar* to a lottery. But I want to make sure that you—the player—understand what this game is, how it works, and how to play it—and that it is *not* a lottery.

This progressive keno game is drawn only once each day. At 6:00 P.M. Pacific time, the keno lounge at Bally's Hotel and Casino in Las Vegas draws the five numbers for the Nevada Numbers game. These are then flashed simultaneously to all casinos around the state where this game is played. These same numbers are also immediately displayed on the Web, at the address www.NevadaNumbers.com. This way, no matter where you are in the state, as long as you are in a casino that offers this game, you can play the ticket and immediately know if you won as soon as the game is drawn. If you are playing Nevada Numbers at one of the casinos elsewhere in the state other than Bally's, you can collect your winnings immediately at that casino, after each drawing. Being drawn only once each day, however, is both a benefit and a detractor. It means you can only play the game once a day, and that's the downside. The upside is, of course, that your "cost" of the ticket is limited to only the $2-per-ticket price for that day. As I have shown earlier, anytime you gamble on Keno, knowing the "cost" of the tickets is important for evaluating your bankroll and the time you spend at the game, as well as understanding your win potential and profitability. This is also actually a blessing in disguise, because it offers you an opportunity to make a day of it in the keno lounge, play some of the keno tickets in the regular games, and then, when the time comes for the drawing of the Nevada Numbers game, pick your favorite 5-spot ticket and play that in the game. Who knows—you could walk away with a $5 million plus jackpot, after having enjoyed a great day in the casino's keno lounge. All these considerations need to be factored into any game, and particularly games like Nevada Numbers. Although in Keno, the frequency is generally the greatest attraction—as I have said earlier—with this game you can combine your shot at the big progressive jackpot along with your day's play at the keno lounge.

The story of Nevada Numbers is very interesting. It was not an easy task to create this game, and not only because Keno was thought of by casinos in general terms as a "dying game." With corporate control over almost all casinos now common, executives are always searching for ways to cut down on labor-intensive games that don't quickly produce large sums of money. Keno has always been a target of such cost-cutting measures. Fortunately, however, there was enough of a groundswell of public resistance to the complete elimination of Keno that the game survived and in recent times has been undergoing a resurgence. This is in no small part due to Nevada Numbers, the game's inventor, Mark Valenti, and his company, Las Vegas Gaming, Inc. They convinced Park Place Entertainment—the corporate giant that owns all of the Bally's casinos as well as Hilton, Paris, and Caesars Palace—to make the Nevada Numbers game available in their casinos, and this resulted in an immediate increase in play for the property's keno lounges. Players were attracted to this game, and for good reasons. In turn, these players were also exposed to the game of Keno in general and soon discovered that it was a game that could be played leisurely, for small stakes, and with high payoff possibilities. Lounge Keno began to post good results, and even players who previously didn't know about casino Keno, or weren't interested in playing it, now found themselves enjoying the game. This not only convinced casinos that Keno should be here to stay, as a regular casino game, but that Nevada Numbers is a great catalyst for attracting regular keno players, and other gamblers as well. Such was the immediate popularity of the game that other casinos throughout Nevada soon came on board, and the game is now available in many casinos.

The game actually came to being as a dream. Its inventor, Mark Valenti, dreamed it. Who says dreams can't be real? His dream first happened back in 1997, when Mark was working for the Hospitality Network and was helping a friend develop Back-to-Back Roulette. He became so interested in this keno game he dreamt about that he left corporate America and invested every dime into starting his own creation—the Nevada Numbers game. In 1997–1998 he formed a company called Las Vegas Gaming, Inc., and raised money to begin the process of making his idea a reality. He started the game on June 25, 2001, with Park Place Entertainment, received the required gaming approval to move forward with the game in November of 2001, and the rest—as they say— is history. As a consequence, we now have another good casino game to play, with a jackpot that's worth $5 million just to start, and grows from there.

Although there are many other progressives available among the various keno lounges in several casinos, most of these are progressives based on 8-spots and are part of only that casino's keno game. Only Nevada Numbers is a statewide progressive. These other in-house progressives are a terrific addition to a keno playing plan and can be played on any keno ticket during any regular keno game, or in accordance with the rules as posted in that casino. Nevada Numbers, however, offers a huge jackpot relative to the cost of playing and also reasonable odds. Some of the odds for the other keno progressives that use 8-spots can actually be far higher for jackpots whose pays aren't nearly in the millions, as is the case with Nevada Numbers. This is the only progressive keno game that starts its jackpot at amounts that are the envy of any other keno progressive—amounts that are very close to many of the starting jackpot amounts for some state lotteries.

The following reasons explain why I think that Nevada Numbers belongs in the "best tickets" category:

- You can play for only $2.
- For that small price, you can win a progressive jackpot that *starts* at $5 million.
- You can play as many tickets for each day's game as you want to buy.
- You can play up to fifty consecutive games, for fifty straight days.
- Payoffs start as low as *any* hit.

Just $2 a game, with a chance for a giant jackpot. That's very good for a keno game. Being paid $1 for even the smallest 1-out-of-5 hit means you get at least something many times you play. Being able to play for fifty straight draws, over fifty days, means you can buy into this game even as you are leaving and then sit back and enjoy the game from your own home. Each night you can call the casino to get the winning numbers, or you can look them up on the Web. Finally, the best—you can play more than one ticket in each day's drawing. This means that although you can't play a keno "way" ticket for Nevada Numbers draws, you can play more than one ticket and use the principles of cores and wheels, such as those you will shortly discover in the next section, where I discuss Video Keno and show you how to make a keno wheel. By being able to do all of this, your ticket in this game can produce more winners, and hit more frequently, than any lottery.

The chart below shows a list of all the pays on the standard straight up Nevada Numbers progressive keno game, along with the odds of hitting.

Although the odds may seem long, remember that the jackpot you are getting is a lot bigger than any other jackpot you can get on any other 5-spot keno ticket. Also remember that in this game you have a much higher hit frequency than on other regular keno 5-spot tickets, whose hit frequency is only at about 6 percent overall (depending on the various and varying payouts per each pay table as offered in the various casinos). Also remember that the overall payback of 72.16 percent is higher than many lounge keno games, such as those listed in chapter 7. The resultant house hold of about 27.84 percent is not that much higher than the average 25 percent hold over most standard keno games, and considerably better than on some keno games that can hold 30 percent or more. To find this game in the casino, just go to the keno lounge and look for the Nevada Numbers logo. You can see what this logo looks like in Photo 1.

Nevada Numbers Progressive Keno 5-Spot Game Pays and Odds

CATCHES	PAYS	ODDS
1	$1	4:1
2	$2	36:1
3	$20	866:1
4	$2,000	64,107:1
5	$5 million +	24,040,016:1

Overall payback:	72.16%
Hit frequency:	28.20%
House hold:	27.84%

Photo 1. The Nevada Numbers logo—look for this in the casino's keno lounge to find out if this casino plays this progressive 5-spot game.

This logo displayed in the keno lounge of the casino where you happen to be signifies that this casino offers the game. If you are planning a trip to Nevada in the near future, here is a list of all the casinos that currently play Nevada Numbers:

Avi Casino	New Frontier
Bally's	Oasis Resort
Binion's Horseshoe	Pahrump Nugget
Bonanza	Paris Las Vegas
Bonanza Inn	The Plaza
Casablanca Resort	Rampart Casino
Castaways	Red Lion
Colorado Belle	Reno Hilton
Edgewater	River Palms
Eldorado	Resort Casino
Flamingo	Riverside Resort Casino
Flamingo Laughlin	Saddle West
Four Queens	Casino Sahara
Fremont	Sam's Town
Golden Phoenix Resort	Sand's Regency
Hotel San Remo	Stardust
Imperial Palace	Stockman's
Jerry's Nugget	Tahoe Biltmore
Joker's Wild	Virgin River Resort
Las Vegas Hilton	

More casinos are adding this game almost on a daily basis, so by the time you read this book, Nevada Numbers will be far more widely available. And with the popularity of this first game, Las Vegas Gaming, Inc. has introduced several other games as well. There is the Million Dollar Ticket, a 10-spot keno game where you can win $1 million for just $1. The hit frequency on this game is at 21.20 percent, and that makes it produce winners of at least some money far more often than many other casino keno games. Another popular new game is a bingo game called Super Bonanza, a bingo progressive game that starts at $100,000. Other games that you may soon find in your casino are America's Numbers and Las Vegas Numbers, both keno-style games similar to Nevada Numbers. Some of these games are already available, while others are still undergoing initial trials. All of these games will soon find their way into the casinos you may visit.

Finally, a note about some strategy for Nevada Numbers.

STRATEGY FOR NEVADA NUMBERS

Since this is a keno game played only once each day, and since you cannot play any way ticket combinations as you would in a regular lounge keno game, this limits some of the strategy options and advice I have offered for the traditional keno game. My best advice is as follows:

Play at Least 5 to 10 Tickets at Once, on a 5- to 10-Day Ticket

This costs $10 to $20, and since you don't have to be present for the collection of your winnings, it's a good ticket to play while you are in town for your vacation or visit, or even from home. If course, if you can afford the $100 investment, the best option is to play the full fifty available games, on a fifty-day cycle. This will assure you of the best bang for your buck, and will often result in significantly diminishing your costs of replaying the ticket, since you will be paid at least something at a far more frequent ratio than for other keno tickets. Plus, of course, you have the chance for that big jackpot—or, at the very least, after the fifty days are over, you have an excuse to plan another vacation—to collect your winnings!

Play More Than One Ticket for Each Game

If you are playing for a few days during your visit, buy more than one ticket for each nightly drawing. This will enable you to make a wheel and exploit some of the strategies you have learned for regular keno. (You will learn how to make a "wheel" in Part Two of this book.) The best use of this is to select a $20 per night investment, and use a 10-ticket wheel for rows or blocks of 5s. This advice will make more sense to you as you read the chapters on how to play *Four Card Keno*™ and *Multi-Card Keno*™. By doing this you will enhance your ability to hit more winners more often, and to make bigger winners out of fewer catches. If your bankroll allows such play, use this multi-ticket wheel to play ten to fifty consecutive games, and this will also enhance your potential to catch bigger winners.

And that, dear friends, is the story of Nevada Numbers, and how to play the game to win. Ready? On your mark (pun intended) and let's find the nearest game for that nice $5 million plus.

Keys to Winning

Before we get to the finer points of strategy, it is important to learn some principles that are keys to winning. If you have read any of my other books, you will be familiar with this concept. Most of my books contain a chapter on keys to winning that provides a list of the most important principles in all gambling. Some of this information is universal—meaning it applies to all gambling games, and not just the one game we happen to be discussing in that particular book. However, there are also points that apply only to the game under discussion—in this case, Keno. If you are a regular reader of the *Powerful Profits* series, you may already be familiar with some of these principles. If not, all of this will be new.

In writing a series of gambling books, I try to strike a balance between information that should be shared and the problem of potentially repeating information from book to book. Short of being assured that each reader will read every book in the series—which would be nice but most likely impractical to expect—I often struggle with how to make this information fresh, yet complete for those who may be reading this for the first time. My aim is to focus each item of knowledge in my "Keys to Winning" chapter on the *specific game* we are discussing, while indicating, wherever possible, that these principles can easily be applied to all other casino games, and indeed to all of your casino gambling.

It's not easy. Keno is not just the simple, dumb game that most people think it is. It is a serious gambling game that has a high house withholding percentage, and a game that can—and will—take your money fast if you don't know how to make it work for you. You need to understand the problems that it presents and the misinformation often presented in the casino's guides to playing, or the brochures and rate card examples. To learn this game takes time, and the willingness not just to learn it, but also to apply the knowledge and skills, and apply them correctly. To help you do this, I have therefore created the Keys to Winning. These are, in order of importance, as follows:

- Knowledge
- Patience
- Bankroll
- Selection
- Discipline
- Win Goals

Simple, right? No problem? I can do that. Can you? Really? Be honest, now. I can tell you from direct personal experience that sticking to these principles—always, all the time, each time—is extremely hard to do. To be a successful player, and win most of the time, you *must* keep to these principles. If you go to a casino, and you leave just one of these principles at home, or take only a portion with you, or you slip and lose one, or more, or a part of one, you're sunk. You're the

Titanic on a collision course with the iceberg, and there's no stopping the final result, or the consequences. And that's no joke. Believe me. I know. Not even I can be this perfect at all times, and I don't expect you to be either. Just *most of the time*, that's all we can ask of each other. There will be times when you will have the best intentions, but you will fail. You will leave home without one or more of these vital principles. And you will regret it.

Any "system," or any advice you may read that says "do this and you will win," is fundamentally flawed, because no human being can be that perfect at all times, each time, all the time. We are frail creatures, mentally, physically, and, most important, emotionally. We get upset. We get angry. We get mad that we have done everything perfectly, and still we lost. It happens. That's also part of life, and certainly part of the gaming experience. Even when you take all these principles with you, and do everything perfectly, there will be times when you will lose. This I also know from direct personal experience. These are statistical anomalies that infect every aspect of gambling, and Keno is certainly one of the games most prone to such visible fluctuations. Other games are equally as prone, but these events are more hidden. Not so in Keno, and that's why you will suffer, sometimes, even when you do it right.

My point here is to let you in on the "secret" that allows you to overcome these problems, these feelings, and these moments of anger. Knowing these principles, as I have outlined them, is important, not because you will become perfect, and a professional gambler, but because *you will become more secure in your gaming*, more steady in your approach, more confident in your end result, and more conscious of your expectations. And these are the real secrets to your keno success. So, in more detail, I will now address each of those principles individually.

KNOWLEDGE

This should be relatively easy. This is the "learning curve," the decision to improve yourself, and probably the reason you bought this book. Knowledge means to learn as much as possible, with as good a direction toward your end goal as possible. Knowledge means to know how to play Keno, but also how to play it *well*. Playing Keno *well* also means incorporating into your knowledge all the other principles of these Keys to Winning. And it also means not stopping here. It means including everything in this book. Knowledge is growth in understanding and in continual improvement. Learning will have a direct and positive impact on your play, on your life, and specifically on how you approach the game the very next time you visit a casino.

PATIENCE

I am often surprised at how easily people get upset. They get upset when they don't hit. They get upset when they do hit, but they don't think it's enough. They get upset if they don't hit the jackpot. When they hit a secondary jackpot, they get upset that they didn't hit the top jackpot. And when they hit the top jackpot, unless it's something in the millions, they get upset as to why they couldn't hit it sooner. Are you this kind of a player? Does this fit your playing profile? If it does, then you aren't patient. You are hyper. You shouldn't play Keno, at least not without a tranquilizer. Playing Keno can be a very prolonged experience, one which will require your utmost patience. Wins will happen, and although sometimes you may be lucky and get that good win right away, most of the time you will have to work for it. This may require you to do several sessions, and perhaps even visit several casinos. Maybe you will have to make several trips before you achieve that desired win goal. Setting achievable win goals is part of the art of patience.

I call it the "art" of patience because that's what it is. Patience is not a skill and it is not science. Skills can be learned. Science can be learned. But you are born with the *ability* to be patient. The vast majority of all of us are born with the ability to learn languages, to deal with our environment through our senses, and to find out how to survive. These are all inherent abilities. We also have the ability to be patient. Unfortunately, the pace of our modern world rarely rewards patience, at least visibly. Although most achievements that we see publicly are the result of hard work and a lot of patience, when we see these achievements they have already happened. To us, they seem to have happened overnight. The old story among actors who finally gain star status goes something like this: "After thirty years of acting, suddenly I'm an overnight success." This is also true for many other disciplines. These examples are here to demonstrate that success playing Keno is not merely that once-in-a-lifetime blind-luck event. You can be successful as a keno player each time you play, overall throughout your career as a player of Keno, but only if you *develop* your art of patience. Notice I said *develop*, rather than acquire. This is because patience is an art, and you already possess that ability. Like the ability to draw, you must practice and learn, learn from doing, and learn from mistakes. It won't be easy, but then nothing worthwhile usually is. Developing patience means that you will curb your natural reactions. These are the emotional bursts, such as exuberance when you win and anger when you lose. Both are the extremes along the scale upon which the pendulum of your keno success swings.

First, the trick to developing the art of patience when playing Keno is to realize that great and glorious wins *will* happen and equally great and horrendous *losses* will happen too. Second, you will learn to develop your ability to curb your reactions to those extremes. Be happy when you win, but remember that this is not an event that will always happen like this. Remember that the money you *don't* lose back today will spend very nicely tomorrow, with a cooler head and a clearer perspective. When you lose, at the other extreme end of the spectrum, curb your reaction equally. Don't start to question yourself beyond reason. If you feel you have forgotten some part of your knowledge, by all means look it up. See if you were correct, and if so, learn from the experience. When you realize that you did everything correctly, and still suffered that great and horrendous loss, then curb your instinct to blame everything and everybody, and try not to destroy yourself, or the solid foundations of your keno-playing abilities. Remember that this is just the other part of the spectrum, and that in this instance, the pendulum of overall probability simply swung against you. It will swing back. It may take what you consider a long time. The phrase "a long time" means to us, as human beings, something entirely different than to the universal event statistics. What you may consider as "a long time" may in reality only be a tiny fraction of a microsecond in the overall scope of universal time. It's all relative. If you play Keno for two hours and you don't reach your win goal, was that losing streak "a long time"? Well, for you, perhaps, but the universe doesn't revolve around your particular perception of reality or time. Patience, therefore, is the art of being able to react to each situation *without overreacting to it*—and that's where the greatest benefit lies. You will have to work this out yourself, because no two people deal with the same set of circumstances in exactly the same way. Therefore, no specific advice is possible. However, a plausible guideline to achieving patience *is* possible, and it's important that you understand that cultivating patience will not only enable you to play Keno better, but will also allow you to reach your comfort level far quicker and with far more positive results. By realizing that patience is a requirement for enjoyment, and profit, from your play, you will become far more at ease with the process. Patience will allow you to relax under a variety of circumstances and situations and to take a far more rational, and less emotional, approach to whatever these situations bring.

BANKROLL

All of these Keys to Winning are important, but bankroll is perhaps the foremost. The reason is quite simple: Without money, you can't gamble. Gambling is all about money. Losing money and, of course, winning money. You must have it to start. You can't start without it. Even credit is money, and so is a credit line at the casino. It doesn't matter how you acquire your money, but whatever money you bring with you, or send to the casino cage, or get in credit at the casino, constitutes your bankroll. This is the money you have designated as your gambling money, your gambling stake. It should not be money for your family's rent, mortgage, food, clothing, health care, and so on. This should be accumulated "spare" money, something you can afford to lose without such loss having a devastating impact on you and your family. Any gambling bankroll should be made up of money that you have designated as *expendable*. This doesn't mean that it should be treated as already lost, and hence treated recklessly. After all, it's still money. You may have worked for it for a year, or more, and saved it up for your casino trip. Or, you may have accumulated it through interest on investments, or from the sale of something you made, or sold, and you don't need the overage for your survival. However it is still your money, and even though it's considered as expendable, it is still *important* money and should be highly regarded. It was your work that made it possible. Just because you designate it as your gambling money, doesn't mean it has suddenly lost its value. It still spends just the same.

Many people make the classic mistake of setting aside their gambling money with the conviction that it's already gone, dead, done, lost, and therefore it means nothing. Wrong! This is a defeatist attitude. Thinking like this will result in two inevitable occurrences. First, you have already convinced yourself that you are a loser, that you will lose, and therefore this money is already lost. Thus, you will gamble recklessly, without thought or regard to the value of the money, or the consequences of your reckless actions. You will lose, and this will reinforce your conviction that "Ah, well, it was already lost. I knew it."

Second, you will not play knowledgeably, and certainly not in concert with these Keys to Winning. So, again, you will lose. When you do, this becomes yet another reinforcement of your initial starting attitude. "So," you now say to yourself, and quite possibly to anyone who will listen, "it was only gambling money. I knew I was gonna lose it, so what? It was my 'mad' money, anyway. Ah, well. Maybe next time." You have now thoroughly convinced yourself that you are a loser, and justified your initial defeatist attitude by making sure that you lost.

Your bankroll is your gambling lifeline. It is essential. It should be protected and handled with care. In addition, it must be sufficient to carry the weight of your action. How much is in this bankroll should be determined by several factors. First, it depends on what this money means to you at that time. If this money is truly unencumbered, then you will feel a lot better about making it a true bankroll. If this money is not completely unencumbered, such as when a portion of it should be used for something else, but that something else is not one of the essentials to survival, then maybe you will not handle the bankroll as well, or it may not be big enough. As a general rule, a gambling bankroll should be made up only of money that is entirely unencumbered, and no part of it is needed, or could be even considered as being needed, for something else. Unencumbered money is free, and not scared. Encumbered money will always be scared money, and in gambling, scared money will fly away quickly. Playing with scared money means you are afraid to lose it. If you have allocated part of your bankroll either as an inadequate amount, or encumbered upon something else, like borrowed from a credit card (which means you will have to pay it back, and probably have to do so at great stress to you, or your family), you have made a bad start to your bankroll. Always start your bankroll with free money, which will become a solid gambling stake and not frightened at the prospect of being lost.

Second, the amount of your bankroll should be determined by the kind of game you intend to play. If you want to play $75 per ticket in Keno, then your bankroll should reflect that action. If you want to play higher limits than that, then your bankroll should certainly be equally higher. If you plan to play $1 Keno, or the Video Keno, which may be nickels but requires you to play $2 per pull (40 coins), or more, then your bankroll should adjust to that. In addition, whatever your action, or intended action, your bankroll should be adequate to withstand fluctuations, not only in your fortunes as you play, but also in your decisions concerning the *kinds* of games you will play. For example, you may have decided to play $1 Keno on this trip, and allocated your bankroll for that action. But when you get to the casino, you discover that the kinds of games you wanted to play have been changed, payoffs reduced, no longer available, or the keno game is gone, or any number of factors that work against your predesigned plan. Now what? Your bankroll should have a "slush" factor, allowing it to withstand the necessity for such on-the-spot decisions. What if you saw another kind of game, perhaps a keno game in a different casino and with different payoffs? Your bankroll should be adaptable to such deviations from your initial starting strategy, and perception of what your action will be.

How do you arrive at the bankroll figure? Hard to say. You know yourself, and your circumstances. I don't. Therefore, all I can do is offer you *guidelines*, with the hope that you will learn enough from reading this book to adapt this guideline to your specific situation. If you plan to play about four hours per day, for an average of three days, then I can offer the guidelines listed in the chart below.

$1 Keno	=	$ 500	minimum
$5 Keno	=	$1,000	minimum
Multi-way at $1 per way	=	$1,500	minimum (depending on tickets)
Multi-way at $0.50 per way	=	$ 750	minimum (depending on tickets)
Progressive Keno at $2 +	=	$ 800	minimum (based on *single* tickets)

Some of these amounts may seem very high to you (or perhaps very low!) but that is because I have no way of knowing exactly how aggressive you may be in your keno game. Perhaps you may have a larger bankroll than others, and decide to use my multi-way ticket examples for really aggressive play, maybe even combining the tickets and adding progressives. You per-game expenditure could easily be $100 per ticket, or even more. For others, perhaps the approach is in the more moderate category. How do you judge? The only sure way to find out is to analyze your own financial situation, your own abilities and dedication to the game, and your goals. Put all of that together with the other Keys to Winning, and the rest of the information and knowledge in this book, and you will be well on your way toward making the best decision possible.

Just to make certain that I make this point quite clear, I

can assure you that you can play Keno very enjoyably for a total $100 bankroll, divided into three sessions of about $33 each. Playing some of my more moderate keno ticket examples, such as the 2/3 and 1/6 ticket at the 50-cent rate, makes your per-game cost only $1.50. Playing this way with a $33 bankroll should assure you about four hours of fun. It's all highly relative to you, and your goals, expectations, and ability to sustain losses while awaiting the wins, and how much you are able to allocate to your bankroll. These factors, combined with all of the others shown here, ultimately determine where you can reasonably expect to be in your bankroll decisions and resultant game and ticket value decisions.

SELECTION

This is the part where "skill" in your play comes into the picture. Many people believe that when playing Keno, winning is purely dependent on luck. While it is correct that Keno is a passive game and, therefore, you cannot control the outcome of the event, it is not correct to say that playing Keno involves no skills. I don't mean merely the skills of being able to mark a ticket. I am referring to skills such as game and ticket selection, how many ways, size of the wager selection, split rates or not, how many split rates and why, reduced rates or not and why, add progressives or not, play small ways conservatively or aggressively, load the bigger pays with higher wagers or not, payoff tables, multi-way and multi-ticket play selections, play methodology selection, size of bankroll, play duration, time *when* to play, casinos *where* to play, and other various applied skills that you will acquire as you continue reading this book. There is a lot more to being a winning keno player than to just show up in the casino, mark a ticket, and hand your money over the counter.

Each of these skills is part of the "learning curve," and "comfort zone," which all of us have to reach. By acquiring these skills, you can become not only more knowledgeable, but also more comfortable. You will find that you are no longer a victim to the mere chance of luckily selecting just the right numbers at the right time, but actually be able to select the right ticket with the right combinations and ways for the right reasons. You will now be able to approach your casino visit with the ability to look for the kinds of situations you know are among the better options, and do so with a solid plan of attack. Not only will this result in more confidence and comfort for you when you play, but it will directly translate to regular profits. Although you won't win every time, or perhaps achieve your win goal every time you play, you will now be able to realize that this is a part of the overall approach to the game. You will no longer be a victim of emotional swings, such as deep disappointment when you don't win or reckless exuberance when you do. Although curbing these emotional reactions is part of patience, as discussed above, and also discipline, discussed below, these Selection skills will contribute to your overall Keys to Winning. You will know what to look for, and how to play the game to your best advantage.

DISCIPLINE

Of all the Keys to Winning, this one sounds the simplest, but is the hardest of them all. Most of us understand the value of discipline, especially when it comes to our money. This is accentuated when we talk about the casino environment. Everything in the casino is designed to separate us from any sense of reality. The casinos are a wondrous land, where everything seems possible, as long as you still have money. The money is the lifeblood of all of this excitement. Without it, you are nothing more than dead wood, and you will be flushed out in a hurry. Having discipline as part of your winning objectives saves you from the inglorious fate of being washed clean, hung out to dry, and tossed away as yet another of the ill-prepared and unwary. Having discipline as part of your tricks of the trade when you gamble simply means to make the commitment to play wisely, with reason, with goals in mind, and with all of the empowering Keys to Winning, as well as all the other information I have shared here. If you want to have your "mad time," that's okay too. Budget for it, realize it, recognize it, place it as part of your overall game plan. That, too, will then become part of your discipline as long as you don't let the thrill overwhelm you, drowning all your plans and your discipline along with it.

Unfortunately, *making* a commitment to self-discipline when going to the casino is very easy. *Keeping to it* once you get to the casino is very hard. So hard, in fact, that the vast majority of people who arrive at the casino completely convinced they will not allow this experience to get the better of them, do just that. And fast—sometimes as soon as they walk through the door. Suddenly, they see all the excitement, games, and flashing lights, and hear the sounds of money and chips—the entire atmosphere captures them. In the door they go, and out the door go all of their well-meaning and carefully conceived plans, their sense of discipline, and their other senses as well. It happens to just about everyone, even hardened veterans of the casino lifestyle. All of us are mere human beings, and we are not perfect. We have failures, and the lack of discipline is the greatest failure of us all. We see it everywhere around us. Schools no longer insist on discipline. Rowdy and disruptive students are no longer punished. They are "counseled" instead. We are producing a society where none of the adults have any idea of what discipline is. When they are faced with it—when they enter the workforce, or the armed services—they are in complete shock. No wonder that most people who go to casinos can't understand what "discipline" really is, and how it applies to their gaming success or financial failure.

Discipline in gambling simply means to remain conscious of the value of your money, and conscious of your desired goals and objectives. It means not allowing yourself to be drawn into the comfortable, but financially deadly, sense of "why not, it's only money" syndrome. Once you have experienced the casino lifestyle a few times, you will often hear many people say things like that. These people are probably trapped in the losses they have incurred, and are now trying to rationalize it for themselves. They don't actually expect anyone to listen to them, or to really understand what expressions such as this really mean. They have just resigned themselves to the loss of all their money, and to the "I no longer care" attitude. That's the danger sign. Once you stop caring about the value of the money you are using to play—or are winning—then you have lost the discipline that comes with realizing that this money is not just coins, tokens, or gaming chips. This money actually spends, buying food, gas for your car, paying bills, and so on. It is real money, and it has real meaning. Therefore, discipline really means just to remember this, and play accordingly.

This *doesn't* mean that you should be a miser. Playing too carefully is also a prescription for disaster. I have already mentioned that "scared" money flies away quickly. Don't play that way. To win, you must play aggressively and with a sufficient bankroll to justify your level of action. All of this is covered in the other Keys to Winning. Discipline is the glue that holds it all together. Once the glue stops holding, it all falls apart.

WIN GOALS

What is a win goal? In simplest terms, a win goal is the realistic expectation of a certain win amount, based on the potential of available wins relative to the bankroll allowed, session stake allocated, expertise at the game, plus time at the game. This simple formula will equal your end-result profitability, in winning situations, and end-result saving of money that would have been lost in negative situations.

For example, most gamblers will say that a 2 percent win goal over and above the session stake is a very great achievement. The casino, for example, has a win goal of around 2 percent for most blackjack games, an average of about 24 percent for Keno, and about 20 percent over all the games they offer. Some games net casinos more money because people will play them badly. Although basic Blackjack, for example, can be played to less than 0.5 percent casino advantage, most players will play the game so badly that the casinos actually yield anywhere from 2 to 6 percent, and often even more, on a game which can actually yield a *player* advantage if played properly and with skill.*

For Keno, the average expectation is around 24 percent to perhaps 48 percent, depending on the casino, where it is located, and what the competition is like. In Las Vegas, the casinos count on around 25 percent as their *average* win goal for all of their keno games. The difference between the casino and the player is that the casino can easily have a much lower win goal because their doors are open 24/7/365. Their games make money all the time—every hour, every day, every week, every month, every year, without ever needing a rest or break. Human players can't play like that. Though the casino can offer a game in which it can reasonably expect

---

*For more information on Blackjack, I refer you to my book *Powerful Profits from Blackjack*.

only less than 1 percent profit, it will get this all the time, always, over the short term as well as the long haul. You, the player, can't play like that. Therefore, whenever gamblers say to me that they expect a 2 percent return and consider this as good, I politely tell them that's great, and quietly chuckle. These "gamblers" are trying to play like the casino, trying to beat the casino at their own game of survival—trying to "outlast" the overall game percentages. This will result in nothing more than the gambler's eventual ruin, and a whole lot of frustration in between. Gamblers in general, and keno players in particular, must have win goals not only commensurate with their bankroll, session stakes, and so on, as listed earlier, but also with the realization that their exposure to the game will only be a very short slice of the game's overall event-reality. Therefore, such win goals cannot— and should not—be measured in percentages relative to the way that the casinos figure their own odds and win goals. Rather, these win goals should be measured in terms of what the game *can yield*, especially if played correctly, and if selected in accordance with the various selection criteria listed earlier. It is also important at this point to introduce a derivative of the win-goal criterion, called the "win expectation."

The win goal is what you have set as your desired objective, realistically based on the various principles already amply demonstrated. The win *expectation*, however, is based within the reality of the game itself and, most specifically, in that very short-term slice of that one specific game's event experience. The point is that throughout your casino visit, no playing session is ever independent of your other sessions. All your keno playing sessions are combined to reveal, in the end as you go home, the entire block of all sessions. Whatever results you have achieved at that point determine your average per session win-expectation percentage, and your win-goal achievement levels. You can then use this information to indicate how well you played, and to modify your goals and expectations for future visits. But you must take *everything* into account, even the value of all the additions you have earned, such as your comps and freebies, and club points. All of this combines to affect your goals, expectations, and final relative results.

This now brings us to the final item in this chapter, and that is the overall win goals and overall win expectation. This is set by you based on bankroll, skill, and other abilities, as well as whatever other information and skills you may have acquired. Your total win goal for your casino visit should be directly relative to your bankroll and comfort level at the games, as well as your other gaming and playing skills, including selection skills.

As a guide, your overall win *goal* should be to double your bankroll. Your win *expectation* should be to come home with 20 percent over and above your bring-in bankroll. If you achieve anything close to this, then you have just beaten the casino, and the keno game, and you have done what fewer than 1 percent of all casino players are able to do. You have become a good, knowledgeable, and responsible player. Congratulations!

Where to Play

In this chapter, I want to share with you some of the "selection" information in greater detail as it applies to the selection of a casino. Many keno games are offered in many casinos throughout the United States, and elsewhere in the world. Even by limiting the "where to play" selection criteria to only the United States, it would be nearly impossible to list every casino and its keno game. There are keno rate cards in every casino in the USA! The purpose of presenting a guide to "where" to play is in the skills it will provide for you to learn how to do this yourself. Once you understand the principles, you will be able to go to any casino and make your decisions immediately, as you read that casino's rate card. If you don't want to go through all of these calculations, simply ask the casino's keno manager, marketing director, or player's representative what their house hold is on their keno game (or games if they have more than one lounge keno game). It is part of their regulatory disclosure, and is public information, so they must tell you. If they don't, insist. It's no secret, and they shouldn't make it one.

The chart below shows the house hold for several casinos. By using this chart for comparison purposes, you will be able to decide whether your particular casino is, or is not, a candidate for your keno play. Since I live in Las Vegas, it is easier for me to use Las Vegas casinos as my examples. However, by simply asking your casino for their keno house hold percentage, you will be able to compare that figure with the figures in this chart. This will provide you with the information you need to make your selection of "where" to play much more intelligently than if you merely showed up at the casino and began to play blindly. It is a useful tool to help you learn just exactly how good, or

Average House Withholding Percentage on Lounge Keno Games in Las Vegas

CASINO	HOUSE HOLD (%)	CASINO	HOUSE HOLD (%)
Silverton	20	Sahara	29
Arizona Charlie's	25	Luxor	30
Frontier	25	Circus Circus	30
Jerry's Nugget	25	Main Street Station	30
Nevada Palace	25	California	30
Orleans	25	Riviera	31
Gold Coast	25	Stardust	31
Sam's Town	25	Plaza	31
Las Vegas Club	27	San Remo	31
Rio	27	Aladdin	32
Mirage	28	Fremont	32
Bellagio	28	Four Queens	32
Golden Nugget	28	Bally's	32
MGM Grand	29	Treasure Island	33
New York-New York	29	Caesars Palace	33
Hilton	29	Station Casinos	33
Fitzgeralds	29	Palms	34
Western	29	Monte Carlo	34

how bad, your casino's payback percentage for Lounge Keno actually is.

It is important to remember that these are averages. At each of these casinos, there are some pays that are better, and other pays that aren't as good as in some of the other casinos. I mentioned this earlier, and it is an important part of your skills and strategy: Check the rate cards at each casino and compare the pays for all the ways you wish to play. Pay particular attention to the smaller pays, because that's where the "meat" of your tickets is, and where the biggest swings are, from casino to casino, in payback percentages. For example, some casinos pay on 8-spots only for hits from 5 out of 8 and higher, while other casinos begin their payback at even money on hits of on 4 out of the 8. These are the casinos with the better payback percentage on this ticket, but be careful also to check the other pays. Often the casino offering the more frequently hit pay will "fudge" by "charging" more than that pay in some other form, such as reducing the pay for the 5 out of 8 and 6 out of 8 to much less than at other casinos, comparatively speaking. This is similar for other pays, including reduced-rate pay schedules.

Your best strategy is first to collect the rate cards from all the casinos you plan to visit, or from all the casinos in your area of interest, or where you are planning to go. You can get them easily: just call the casino, ask for the Keno Department, and request that they mail you their keno pay rate brochure. Or, if you are already in the gaming city, you can go to all the casinos yourself and get these brochures, or even ask the casinos to send them to where you are staying. Once you have all the rate cards, compare them with each other and then compare your selections to the house withholding percentage chart. If your selected casino is among the top ten or better listed here, then you have a good game. If not, then you will have to choose more carefully, and perhaps select only those tickets from that casino's brochure that actually are the better pays. Always remember that the chart in this book is only the average house hold, and that even casinos that are at the bottom of that scale sometimes have tickets that are very good candidates for your play.

The way these house hold percentages are calculated is to take a section of the most common paybacks for the average tickets combined and then fractionalize them to arrive at the average house hold over the entire game, as opposed to any individual ticket or payback. Although these percentages are actually fractions, I have rounded them off to the nearest whole number equivalent. Many of the casinos listed as, for example, a house hold of 25 percent, are within less than 1 percent of each other in terms of fractions. One casino among these may have a house hold of 25.2 percent, while the next one can have 24.87 percent, and so on, but they are statistically so close that it is easier to represent their average house hold in whole numbers. By this being the average, this also means that some of their tickets may actually have a much lower house edge on them, while some of the other tickets may have a higher house edge than could be considered normal. It all depends, and that's why your investigation of exactly what pays what is important, particularly the comparison of these pay rate brochures among all the casinos you plan to visit.

Some of these casinos may have bad pays on the more frequently played and more popular tickets, while they have extremely lucrative pays on the less-popular, or more complex tickets. Other casinos may have better paybacks and lower house hold on some of their reduced-rate tickets, as I mentioned earlier, where the calculation of the correct payback fractions may not be exact and, as a result, some of these lower rates on some tickets may be actually a better bet than on the full rates. A lot of this will depend on you, and must depend on you, because the situations change, the casinos change, and so do their pay schedules and house hold percentages. Your skills in being able to adapt and make this research and information work for you is what will differentiate you from the regular keno crowd. You'll be able to substantially reduce the house withholding percentage on many of your tickets, even as far as making the game actually yield you a positive profit when you play the good tickets well, and in casinos where the payback is the best and highest for such tickets and rates.

Generally, your best guide is to first look at the casino's pay rate brochure. Even without all of the comparisons—which you really should do, but many of you may not wish to do because "it sounds too much like real work and too much effort"—the brochure can give you an indication of whether this casino is, or is not, a good one in which to play your lounge keno tickets. To accomplish this, the chart below shows what to look for in the pays on the key tickets, all based on the $1 rate.

If the 8-spot ticket does not pay at least as shown, it's not your best casino. However, if this casino only starts with a 5-out-of-8 pay, but pays $5 or more for 5 out of 8, and $100 or more for 6 out of 8, then you may consider playing there, but understand that this is a casino that is "top heavy," meaning one whose majority payback is in the harder-to-hit higher pays, and the majority of its house hold percentage is in the low pays, or they don't pay anything at all for the small pay. Also be wary of casinos that will pay for 4 out of

TYPE OF TICKET	KEY HITS	SHOULD PAY
8-spot	4	$1 for 4 out of 8 (or even money)
	5	$3–$5 for 5 out of 8
	6	$75–$100 for 6 out of 8

8, but only pay less than $1—or less than even money. That's a clear indication this casino is trying to hide something, and make their pays look good, when in fact they are making you pay for the win.

TYPE OF TICKET	KEY HITS	SHOULD PAY
6-spot	3	$1 for 3 out of 6 (or even money)
	4	$3–$5 for 4 out of 6
	5	$75–$120 for 5 out of 6

If the 6-spot doesn't pay anything for the 3-out-of-6 hit, or pays less than even money back, don't play this ticket or any 6-spot ticket in that casino. Look carefully at all the other tickets and pays as well. This could be one among those casinos that try to get most of their profits from this game by eliminating, or lowering, some of the very common and frequent pays on the most popular and often-recommended tickets.

TYPE OF TICKET	KEY HITS	SHOULD PAY
7-spot	4	$1 for 4 out of 7 (or even money)
	5	$20–$50 for 5 out of 7
	6	$400 for 6 out of 7 (minimum)

Your keys to look for in these tickets are the pays for the 5 and 6, because you may need to compare the differences. Some casinos may pay $30, or $40, or even $50 for the 5-out-of-7 hit, but then reduce the pay on the 6-out-of-7 hit to only $325, $350, or $375. This may make the 7-spot ticket a more viable candidate for some of the way tickets in my "Best Tickets" examples (chapter 4) where we have a choice of playing more, or fewer, 7-spots on the multi-way tickets. However, the lower pays on 6 out of 7 may not fully compensate for this, so be careful as to how and *why* you select the 7-spots.

TYPE OF TICKET	KEY HITS	SHOULD PAY
10-spot	5	$1 for 5 out of 10 (or even money)
	6	$12–$25 for 6 out of 10
	7	$142–$180 for 7 out of 10
	8	$1,000 for 8 out of 10 (minimum)

The indicators of this ticket are mostly in the 7 and 8 hits out of 10. If this casino doesn't pay at least $142 for the 7-out-of-8 hit, then you are better off not playing there, and perhaps better off playing the 10-spot straight up ticket on a video keno machine. If this casino doesn't pay at least a minimum of $1,000 for 8 out of 10, then there's no excuse for this, and you should not play there, and certainly not play these tickets. Also take a close look at the smaller pays, because some casinos often drop the 5-out-of-10 pay in the same manner as they drop the 5-out-of-8 pay, further increasing their overall average house hold over their keno game.

These four selections—the 6-spot, the 7-spot, the 8-spot, and the 10-spot examples—are the keys by which you can quickly determine whether this casino's keno game is, or is not, among the better games to play. These pays are a window into the rest of the game and that game's payback percentage and, conversely, the house withholding percentage over the average. Make no mistake about it:—If you don't know this, or don't know what this means and how it will affect you, your money, your bankroll, and your profitability, then you will not be able to make those powerful profits from Keno to which you can easily be entitled. This is not a mystery—simply some brain work and application of the other information and skills I have shown you in this book. Even if you don't wish to go through the grind of getting all those pay schedules from all those casinos, and then charting the comparisons of all their pays, you can make a quick decision and determination simply by checking these key indicators on these four tickets, and those rates. If the casino where you are has pays that are close to these, then you are playing in a casino whose average house withholding percentage over this keno game is about 25 percent, and certainly in the range of between 25 and 30 percent. This is about as close as you can get to making such a quick determination, without additional analyses and comparisons of individual items, but this will help. It will make it possible for you to make these judgments quickly, and you will generally be able to play in such casinos. Nevertheless, I would like to advise you that a little more information, in addition to this "quick glance," will serve you well. Take a little more time, and investigate a little closer, look at the fractions of paybacks for reduced rates. Those efforts will provide you with an even bigger opportunity to make more powerful, and more powerfully profitable, keno plays.

Strategy for Lounge Keno

I know several people who claim that there is no such thing as a strategy for Keno. Mostly, these are the same people who claim that a negative-expectation game can never be beaten for profit, no matter what, and because of that no strategy for such games is possible. Unfortunately, these are often the same people who habitually play casino games in an effort to validate the game's statistics, blissfully ignorant of the fact that the statistics and probabilities they hold so dear are the result of an infinite sampling of events and therefore none of their short-term event slices of that experience will ever mirror exactly their perceived and expected probability of success. These people are so trapped inside their small box of dogmas that they fail to consider the possibility that something may exist outside of their box, or that they actually *are* inside a small box, limiting their understanding of everything. Any challenge to what they consider as the absolute truth leaves them cold. They are comfortable in the dogma, secure in the limitations of what they think is knowledge, and viciously defend anything they perceive as an attack on these "truths," conveniently for-getting even their own admission that there can be no such thing as a defined truth. Although they think that truth is something real, tangible, and understandable—something that can be delineated, such as mathematical equations—they are willing to accept it *only in so far as it fits within their perceptions, and their understanding.* Thinking within these walls of their box makes it easy for them to function. As a result they often refuse to even discuss, much less consider, the *possibility* that something else may exist, or that it could be useful in some way.

Our world is literally plagued by this sort of limited think-ing. You can see it everywhere, in magazines, newspapers, schools, science, and—most clearly—in gambling and gam-bling literature. Nearly everything you read will be presented from within limitations and box-like thinking, particularly a slavish reliance on mathematics, percentages and proba-bilities.

Though I have said many times that strategizing and an-alyzing of casino games *is very useful as a guideline*, I have also clearly stated that *overreliance on this* is equally as foolhardy as ignoring it. Knowing what pays what, how much, under what circumstances, and what the odds are against, or what the percentage payback may be are important as-pects of your overall gambling knowledge, and of your ex-pertise in the game. These items of knowledge we can all share in common, and *knowing* this is better than *not* know-ing it. Unfortunately, for most people—readers and authors—that's where the story of gambling and gambling games begins and ends. It either *is* a mathematically beatable game, or it's *not*. That's it, and that's as far as everything usually goes.

As a result, all strategies require players to play in a man-ner that validates the stats, rather than in a manner that makes money. Although playing that way and making money are not always mutually exclusive, the greatest fallacy in all mathematically based strategies for casino games is that no player will ever play any such games precisely and exactly to the laboratory conditions that were the basis for the mathematical and probability calculation analysis, nor will they ever play any of these games for anything even close to the number of events that are required to provide even the most rudimentary of statistical samplings. As a direct consequence of this, virtually all strategies that use probabilities and statistics *as their foundation* are in error unless they are used merely as guidelines upon which workability and adaptability can be hinged.

I am *not* anti-mathematics, anti-statistics, or anti-probabilicist—in fact, I am not anti-anything. On the contrary, I have always stated that more knowledge is always better, and even the knowledge of the math, stats, and probabilities and odds is better than none. But these are *not the only items of knowledge* you ought to consider when making strategy decisions for your gambling, nor the only means by which you can secure a profit playing these games.

As with most things in life, there are more ways than one to look at the same thing. So it is with gambling games, and so it is with Keno. Although Keno may be considered by most math-oriented players as a terrible house game, it need not be so. Even the worst-paying slots have to pay off sometimes, otherwise no one would ever play them and, consequently, they would not be on the casino floor taking up valuable space. Keno *does* pay. And yes, Keno can, and does, have a high house edge and high odds against for many of the big-money hits. But it also has comparatively better odds than some other games.

Let's revisit the video poker example: For a standard video poker game, on a quarter machine, the investment per hand is $1.25—five quarters. The top jackpot is $1,000. The odds against are about 40,400:1. In Keno, playing a 10-spot, you can wager a mere $1 per game. The odds of hitting 8 out of 10 are about 7,384:1 against, for a pay of $1,000. This is the same $1,000 pay that costs $1.25 per hand on Video Poker, with odds of 40,400:1 against. So, let us think along with the mathematicians, and ask: Which is the "better" game, odds wise? Even the math experts and statisticians would agree that given the objective of achieving a $1,000 pay, the game that costs only $1 and faces odds of only 7,384:1 is better than the game that costs $1.25 per hand and faces odds of 40,400:1 against for the same value jackpot.

I mention this example again to illustrate just how flawed the many erroneous perceptions about Keno are, and how deeply rooted they can be even among those experts whose own numbers refute that dogmatically entrenched perception. Even when considering Keno from within the statistical model of understanding, it should be obvious that while Keno is not among the *best* casino games—odds wise—it certainly is not among the worst, particularly when it can be very favorably compared with games that even experts agree can be positive-expectation games, such as Video Poker.

All that you have read so far has been necessary as background for the strategy information that now follows. Because Keno has a "bad rap" in the casinos, players have come to think of it only as a diversion, a costly game with little or no potential for wins, and a terrible house game to boot. As a result, casinos have come to think of the game as a necessary evil, because it is so labor intensive and so slow and played by so few players. Misperceptions about the game cause players to think they can't win, and casinos to think they won't make enough money to warrant keeping the game, or at least keeping it at the forefront of their gaming mix.

I am writing for the players, not the casinos, and I urge you to learn to select your tickets wisely and play smart tickets intelligently. If you do that you can substantially enhance your win potential, reduce the odds against you and the costs of your gambling sessions, and provide yourself with the best chances to make a lot of money from small stakes. To that end, some strategy guidelines follow to help you with those decisions.

SIMPLE STRATEGY GUIDELINES FOR LOUNGE KENO

• Play way tickets only. Use groups (as shown in the chapter on Best Tickets), and learn to make your own tickets to adapt to the game as it is being played, to circumstances as they change, and to your own abilities, goals, objectives, and financial situations.

• Be flexible. Change your method of play as the circumstances warrant. Be more aggressive and play more tickets and more ways when you are hitting frequently and making more wins. Play higher value win ways for higher per way amounts when you are ahead, and reduce your costs when you are not hitting and are falling behind.

• Start by selecting tickets with the greatest potential to pay for themselves along the way, while you are waiting for the big hit. All of the tickets shown as samples in the chapter on Best Tickets were designed precisely for that purpose. Adapt them as you go along.

• Experiment. Don't be afraid to try different tickets differently, particularly if you spot a trend in the game you are playing. Try to do this after you have had some wins so you play with money won, rather than money brought with you. It is easier to try new things when you do so with winnings rather than with your own original bring-in bankroll.

• Keno numbers tend to run in groups. Look at the groups they form on the flashboard, or TV screen display. Sometimes they will run top to bottom, making vertical groups.

Sometimes they will run side to side, making horizontal groups. And sometimes they may run in groups of three, like a triangle, or as groups of twos, either horizontally, or vertically. While neither the Keno game nor the numbers have any "memory," and as a result each game is an independent event, as you play the game and gain familiarity with it you will see that there are *patterns* that happen, and while you may not be able to pick exactly which numbers will come up, you may be able to exploit the patterns as you recognize them and to adapt your tickets accordingly. This is particularly useful when you are playing way tickets, because these tickets give you the opportunity to do this. Although you may not wish to change the ticket you happen to be playing, you may want to add another ticket to it where you use the new number combinations you have been seeing in those patterns during the games. These observational skills are similar to those used by blackjack players, poker players, dice players—in fact all kinds of gamblers, including professionals.

• Before starting your session, ask the keno writer for a printout of the last twenty games. Many times they will have a punch-card copy on a hook, or spike, behind the keno counter and they will let you look at it. If they don't, they will print out a series of past games tickets, although you may have to settle for only ten. Try to ask for the punch-card copies first, because there you may be able to see more than the past twenty games. This is useful if you wish to see the kinds of patterns that the keno numbers have been forming before you start playing. While useful as an example of the recent history of the game, do not become too attached to it. Remember that *this is only information about past events, and that past events have no bearing on the present or the future.* This exercise is useful as another means of acquiring additional knowledge. I do this myself, because I have found it to be of great advantage when facing a decision about which kinds of tickets to play. Sometimes it tells me that the horizontal groups may be better, or the vertical, and so on—or perhaps a combination.

• Request a "hit frequency" printout. This is a computerized printout of the last twenty games or so—more if you can get them—that shows how many times each number was drawn. Again, this is useful as an example of what may be happening in that short term. Theoretically, any of the eighty numbers in the bubble, or bird cage, should have the exact same chance of being selected during any one game. *Theoretically.* However, as I hope you have learned by now, what the theory *says* and what actually *happens* in the real world are very different situations.

In the real world, nothing is perfect. The blowers and tumblers may not be exactly precise, and may be selecting certain numbers more often simply by the accident of their imperfection, no matter how tiny. In the real world, keno balls get dirty. Although they are cleaned every twenty-four hours, and even replaced once a month (or even more frequently), the fact remains that they aren't perfect. Some may have manufacturing flaws, or be heavier or lighter than others, even by a micron. All of this—and many other such situations—make the game far from that nice, clean theory. In the real world some numbers are drawn more frequently than others—whatever the cumulative reasons may be. By obtaining a printout of the hit frequency of numbers for as many games as you can, you will be able to see which of these numbers may currently be among such anomalous draws. As you play the game, you can continually update your list and see how this is bearing out. Then you can decide either to add these numbers to your selections or to delete them in favor of others.

Playing Keno for profit also means you discard any preconceived notions of playing numbers such as birthdays, anniversaries, and such. None of this should have any bearing on your keno number selections. You should pick numbers and number groups for your way tickets based on as much information as you can get, and then work the game as it happens and adapt accordingly. That's your ticket to profits: eliminating as much of the chance as you possibly can, while realizing that it is still a random event. However, by using this information you will be able to make better decisions more often, which will help defray your costs and increase your wins.

• Never play for 2s and 3s unless they are part of the sample tickets I have shown in the chapter on Best Tickets.

• Never play fewer than five numbers, or more than ten numbers, unless they are in groups on way tickets.

• When making groups on way tickets, never make more groups than you can afford to bet, or bet low-value groups, or make multiple-way groups that will result in too many ways. Multi-way tickets are good as long as you keep them simple and play only those groups with the highest replay value and highest win value. (Again see my sample tickets, which can be adapted to additional ways and groups.)

• Wheel your tickets. Wheeling, a lottery concept, means to select core groups of numbers that will remain the same for multiple tickets. For example, if you are playing a group ticket with one of my sample 6-spots, and you also want to play another ticket with one of my sample 8-spots, plus perhaps my sample 9-spot and even perhaps my sample 10-spot, then use the original 6-spot numbers in *all* your tickets—meaning you "wheel" them as your "core" numbers, so that if any of them hit they will also hit on all of your other tickets. Of course if they all hit, you have multiple winners on all of your tickets, and this is why wheeling numbers is always a good idea. This is also the best way to play Video Keno in a game called Four Card Keno, which I will discuss in Part Two of this book.

- Cross-bet your way tickets. In addition to "wheeling" your numbers, it is also often profitable to cross-bet your way tickets. For example, you may be playing 8-spot tickets such as the ones previously shown in Figures 12 and 13 using the "columns method" of playing, a method whereby all your eight numbers are along the *columns*, vertically from top to bottom. There are ten such columns, the first starting with the number 1 at the top and the number 71 at the bottom, making a total of eight numbers in that column. This is the "ones" column. There are a total of ten such columns of eight on a standard keno ticket, from numbers 1 through 10. By placing your 8-spot groups all in such a column, you are enhancing the value of your ticket, because keno numbers often group in such columns. Although statistically no number selections have any more chance to be drawn than any other (as I have said numerous times) over-reliance on purely statistical theories is not the only skill to making powerful profits from Keno. Trend spotting is at the very core of many time-honored and established gambling strategies, even for games often cited by theoretical purists.

As you play keno, you will see groupings of hits of 5, 6, and 7—and even 8—numbers all in a column, top to bottom along the same vertical lineup. If you see such groupings in your keno game, it may be advisable to add such a ticket to your play, using one or both of the 8-spot examples as shown in Figures 12 and 13. Furthermore, you may wish to expand your play into a more aggressive form, by playing such tickets for *all* these columns. This would require ten total tickets (at ten times the price, of course). Additionally, if you can afford it, you could play both versions of the 8-spot tickets shown in Figures 12 and 13, for all the ten columns, thereby truly maximizing your value and hit frequency. This will get expensive, but you will be hitting many pays, and even a small pay will be enough to reduce the cost of replay on these tickets.

Additionally, even if you do not wish to get this aggressive in your play, you can often use the "wheeling" and "cross-betting" concepts together by playing more than one ticket, and then making some of the numbers, or groups, not only "core" among the tickets, but also in cross-bets, such as when on one ticket your group of three numbers will be cross-bet on another ticket as a group of two, perhaps with the third number as a king. And so on. This can get tricky, but it will make abundant sense to you once you become more familiar with Keno. Once you learn how to make and mark your tickets, you will be far more able to make these decisions. You will discover that using four "way tickets" in cross-bet groups, with a core wheel, is the most profitable combination you will ever find. Precisely which numbers and groups will depend on you—your abilities to observe and adapt; your bankroll, goals, and objectives; your skills, win expectations, and patience; and all the other Keys to Winning, as well as your ability to select the tickets, pay tables, rates, and so on, all of which combine to make you a very good keno player.

Well, that's about it. Even though the advice I've given you may not contain a whole bunch of numbers and statistics and "do this and then do that" instructions, it's a good strategy for Lounge Keno. What defines a good strategy—in my mind—is applicability, workability, flexibility, adaptability, and general usefulness in actual playing experience. Many of the tickets in my Best Tickets samples produce thousands of dollars in frequent wins. Your ability to make these powerful profits is directly related not just to your skills, abilities, knowledge, patience, and bankroll, but also to these points of strategy. That entire advice package will differentiate you from players who smirk at Keno, or who play it badly and then wonder why they lose while you smile as you cash in on the same game.

My final piece of advice for Lounge Keno is perhaps the most important: *be patient*. Patience is always a virtue and certainly so in Lounge Keno. Always keep in mind that this game plays only about six to twelve games per hour, on average. Sometimes more, sometimes less. If you can find a casino that plays a fast game, so much the better, but a game once every five to ten minutes or so is about the best you'll get. Don't fret, become angry, frustrated, impatient. Don't overbet your game and tickets in a mad dash to hit the big pay all at once. Making regular profits from Keno means to patiently await the big hit while playing tickets that mostly pay for themselves, or at the very worst make enough frequent hits so that their replay costs are significantly reduced. It also means to accumulate smaller profits more regularly—and to keep them, not spending then on other games or other entertainment or purchases. *Small wins more often will equal bigger wins, and more money to play with.* Less cost is just as important as big wins. Keeping your play to smart tickets assures you of such success.

PART TWO

Video Keno

Introduction to Video Keno

Video Keno is a hugely misunderstood game, often needlessly shunned by casual players. To many slot players, Video Keno either looks foreboding, intimidating, too complicated, or it looks too simple and too boring. None of this is true. Unfortunately, many people will not take the time to investigate just how good a game this really is, or how profitable it can be. Still others don't even realize that Video Keno is a slot machine, and one that can easily provide great pays—and big jackpots—for a very small investment. Unfamiliarity and misunderstanding are the two greatest problems that manufacturers of video keno games must overcome. Then they must convince casinos that these games should be placed on the casino floor as part of the casino's slot mix. In the not-so-distant past—merely a few years ago by the calendar, but light years ago by technological standards—video keno machines were huge pillars with two cathode ray tube (CRT) screens. They were colossal, imposing, and looked very complicated. "Wands" were used to select the numbers, and the games played slowly and with

Photo 2. The multi-game *Game King®* machine with multiple games in the on-screen menu.

loud chimes. It all looked like something from Buck Rogers. Fast-forward now a few years. A well-known slot machine manufacturer, International Game Technology (IGT), started to make small cabinet-sized games with screens that could be touched with a finger. This was the beginning of a line of multi-game video machines that are called *Game King®*. (See Photo 2.)

Among these games was one of the first touch-screen video keno games. Instead of the large, bulky machines with wands, these were compact games, easily activated by a finger, and with play buttons that helped the other functions. There was also a "re-bet" button so that players could easily replay the last game without having to go through the process of putting in more coins and pushing other buttons. The effect was electrifying. Instead of having to put in coins, select numbers, push a bunch of buttons and then wait forever for the game to finish, players are able to play a fast game with only one button to push. This meant that many games could be played in the span of a minute, and hundreds of games per hour. Speed and efficiency are the keys to the success of these games, particularly Video Keno. Players soon realized that these video keno games had two huge advantages that other games did not have:

- A big jackpot could be won with only one coin played.
- The faster the game played, the more chances there were to hit such a pay.

These are the two biggest factors contributing to the profitability of Video Keno. There is a third, and that is the availability of modifying the player's selection. In later game models, there is a game called *Four Card Keno*™, which allows players to play multiple cards and even "wheel" their numbers. (More on this later.) At the time IGT introduced the first *Game King* models of multi-game video machines, there was still quite a bit of resistance from many casual players. The ability to comprehend the benefits of these games was yet to catch up to the technology. The result was that these games became hugely popular among the locals' places around Las Vegas—the off-Strip casinos that normally cater to people who live and work in Las Vegas. Later, smaller casinos elsewhere in the country, tribal casinos in particular, that were located in remote areas and had a steady clientele from nearby residents also found that these games were extraordinarily popular. This was due to the familiarity factor, born out of experimentation, and resulting in players' overcoming their fear of the machine. These local players began to understand the technology and benefits of games like Video Keno. They realized that there was money to be won here, and for a much smaller investment than—for example—was required on the vastly more popular video poker games that had been hugely popular in casinos everywhere for quite some time. Even regular slot players soon discovered these *Game King*® machines, and in their game menus discovered Video Keno. Now they could play longer, for less money, and have a chance at really big wins. What could be better?

Nevertheless, many casual players still shy away from Video Keno due to the seeming complexity of the game and the apparent boredom it can elicit from players who don't understand it. Another factor is the longevity requirement. Like Lounge Keno, Video Keno requires time and patience. Hits are frequent, but to maximize the benefit of the game the player must be able to sustain play for a long time. I have played video keno games anywhere from three to sixteen hours at a time before I hit the jackpot!

Patience pays if you play any kind of keno game. Unfortunately many casual casino visitors either do not have it or don't want to "waste" their time. This is understandable, because many casual players come to casinos infrequently, perhaps once or twice a year on a vacation or holiday trip. They stay only three or four days, and in that time they try to pack in as much activity as they can. This is too bad, because it always costs a lot more money than it would, if they used their heads and thought about it for a while. I have been to casinos as a visitor—to Reno, Sparks, Lake Tahoe, Laughlin (even as a guest in Las Vegas hotels), the Midwest, and Connecticut. As a tourist, there for only four days or so, I understand the desire to play everything, everywhere, do everything, be everywhere, try everything everywhere and all the time. It's overwhelming. And it costs money. That's why casinos can rake in hundreds of billions of dollars every year, nationwide. Video Keno is the ideal alternative to this hustle and bustle.

Whenever you are in a casino, and if you are one of those casual players, by all means do all those things you wish to, and experience all those games that casinos provide for your entertainment. Then, take a rest, and find a video keno machine. Learn the game from the information in this book, read the help and pay table screens on the machine, then pick your selections, sit back and relax, and enjoy a restful, entertaining experience in front of a game that can provide you with terrific profits. Use your video keno playing time not only to relax, but also to make some money as you get ready for all those other activities you want to enjoy on your vacation. Of course if you are a local, or a frequent and regular casino visitor, then it is even more important for you to learn about this game and experience it. There is a lot more to Video Keno than first meets the eye. It is one of the very few casino games that can—and does—provide truly powerful profits, often for a very small investment. As a casino player of all the various and great casino games, I wish to tell you that I play Video Keno almost exclusively now, simply because this is the game that provides very big hits and large profits very regularly.

Here, I will show you how.

BASICS OF VIDEO KENO

Before we get into the details of the various video keno games, I think a short introduction to the game, in addition to the brief overview I just presented, is necessary for those of you who are not familiar with the game. Even if you have played the game before, this chapter may provide information that can enhance your understanding of the game. It is important that all of us know the same things in the same manner, so that later we can discuss the games and their play methods and to discuss the finer points of profitable keno play. So I ask you to read through these few pages, even if some of this information seems obvious to you. If we go through all these steps together, we will all be able to proceed and progress, in later chapters, to an understanding far deeper and greater than most people who have not taken these steps. And so, we begin.

The game of Video Keno looks the same and plays the same as Lounge Keno. The differences lie in the speed of the game and the payoff schedules. Lounge Keno is mostly a slow game, with one game played on average about every five minutes. Each game in Video Keno lasts only a few seconds, and this makes the game more exciting. This frequency also gives you more chances at winners. In Lounge Keno the minimum bet is usually $1, but Video Keno is offered in a variety of denominations from nickels to dollars, and even more such options on the modern multi-denominational *Game King*® machines. Most traditional Video Keno machines are of the 25-cent variety, and you can play from one quarter to four quarters. There are, however, machines that offer lower coin values, such as nickels, although *coin*-specified denominations are now mostly relegated to slot machine history. Most of the modern machines, such as the *Game King*® multi-game machines, now use on-screen menus that allow you to *choose the value* of your *credits*. These choices can be from as low as 1 cent per credit to as high as $5 per credit, with anywhere from 4 credits to 100 credits as maximum bet. Most of these choices are controlled by you and your selections. Therefore, you can not only choose the game you want to play, but also for how much—the credit value—and for how many credits per event. This gives you much greater control over the game, and over your costs as well as winnings. You can see what the *Game King*® video keno machine looks like in Photo 3.

In slot play it is always advisable to play the maximum coins, but *in Video Keno the advantage lies in exactly the opposite*. Video keno machines offer many big pays even when betting the minimum one-coin requirement or minimum credits required. A player can easily spot three styles of video keno machines. The first kind are the older-style machines that can still be found in some casinos. They are very tall, green in color, and have two CRT video display screens. The second kind are slant-top video keno machines, not found so often. The third kind are the modern multi-game and multi-denominational machines, such as the *Game King®*. Please look again at Photo 2, on page 164 to see exactly what a multi-denominational machine looks like.

If you visit some of the older casinos, perhaps locals' casinos, or some smaller tribal casinos, you may still find several older-style video keno machines, those tall stand-up types where the top screen shows the payoff schedules and the bottom screen—the one at eye level—shows the same eighty-number

Photo 3. The multi-game *Game King®* machine showing the video keno screen.

display that you find on the main board at Lounge Keno. The payoff schedules on the top screen alter depending on the number of spots you mark and the number of coins you play. This is different from Video Poker and Keno where the payoff schedules are fixed. On the slant-top machines, this schedule is usually available on a screen mounted vertically over the "slanted" main display screen. On the newer multi-game machines, the screen has been replaced by a side bar—like a computer "window"—in which the same payoff combinations appear and change as you select your number and deposit your coins, or, on the very newest ones, by a separate pay table screen that can be accessed by touching the on-screen icon saying "See Pays." To see what the older style video keno machine looks like, please look at Photo 4.

Even though some casinos have a lot of different-looking video keno machines, remember that the video keno game *in* them is almost always the same. There are however significant differences in the actual game-*content* of the game itself, so it is important for you to learn which are the best. I have chosen the *Game King®* machines as an example of the video keno games with the best choices, best pays, and best options. These are player-friendly, and fast, as well as attractive.

Any video keno slot machine looks very similar to the keno board in the keno lounge, and the game works almost exactly the same. There are eighty numbers on the screen and you can pick from one to ten numbers at a time. If your machine still uses coins, you first deposit your coins in the same manner as you would if you were to play any slot machine. Then you press the "erase" button to clear the screen. Use the "magic wand" if this is one of the older style machines; use your finger on the more modern touch-screen machines like *Game King®*. Touch the screen over the numbers you wish to select, pick one to ten

Photo 4. The old-style upright two-screen video keno machine, now rarely found in major casinos.

numbers, depending on your taste, then press the "start" button and the machine does the rest.

The "erase" button is mounted directly in front of you as you sit at the machine and works on the same principle as the "hold" buttons on Video Poker. It is used to give the machine a command telling it what your decision is. On the newer machines, this is a touch-screen display. By pressing or touching it—after first either depositing your coins or inserting currency into the bill acceptor and making your wager—you wipe out all the numbers selected by the player who previously played the machine. Of course if you wish to play exactly the same numbers that were already selected by the previous player, all you have to do is make your wager and then press the "start" button instead of the "erase" button. The machine will then play the same game, and your win/loss results depend on how many of the selected numbers the machine hits.

The "start" button starts the game. After you have deposited your coins or inserted the currency and made your wager, then pressed the erase button and marked your numbers, you can press the start button and the machine plays the game. The machine will randomly pick twenty numbers, and your goal is to select numbers that the machine will "hit." Most people play 6 spots, and the payoffs are quite remarkable. For a $1 bet—four quarters—if you hit all six numbers you win $1,600!! The payoffs for other number combinations are equally as impressive. For example, if you pick the 6-spot, and play only one quarter, you will still be paid $400 if all your six numbers are hit. This is a very high payoff relative to the investment. The fact that you can get a high pay like this, relative to the amount at risk, makes Video Keno a good moneymaker when you hit *your* combination of numbers. Granted, it is not easy to hit the total numbers, but then no slot play is an easy proposition. But unlike other slots where for four quarters you may win, say,

1,600 *quarters*, on the Keno Slot you win 1,600 *dollars*. A big difference. The smaller payoffs are not bad either. The chart below shows the pay table using the example of a 6-spot, for a 25-cent bet, video keno machine.

0	out of 6	=	no pay
1	out of 6	=	no pay
2	out of 6	=	no pay
3	out of 6	=	$0.75
4	out of 6	=	$1.00
5	out of 6	=	$17.50
6	out of 6	=	$400.00

These pays are *doubled* for the *next* coin played. So, if you play 50 cents, your 6-out-of-6 jackpot is $800 instead of $400. For each additional coin thereafter the jackpot grows by an added $400. A bet of 75 cents will therefore pay $1,200, and a bet of four quarters . . . $1 . . . will pay $1,600. The same applies to all the little pays in between.

In some casinos the 75-cent bet will pay $1,199.75 instead of the $1,200. This is done to keep the jackpot under the $1,200 IRS-imposed tax limit. As a smart player you should look for this option on the video keno machines you are playing. This offers you a jackpot without the immediate necessity of having it officially listed as taxable income and automatically reported by the casino to the IRS . . . in *your* name! It should be noted, however, that *all* your wins must and should—according to the hard-and-fast rules—be reported as taxable income, regardless of their amount. You can deduct your losses up to the amount of your accumulated wins for any one tax year, but in order to do that you must keep very accurate records. Using your slot club card will provide you with a good and clear record of all your activity, a very useful tool to keep accurate records for filing your taxes. It is very important that you always report your wins as taxable income, because only then can you likewise request a deduction on applicable losses. It is also *always* a good idea to accurately list all your gaming wins and activity.

In my opinion, video keno machines are by far the most underappreciated slot machines in the casinos today and they seem to be almost exclusively the playing property of the local players. Many of the "local Las Vegas spots," like Arizona Charlie's, The Palms, Coast Resorts, Rampart, Cannery, Station Casinos, and Sam's Town have dozens of these machines, testifying to their popularity, yet most visitors to Las Vegas shy away from them because they look so intimidating. Nothing of the sort.

Notice that on a 6-spot, video keno machines pay 3:1 for hitting 3 out of 6. This is very good because it occurs quite frequently and provides you with a good return even when you don't hit the top jackpot. You will also notice that on a 6-spot there are *four* ways, out of six possible, that provide you with a win, and only three ways in which there is no win. These combined factors make a 6-spot the preferred favorite among smart video keno players. Although you can pick up to 10 spots, generally the fewer spots you pick the better your chances of a win.

Often I see people play one, two, and three spots, spend a good deal of their money, and even when they hit their numbers wind up not even recouping their investment. The chart on the next page shows, in order of suggested value on regular video keno games—those that are not multi-card or way-ticket games, which we will discuss later—your best bets in Video Keno.

Some casinos offer bigger payoffs on some of their video keno machines. For example, a solid 9-spot at these casinos may pay $2,750 for a 25-cent bet, as opposed to the regular $2,500. This extra $250 is quite worth it! The best news is that these better payoffs also apply to the smaller jackpots on Video Keno. Applying the same example, a hit of 8 out of

6-spot	pays $ 400.00	for a 25-cent bet when all are hit
8-spot	pays $2,500.00	for a 25-cent bet when all are hit
7-spot	pays $1,750.00	for a 25-cent bet when all are hit
5-spot	pays $ 205.50	for a 25-cent bet when all are hit
4-spot	pays $ 22.75	for a 25-cent bet when all are hit
9-spot	pays $2,500.00	for a 25-cent bet when all are hit
10-spot	pays $2,500.00	for a 25-cent bet when all are hit

9 will pay $1,199.75 as opposed to the regular $1,175. This is bonus money, but be wary of reductions in pay schedules elsewhere in the pay table (as we will discuss shortly). The 6-spot is the best option in any casino because it offers the most chance and the highest payoff relative to the investment required and degree of difficulty necessary to hit it.

Video keno machines have 80 spots from which you can choose. The machine then draws 20 numbers total. Picking 6 out of those 20 drawn by the machine is easier than picking, say, 10. To hit 10 numbers out of the 20 drawn by the machine requires you to hit half of all the numbers drawn by the machine during the game. This is very hard, but it is possible. I have personally hit 10 out of 10 many times, recently more often than before when playing *Four Card Keno™* (more on this later). But in general, picking 6 numbers represents slightly less than one-third of the numbers drawn by the machine, thereby increasing your odds of hitting them. In playing the 6-spot, most of the time you will receive pays up to 5 out of 6, but the solid 6 will hit more often than many other number combinations available on Video Keno. With odds against a solid 6-spot hit of only about 7,753-to-1 it isn't hard to see why the 6-spot tends to be the most popular and most frequently played ticket, in both Lounge Keno and Video Keno.

The 8-spot is good to play because a lot of the time you can expect to hit the 6 out of 8 for $24.75, giving you additional playing money. As I've often stated, playing with casino money is better than playing with your own. In this way the higher non-jackpot wins offered by the 8-spot serve you well. However you should not expect to hit the solid 8. This is very rare, and with odds against a solid 8-spot hit of about 230,115-to-1 it isn't hard to see why. Most of the time you should look for the 7 out of 8, which will pay you $413.50 for a 25-cent bet. This occurs about as often as a solid 6, but the advantage of playing the 8-spot is that you still do have the chance of hitting the solid 8. By playing the 6-spot you only have a chance for a solid 6. Nonetheless, as far as strategy advice goes, the 6-spot is still the best option on standard, traditional, single-screen video keno games.

The 7-spot usually provides the best chance for hitting 6 out of 7, which pays $100 for a 25-cent bet. A solid 7 is just as rare as any solid hit, other than a solid 6-spot, but does happen more frequently than the solid 8. A solid 7-spot faces odds against of only about 40,979:1.

Playing a 5-spot is fun if all you're after is a small jackpot, or just want to pass some time. Otherwise it provides little opportunity for some decent dollars. Same goes for the 4-spot, which is best employed if you wish to win some casino money first before playing for the bigger jackpots. But be careful not to blow your whole bankroll chasing a 4-spot. Most of the time if the machine you are playing will hit the 4-spot, it very likely could have hit a 6, 7, or even 8, so normally you are better off starting with the bigger jackpot combinations and sticking to them.

On the 9-spot you can expect a 7-out-of-9 hit with more frequency than 8 or solid 9. This pays $83.75 for a 25-cent bet and will happen more often than the higher payoff combinations. The 8 out of 9 also hits quite frequently, but a solid 9 is, of course, harder to hit than a solid 8. A 9-spot is a good option if you have lots of time and patience, and also is good because the 7-out-of-9 win provides some decent play money. Often you can hit this $83.50 payoff and then go to a 6- or 7-spot and play for more than 25-cents per bet. This increases your chances for a bigger "pay day."

The 10-spot is advisable only with an 8-out-of-10 win expectation. This happens more often than even a solid 6 and appears to be a quirk in the machines. I have hit this for the $250 (per 25-cent bet) more times than any other combination in Video Keno. Logically there appears to be no reason for this startling frequency, but it is a fact of how the machines play. The odds against a hit of 8 out of 10 are only 7,385:1, which is a lot better than comparable video poker odds. My experience has been that this hit is far more common than indicated even by these odds-against, particularly so on the *Four Card Keno*™ machines I will discuss a little later on. I usually play a straight 10-spot for 50 cents per game, and this yields a jackpot of $500 for that 8-out-of-10 hit. Sometimes I also play $1, and this makes for the $1,000 hit I mentioned earlier when I was comparing keno hits to video poker hits. I have also hit many 9 out of 10s with the 50-cent and $1 bets, and these are very good jackpots indeed.

HOT HINTS FOR VIDEO KENO

Although this is not the strategy section, it's a good moment to show you how you should approach the traditional single-screen video keno game. These "hot hints" will lay a solid foundation for your continued good play when you start to explore and exploit some of the more modern, and more complex, new video keno games. If you take this advice to heart, you will be better able to adapt these skills to the many varieties of video keno games that are now available as part of the *Game King*® platform.

Remember that these recommendations and suggestions are based on playing the traditional single-screen game, and that I am using the example of the 25-cent credit as the basis for all wager calculations. As you will shortly find out, many of the newest video keno games can be played for as little as 1 cent per credit, with 10 credits as an average maximum wager. It will then be necessary to adapt these recommendations to those particular games, but first you need to know how to play the standard traditional video keno game to your best advantage. To that end, here are some play recommendations to help you make the most from traditional video keno.

• Play 25 cents per bet until you win. Then double your bet to 50 cents. If you win again, add another quarter and play for 75 cents per bet, and if you win again, up this to the maximum bet of $1. If you play at a higher per-credit level or a lower-credit value—nickels on a standard video keno machine—then this will also apply. If this is a multi-card game, or a way-ticket game, an entirely different strategy often applies (more on that later).

• If you have three losers in a row, go back to 25 cents per bet.

• Play a 6-spot more than any other combination. Look at the list of suggested play options I provided earlier and select which jackpot you *realistically* wish to go for. Then stick to this combination for your entire period of play. For multi-card and multi-way games, this advice changes slightly to reflect those game options (more on that later).

• Group your numbers. Video keno machines have a tendency to group numbers. For example, a 6-spot combination of: 25, 26, 27, 35, 36, and 37 hits more often than many other combinations on video keno machines. This is another quirk of the machine's program, but one you can exploit to your advantage. Same goes for any other number combinations you select. Grouping them will give you a better chance of winning. On the newer touch-screen machines, a 6-spot of 78, 79, 80, 68, 69, and 70 works that way too.

• Have patience; Video Keno requires a lot of it. It can be a very frustrating game, and quite time consuming. If you have no time and no patience, don't play this game. But if you wish to relax, gamble with little to win a lot, and you have the time to enjoy the casino and free cocktails, settle yourself down in front of a video keno machine for a few hours and you're likely to walk away with a sizable win.

• Changing your numbers is keno suicide. Whatever numbers you pick, stick to them for the entire duration of your play. Even if the numbers are not hitting, eventually they will. The more they are *not* hitting, the better chance you have that they will all come in. There are some books that advise you to constantly erase and re-mark your numbers on the theory that this has some kind of a "re-set" effect on the machine. This is plainly not so, and is merely a superstition seemingly reinforced by a few lucky hits by players who did this and it happened to so work out. The truth is that the machines work on a binary numerical sequencing algorithm, the randomness of the events is provided by the linear feedback shift register, and the event is determined in a microsecond after the first credit triggers the program to stop the random selections of billions of bits.* (See the chapter on Superstitions.)

• Select your bankroll for Video Keno play before you begin, and then buy all the change for your entire bankroll and put it all in the machine. The machine employs a "credits" display, like most slot machines. All winning pays will run up on this credit meter. If, after you have put in all your bankroll for this session, your credits are close to even, even, or greater than the amount of your bankroll, your machine is playing well and will likely hit you a jackpot. Continue to play it to either half your session stake or twice your money.

*For more information on this, please refer to my book *Powerful Profits from Slots*, chapter 10.

Or, of course, the top jackpot. This may not be possible *on the newest coinless machines*, where *only credits* are used, and currency is inserted into the currency acceptor instead of coins. In this case, use your bankroll as your buy-in for that session, and keep your eye out on how much you are winning or losing. Try to gauge how many games you play. After each 100 games, or as close to this as you can count, look at your credits. If you have lost 25 percent or more of your own starting bankroll, stop. Otherwise, continue to play until you either hit the jackpot, or double your bankroll—then stop.

• Don't chase your money. Video Keno is a slot machine just like all the others. If the machine is "cold," meaning it's not paying, move to another, or quit for this session. In my *Slots* book there is a chapter on machine selection, and game and play selection principles that can easily be adapted to this item. You may wish to read that as well, since it will provide you with a greater overview of slot machines and selection skills. After all, Video Keno *is* a slot machine.

• Be wary of machines that have had their payoff programs slightly altered. These machines have been "chipped," which is a slang term for having their programming chip replaced with one that pays less well. This also means that the casinos that did this had to show the altered payoff schedule, so this is not exactly "hidden." However, many people simply don't know what to look for, so it can be considered a "sly" trick. To find out if your video keno machine has been so altered, take a look the at 6-spot payoff for a one-coin bet (25 cents in case of the most widely available quarter machines). If this payout for this 6-spot isn't the same as that which I listed previously, then that machine's program has been altered. You should avoid playing it, and play the same game on a different machine, or elsewhere in a different casino. However, don't confuse this with "bonus keno" games, or some of the other keno multi-game derivatives. On these games, the payouts may be different from those I have listed because they are a different kind of game, with different rules. I am telling you here about the most widely popular video keno games, and how to find out if that machine's program is indeed set for the optimum pay program. The "bonus keno" or multi-game keno machines are a little different, but you can still apply this method of selection to make the correct wagering and selection choices for all kinds of video keno games.

While Video Keno pays back at an average rate of about 92.3 percent, even the high house hold of around 25 percent for Lounge Keno can be drastically reduced with the smart use of way tickets, as you learned in part one of this book. The attractiveness of Keno lies in the large pays it provides when the total numbers you picked all hit. Treated this way, your approach to Keno will provide you with a good gaming experience and can provide considerable and memorable wins. You should however be very aware that—as with any gambling game—committing your entire vacation bankroll to Keno is just as bad as committing it to any other single game.

Video Keno is a good alternative to fast action in the casino. So is Lounge Keno. Both require relatively small investments, but lots of time and a great deal of patience. By keeping this in mind, you will provide yourself with the correct mind-set and win-loss expectation. Also don't forget, or undervalue, the importance of the "fun factor," or of variety. Although many books are written as if the readers were interested only in becoming professional gamblers, in reality the vast majority of casino players simply want to have a good time and to have fun with the games. Sadly, many of these players place the "fun factor" high on their list and leave "knowledge" at home. What is even worse is that many thousands of players simply don't know that there is information available to show them how to have a great time, and lots of fun, without the expense of playing willy-nilly, and wasting money for little or no gain or win potential. In all of my books, I stress the importance of fun. Casino gambling should be fun, and should not have to be treated as a job. Even if you *do* wish to become a professional gambler, your job should be fun, because the day it starts to become only a grind is the day you will lose your focus—and in gambling, this will mean inevitable ruin. Never forget the value of fun and the thrill of the experience. They are important, but should be tempered with at least some knowledge.

Another important factor to consider is variety. For people who play in casinos infrequently, only a few times a year on trips and vacations, variety is very important. They want to try everything, everywhere, and usually all at the same time. This inevitably leads to a little bit of money lost here, another bit there, some more over there, and so on. Soon, the players are broke, or having to get more money, and don't even know where it all went, or how. Such a wide variety is very expensive. The variety I recommend is more directed to the game that you select. By choosing Video Keno as your game, you have found a game that can be played well, and often very profitably. You can select a variety of keno games and have a great time, thereby keeping your costs down and your win expectations up.

I will shortly discuss some of the various video keno games that are available in *Game King®* machines, such as *Caveman Keno®*, *Cleopatra® Keno*, *Four Card Keno™*, *Way Keno*, and others. All of these are usually found in the one multi-game machine, and all you have to do is first look for a *Game King®* machine and then look at the menu to find those that contain mostly video keno games. Many of these machines also have video slots and video poker games as part of their menu variety, but since this book is about Keno, I will now continue with describing the various video keno games you can find in these machines.

There is a series of these machines that contain *only* video keno games in their menus, and these are the ones I'd like you to look for. If you can't find one in your casino, ask them to get one. I have hit the majority of my wins in video keno precisely on exactly these kinds of machines. That's why I like them so much and wish to show them to you so that you can benefit from my experiences and win on them as well.

Video Keno by the Numbers

Knowing the pay tables for machine-based gambling games is essential and paramount to your ability to win money. Although powerful profits are possible even on games whose statistical profile distinctly classifies them in the "not so good" category, *knowing* this *before* playing is equally as important as knowing the information that statistically so classifies them. Just as important is knowing the odds and the payback percentages on such machines. These are the best possible *guidelines* that can enable you to make better decisions with your gambling. Although (as I have stated numerous times) overreliance on mathematical and statistical profiles of gambling games is not necessarily conducive to the making of profits, I have also stated many times that knowing such information is crucial. It is crucial not just to the understanding of the game, and how it plays, what does what, how, when, and why—but primarily because it allows you to make your own decisions regarding how to play it, for what goals, which bankroll, how long per session, and what you can hope to achieve as your profit in the limited slice of your exposure to the game. While some games are called statistically "bad" because their pay tables and payback percentages are not very good, either by themselves or in comparison to other gambling games, this does not automatically exclude them from profitable play. The biggest mistake made most often by players who read something about casino games is to immediately become enthralled with the stats and forget everything to do with winning money. Trying to play casino games in accordance purely and only with the stats is bound to be an exercise in frustration. The greatest fallacy of gambling, and gambling literature, is the promotion of total reliance on math and stats and probabilities.

This fallacy is dangerous if players and readers accept it as "gospel" and as "absolute truth," instead of merely a useful guideline. The truth lies in something far less definable and far less enumerated. The stats will come "close" to the expected theory, but just precisely *when* no one knows.

The point—as it applies to Video Keno—is that, while many of the payback percentages for video keno games are in the "bad" category, when viewed statistically, this is useful *only* as a *guideline*, and should be treated as such. Being a statistically "lousy" game is not the domain of Video Keno only. All casino games can easily fall into this category, even those that are—or can become—player-positive expectation games. Playing a machine game that can pay back over 100 percent if played correctly doesn't mean that we will always, each time, get back more than 100 percent of the money we play in it! Playing a table game wherein we can expect a positive payback percentage because of skill doesn't mean that it will always so happen. Even games considered "good" by the math experts don't always pay, and those who are skilled players of positive-expectation skill-based games don't always win. A good payback percentage is better than something lower because this payback percentage is a good *guide* and shows the *potential* for greater hit frequency and greater pays, requiring an overall lower bankroll. However, this doesn't mean that a game whose payback percentage is slightly lower should automatically be excluded from your game selection mix.

Some video keno games pay back as low as 90 percent, and sometimes lower. Is this "bad"? Well, how do we consider it? There are video keno games that pay back 94 percent, and better. Is that "good"? Well, how do we consider *that*? Quarter Reel Slots pay back around 88 percent, and can sometimes pay back as low as 75 percent. Dollar Reel Slots usually pay back around 94.7 percent, and many pay back around 98 percent, with some even paying back 99 percent. Is that "good"? Comparatively speaking, as a guideline, absolutely, yes, it is very useful. I would be more than likely to play a machine that I knew had a 98 percent payback potential than a machine with only an 88 percent payback potential. But that's also an arbitrary decision, however intelligently made. There are many other factors involved here, most of which cannot be so neatly quantified in the math. What kind of a machine, where is it, and how well can you play it? Well, on Reel Slots, I'd always go for the most visible slot island, and play the best payback percentage machine I can find. This makes sense because my profitability is enhanced by my knowledge of these factors. But what about Video Keno? This game is not the same as Reel Slots, and it is not the same as Video Poker, and not the same as any other game. It is incredibly different. Since there are so many possibilities in Video Keno, a machine that may have a really "bad" payback percentage—perhaps as compared with other machines, such as the reel machines with a 98 percent payback percentage—it can actually yield better *financial* results and "pays," and more often. On Reel Slots, all you have at your disposal are the combinations as preprogrammed. In Video Keno, however, you have an eighty-number total pool, out of which you can select from one to

ten numbers to match the picks, and the machine picks twenty
new numbers each game for you to match. While the overall
math may indicate long odds, the fact remains that you can
select numbers and number combinations based on several
recurring factors. What the mathematics cannot quantify is
the human ability to play by patterns.

Video Keno is primarily a "numbers" game, but playing
it profitably is a "patterns" game. I'll get to the discussion of
video keno patterns in the chapter on strategy. For now, remember that while this chapter is all about the numbers,
and all about the odds, payback percentages, hit frequency,
and overall expected percentage of return—these are all the
guidelines by which you can navigate the many selection
criteria and play options you will encounter in Video Keno.
I am presenting this information here to enable you to have
that knowledge and to assist you in gaining the expertise
and familiarity with the game, both designed to enhance
your ability to turn a profit.

All video keno games are fairly simple to play, at least
initially. There are, however, many differences in the games
themselves, how they play and pay, and their pays, payoffs,
and payback percentages. Before you select which game
you wish to play, you should always consider the fun-and-
win factors. Which is your primary goal? Is it to be enter-
tained or to make a profit? Although neither necessarily
excludes the other, in Video Keno some games are more fun,
while others are more profitable. Creating a balance among
these games can be difficult. Fortunately, many different
video keno games available, including those in the IGT
Game King® series of multi-game and multi-denominational
machines, provide such a balance. I begin with *Cleopatra*®
Keno, an Egyptian-themed game resembling the very popular *Cleopatra*® video slot game, also from IGT.

CLEOPATRA® KENO

The base game is Video Keno, as I have described it earlier. The difference lies in the last ball drawn (the last number, displayed on a ball that you can see being drawn from a device that looks like the lounge keno "blower" or "tumbler"). If this last number matches your selected numbers, and if this makes it into a winner for you, in addition to the wins you get for this hit you will now also receive twelve free games. During these free games any wins you get are doubled, so you win twice the amount you would have normally won, and for free. This is a kind of "bonus" game, similar to the many such bonusing features you often find on Video Slots.

Naturally there are some decreases in the base payoffs of this game to accommodate this extra bonusing feature. This is also the case for all slots that offer such bonusing features, although in many traditional Reel Slots, or the newer Video Slots, these "costs" of the bonus hits are more hidden and less visible. In Video Keno you can tell by looking at the pay table exactly what you are giving up to achieve these extra wins. Nevertheless, hits of this kind happen quite frequently. Many times you will get a winner with the last number drawn, and on this game it means that you have entered the bonus round. Now you can sit back and wait to see what great pays you will get as the game plays those twelve free games. This is very similar in principle to the *Cleopatra*® video slot game and to another IGT video slot machine called *Leopard Spots*® (which I also like to play). Of course, while you are in the twelve free games mode, you can't win any more free games even if you get more of the "last ball" hits, and if the game is also a progressive, that progressive feature doesn't apply. But you do get double the pays, and so as the game plays the same card that activated this bonus

Photo 5. The *Cleopatra® Keno* main game screen.

feature, you have a good chance to make some nice wins. You can see the actual game screen in Photo 5.

As with all video-based slots there are many different payback schedules available. The casinos have options of selecting which kinds of paybacks they will put on their casino floor. There are four basic versions of the Cleopatra keno game. The chart below is a list of the available payback percentages for this game, from best to the last.

When you are looking at these payback percentages, remember that it is the *casino*, and not the game's manufacturer, who decides which they want. The makers of this game merely provide options for the casinos to select. In the final tally, it is **you**—the player—who decides if the casinos can get away with having the lower-payback percentage games or will have to offer the best possible game. The more knowledgeable you are, as a player, the more the casinos will have to offer the better payback machines, because knowledgeable players won't play games that take more money than they should, given the availability of better paybacks. This applies to all slots, and not just Video Keno. The chart below shows a typical pay table for the best payback percentage for the Cleopatra keno game, the one that pays back 94.947 percent. Remember that this payback means that the casino has a "house hold" of 5.053 percent on this game, which is not too bad. Many Reel Slots don't pay nearly so well, certainly not quarter Reel Slots whose average payback is in the 88 percent to 92 percent range. Many video poker machines are comparable to this payback percentage as well, so don't automatically dismiss Video Keno as a "bad game" because it initially shows what appear to be higher house withholding percentages, and hence lower overall payback.

The pay table, hit frequency, payback percentage, and the average payback as shown are the exact numbers as approved by the gaming regulators in Nevada, supplied to me directly from the game's manufacturer, IGT of Reno, Nevada. This also applies for all the other charts and pay tables, payback percentages, and hit frequencies as I list them throughout this book. The numbers you are reading here, and the games you are reading about, are the exact, actual numbers and games as they really are—"directly from the horse's mouth." I am proud to be able to share this information that was made available to me through the courtesy of the game's makers, IGT. A large portion of this information has never

CLEOPATRA® KENO PAYBACK	PERCENT
Best	94.947
Next best	94.120
Third best	92.095
Least	90.110

before been made available, at least not directly from the source itself. This is an invaluable guide to the games and your ability to play them for good wins.

The pay table for *Cleopatra® Keno* is the best that is currently available. Always check this pay table when you see one of these games in your favorite casino. Each of these games show the pay table on a separate screen, which you can access by touching the "pays" icon on the screen menu. Once you see the pay table, compare it to this one. If the game in your casino has this exact same pay table, then you know you have the best version of this game currently available. If not, compare the differences, and look in particular at the small differences in some of the pays. For example, if you see a version of this game that shows pays for the 3-of-3 hit as 43 instead of 45 credits, and the pay for the 4-of-4 hit as 230 instead of 240 credits, then you know you are playing a lower-payback machine. This one actually pays back at the average rate of 94.120 percent, as opposed to the better 94.947 percent, which is the table I have shown. On another version of this game, these same two pays may only be shown as paying back 17 and 35 credits, respectively, and this means that machine only pays back at the average rate of 90.110 percent. As with Video Poker, the major differences lie in the most frequently hit pays. You should look carefully at these pays and find out precisely what it is you are about to play. Just because video keno machines do not appear to be same as other slots, or play in the same manner, doesn't mean they aren't slots; that's what they are. Video keno games are a video slot machine, with numbers instead of reels. Practicing the same kinds of skills as you can learn from my *Slots* book, and my *Video Poker* book, will help you here as well.

Pay Table Chart for *Cleopatra® Keno* with 94.947 Percent Payback Average

(starts with minimum 3 spots selected—hit frequency and payback shown for solid hits only)

SPOTS MARKED	HITS	PAYS
3	0	0
	1	0
	2	3
	3	19

Hit Frequency: 15.263%
Payback Percentage: 94.026%

■ ■ ■ ■

SPOTS MARKED	HITS	PAYS
4	0	0
	1	0
	2	1
	3	5
	4	45

Hit Frequency: 25.895%
Payback Percentage: 95.251%

■ ■ ■ ■

SPOTS MARKED	HITS	PAYS
5	0	0
	1	0
	2	0
	3	3
	4	24
	5	240

Hit Frequency: 9.667%
Payback Percentage: 95.049%

■ ■ ■ ■

SPOTS MARKED	HITS	PAYS
6	0	0
	1	0
	2	0
	3	2
	4	5
	5	42
	6	410

Hit Frequency: 16.158%
Payback Percentage: 95.032%

— — — —

SPOTS MARKED	HITS	PAYS
7	0	0
	1	0
	2	0
	3	1
	4	3
	5	7
	6	118
	7	500

Hit Frequency: 23.658%
Payback Percentage: 95.073%

— — — —

SPOTS MARKED	HITS	PAYS
8	0	0
	1	0
	2	0
	3	0
	4	3
	5	10
	6	65
	7	250
	8	1,000

Hit Frequency: 20.234%
Payback Percentage: 95.093%

— — — —

SPOTS MARKED	HITS	PAYS
9	0	0
	1	0
	2	0
	3	0
	4	2
	5	5
	6	12
	7	108
	8	200
	9	1,000

Hit Frequency: 15.305%
Payback Percentage: 95.037%

▬ ▬ ▬ ▬

SPOTS MARKED	HITS	PAYS
10	0	0
	1	0
	2	0
	3	0
	4	1
	5	3
	6	5
	7	35
	8	206
	9	1,000
	10	2,000

Hit Frequency: 21.198%
Payback Percentage: 95.018%

CAVEMAN KENO®

This is a video keno game where a volcano blows the numbers out through the lava funnel at the top, spewing out virtual smoke, fire, stones, and ash along with your winning numbers. This is accompanied by loud rumbling sounds, often so loud that the machine shakes as if in an earthquake. Many times I have seen players near these machines jump out of their seats as one of these rumbling and very loud events takes place. Although I like this game, I don't play it because of these loud sounds. I like things quiet, so I can concentrate on my game. You may not believe it, but Video Keno does require concentration. Most people think of it as a mind-numbing, repetitive, and largely pointless game, but they are wrong. Although all casino games can be played with a mind-numbing disregard for what's going on, as surely as that approach is a prescription for financial ruin in traditionally understood skill-based games such as Blackjack, Video Poker, and Live Poker, so it is with Slots, Keno, other casino games, and Video Keno. Photo 6 shows the actual game screen of *Caveman Keno®*.

Photo 6. The *Caveman Keno®* main game screen.

Caveman Keno® features Paleolithic graphics, kind of like the newspaper cartoon strip "B.C." It's all about the "dinosaur age"; some of these games may even have little caveman characters poking out and about. The main features of the game are the dinosaur eggs—dino eggs for short. The base game is Video Keno, formatted around the same principle that plays all other video keno games. The dino eggs in this game act as the bonusing feature, similar to what happens in the Cleopatra keno game. In *Caveman Keno®*, however, the bonus does not require that the last number drawn is part of the win. Some games can have as many as four dino eggs; the game I describe here has three. The dino eggs act as multipliers, which is the same principle as the "bonus symbols" on slot machines. In this video keno game, if two dino eggs turn into dinosaurs—"hatch" would be a better description—the total win achieved is multiplied by a factor of four, meaning four times the win amount. If all three of the dino eggs hatch, your win is multiplied eight times. Some of these games are also available with a ten-times pay for the hit of all dino eggs hatched.

A further feature of this game is the availability of multicards. Some of these games can be played with as many as twenty keno cards, which provide you with an awesome potential to "wheel" your numbers for some great wins. Unfortunately this multi-card feature isn't available in most casinos. Nevertheless, the fact that dino eggs act as large-value multipliers means you can get very good wins as you play. As is the case with all games that offer such bonuses, however, here too you will find that the base keno pay schedule has been reduced to compensate for the occurrences of the bonus wins and the occurrences of more frequent wins. This is not necessarily a disadvantage, because you have to take into account the extra money you get by those dino-egg hits. There are many variances in this game and its overall payback. This is standard for all slots, because the more popular they are, the more versions of them there will be for the casinos to choose from. With *Caveman Keno®* there are nine popular versions, each with a different payback. The chart below shows a list of the various percentage payback options available with the Caveman keno game.

CAVEMAN KENO® PAYBACK	PERCENT
Best	95.112
Next best	94.008
Third best	94.022
Fourth best	92.070
Fifth best	91.438
Sixth best	90.052
Seventh best	89.885
Eighth best	88.017
Least	88.004

As you can see, the variety of available paybacks and options is quite staggering, as are the differences in the games. I again remind you that it is the casinos who ask for these paybacks, and the maker of the game merely makes it to the specifications of the casino that is ordering the game. In the end it is wholly up to you to make sure you are playing the better games, and not those that aren't as good—percentage payback wise. Casinos will put the lower-payback machines on the floor just to see if people will play them. If they do, the casino will leave them there because they will make all that extra money. However, if players are smart, they will refuse to play games with bad payback percentages and instead demand that casinos order the better-paying machines and games that are available. As a player of casino games, it is you, therefore, who controls your destiny, not only in how much you will *spend*, but more important in how much you will *win*. Choosing the better games will make your casino experience better and will also help your favorite casino attract more players. As with all casino games, you control what games the casino will be able to carry, and which they won't. Ask your casino to get the better games, and choose to play in casinos where you can find them. Since there are so many versions of *Caveman Keno®*, I will again list in the chart below only the best payback table and then show some of the differences you should look for when deciding which game to play.

Pay Table Chart for *Caveman Keno®* with 95.112 Percent Payback Average

Starts with minimum 2 spots selected

Hit Frequency and Payback shown for solid hits only

SPOTS MARKED	HITS	PAYS
2	0	0
	1	0
	2	11

Hit Frequency: 6.013%

Payback Percentage: 95.048%

— — — —

SPOTS MARKED	HITS	PAYS
3	0	0
	1	0
	2	3
	3	18

Hit Frequency: 15.263%

Payback Percentage: 94.246%

— — — —

SPOTS MARKED	HITS	PAYS
4	0	0
	1	0
	2	1
	3	5
	4	81

Hit Frequency: 25.895%
Payback Percentage: 95.357%

— — — —

SPOTS MARKED	HITS	PAYS
5	0	0
	1	0
	2	1
	3	2
	4	15
	5	75

Hit Frequency: 36.713%
Payback Percentage: 94.982%

— — — —

SPOTS MARKED	HITS	PAYS
6	0	0
	1	0
	2	0
	3	2
	4	6
	5	77
	6	150

Hit Frequency: 16.158%
Payback Percentage: 95.200%

— — — —

SPOTS MARKED	HITS	PAYS
7	0	0
	1	0
	2	0
	3	1
	4	3
	5	14
	6	300
	7	1,000

Hit Frequency: 23.658%
Payback Percentage: 94.962%

━━ ━━ ━━ ━━

SPOTS MARKED	HITS	PAYS
8	0	0
	1	0
	2	0
	3	1
	4	2
	5	5
	6	77
	7	200
	8	1,000

Hit Frequency: 31.712%
Payback Percentage: 94.984%

━━ ━━ ━━

SPOTS MARKED	HITS	PAYS
9	0	0
	1	0
	2	0
	3	0
	4	1
	5	6
	6	50
	7	166
	8	500
	9	1,000

Hit Frequency: 15.305%
Payback Percentage: 95.037%

━━ ━━ ━━

SPOTS MARKED	HITS	PAYS
10	0	0
	1	0
	2	0
	3	0
	4	1
	5	5
	6	10
	7	90
	8	275
	9	500
	10	1,000

Hit Frequency: 21.198%
Payback Percentage: 95.140%

If you compare this pay table with the one for *Cleopatra®* *Keno*, you will find quite a few differences. *Caveman Keno®* pays more on some of the smaller hits and less on several of the big hits, which makes *Caveman Keno®* a "meatier" game, because more of the frequently occurring hits will happen more often, as well as many hits that pay in this game but don't pay in others. I will now show you some of the differences to look for among the various pay tables. The game I have shown here—the one with the pay table of 95.112 percent as the average—is the best available. Some of the other pay tables are close to this one, certainly enough to warrant play even with just small fractionally fewer pays in certain instances. This game holds only 4.88 percent for the house and is therefore among the very best slot machines you can find. There are, however, other versions of this game that aren't nearly as loose. The second to last in my list is an 88.017 percent payback version of *Caveman Keno®*, and this one holds a whopping 11.98 percent for the house. Again, you, the player are the only one who can decide and determine whether the casinos will stock the better games, or the not-so-good payback games. Here's how you can tell the difference: Look at the payback schedule of the game you are considering. If it is a *Caveman Keno®* game, it should have a pay table as I have shown it. If, however, the 4 of 4 pays only 60, instead of 81, and the 4 of 5 pays only 4, instead of 15, and the 5 of 6 pays only 46, instead of 77, you have an 88.017 percent payback game, with that high 11.89 percent house edge, and that is just too much to overcome. Although in this game you will see much higher pays for the solid top hits, and even the top two hits on some pays, this game is what we call "top heavy," meaning that it takes away a lot of the smaller, more frequently hit pays, and "loads up" on the top, harder-to-hit pays as a compensator. The inevitable result is that the game winds up eating your money and turns what was otherwise a really good game into a bad one—not because of the game itself, but because your casino decided to try to get more of your money faster by ordering this low payback. Simply put, if you see a *Caveman Keno®* game, and its pay table isn't at least close to the one I show here, you'd probably be better off playing another video keno game altogether. Just because this casino may have a "bad" *Caveman Keno®* game doesn't mean that all of their video keno games may be of this kind. Casinos tend to mix the games up, some with the really good pay tables and payback percentages, and other with ones not so good. This is done not only to confuse the players, but also because casinos know that players will not take the time to look carefully at the payback schedules; if they see one *Caveman Keno®* game and then another, they think both are the same. It's up to you to look it up, to understand what it is you are seeing, and to know what it really means to your bottom line. I can't help you win, or make powerful profits, if you ignore these hints and this advice and play bad games without looking at the pay tables. If you lose playing a not-so-good payback game, blame yourself and no one else. Here you have the knowledge, and the pay tables, with which to make these decisions and choices, easily and with little effort. Take it to heart, and remember this as we move on through some other games.

SUPER "POWER" KENO®

This game is often called "Power Keno," because it has a bonus feature on the last number drawn—kind of like a "powerball." There is another game called "Super Way Keno," but that is an entirely different game, and I will describe it next. In this game—called *Super Keno*™—the bonus pay is activated when the last number drawn makes the game into a winner, or makes the winner into a bigger one. This is similar to the *Cleopatra Keno*® game, but in this *Super Keno*™ the winning event is multiplied by four. What makes this game different from many of the others is that this particular IGT version comes with some pretty good pay tables. All of these bonus-type games have a reduced pay table to accommodate the super wins, which usually detracts from the game's popularity, but this particular version of *Super Keno*™ comes with a payback program of 94.06 percent, making it a very good game. Photo 7 shows an actual game screen for *Super Keno*™.

Photo 7. The *Super "Power" Keno*™ main game screen.

The base game is, of course, just like the standard video keno games. The only difference in *Super Keno*™ is the fact of the extra four-times bonus pay if the winning event was achieved with the hit of the last number draw. The chart below shows the standard pay table for the 94.06 percent payback *Super Keno*™ game.

Pay Table Chart for *Super "Power" Keno*™ with 94.06 Percent Payback Average

Starts with minimum 1 spot selected

Hit frequency and payback shown for solid hits only

STANDARD PAYS			PAYS WITH POWER HIT
SPOTS MARKED	HITS	PAYS	POWER PAYS
1	0	0	0
	1	3	12

Hit Frequency:	25.00%		Hit Frequency:	25.00%
Payback Percentage:	75.00%		Payback Percentage:	300.00%
Total Hit Frequency:	25.00%		Total Payback:	86.25%

— — — —

	HITS	PAYS	POWER PAYS
SPOTS MARKED			
2	0	0	0
	1	0	0
	2	12	48

Hit Frequency:	6.01%		Hit Frequency:	6.01%
Payback Percentage:	72.15%		Payback Percentage:	288.61%
Total Hit Frequency:	6.01%		Total Payback:	93.80%

— — — —

STANDARD PAYS			PAYS WITH POWER HIT
SPOTS MARKED	HITS	PAYS	POWER PAYS
3	0	0	0
	1	0	0
	2	1	4
	3	38	152

Hit Frequency:	15.26%		Hit Frequency:	15.26%
Payback Percentage:	66.60%		Payback Percentage:	266.41%
Total Hit Frequency:	15.26%		Total Payback:	94.49%

— — — —

SPOTS MARKED	HITS	PAYS	POWER PAYS
4	0	0	0
	1	0	0
	2	1	4
	3	4	16
	4	84	336

Hit Frequency:	25.89%		Hit Frequency:	25.89%
Payback Percentage:	64.30%		Payback Percentage:	257.18%
Total Hit Frequency:	25.89%		Total Payback:	93.90%

— — — —

SPOTS MARKED	HITS	PAYS	POWER PAYS
5	0	0	0
	1	0	0
	2	0	0
	3	2	8
	4	13	52
	5	395	1,580

Hit Frequency:	9.67%		Hit Frequency:	9.67%
Payback Percentage:	57.98%		Payback Percentage:	231.93%
Total Hit Frequency:	9.67%		Total Payback:	94.07%

— — — —

STANDARD PAYS			PAYS WITH POWER HIT	
SPOTS MARKED	HITS	PAYS	POWER PAYS	
6	0	0	0	
	1	0	0	
	2	0	0	
	3	1	4	
	4	6	24	
	5	52	208	
	6	800	3,200	

Hit Frequency:	16.16%	Hit Frequency:	16.16%
Payback Percentage:	56.52%	Payback Percentage:	226.08%
Total Hit Frequency:	16.16%	Total Payback:	94.00%

--- --- --- ---

SPOTS MARKED	HITS	PAYS	POWER PAYS	
7	0	0	0	
	1	0	0	
	2	0	0	
	3	1	4	
	4	2	8	
	5	12	48	
	6	216	864	
	7	800	3,200	

Hit Frequency:	23.66%	Hit Frequency:	23.66%
Payback Percentage:	56.07%	Payback Percentage:	224.28%
Total Hit Frequency:	23.66%	Total Payback:	94.26%

--- --- --- ---

SPOTS MARKED	HITS	PAYS	POWER PAYS	
8	0	0	0	
	1	0	0	
	2	0	0	
	3	0	0	
	4	2	8	
	5	5	20	
	6	52	208	
	7	800	3,200	
	8	2,500	10,000	

Hit Frequency:	10.23%	Hit Frequency:	10.23%
Payback Percentage:	51.68%	Payback Percentage:	206.73%
Total Hit Frequency:	10.23%	Total Payback:	94.18%

STANDARD PAYS			PAYS WITH POWER HIT
SPOTS MARKED	HITS	PAYS	POWER PAYS
9	0	0	0
	1	0	0
	2	0	0
	3	0	0
	4	1	4
	5	4	16
	6	12	48
	7	254	1,016
	8	1,200	4,800
	9	2,500	10,000

Hit Frequency:	15.31%	Hit Frequency:	15.31%
Payback Percentage:	50.44%	Payback Percentage:	201.74%
Total Hit Frequency:	15.31%	Total Payback:	93.96%

— — — —

SPOTS MARKED	HITS	PAYS	POWER PAYS
10	0	0	0
	1	0	0
	2	0	0
	3	0	0
	4	0	0
	5	1	4
	6	15	60
	7	75	300
	8	860	3,440
	9	1,200	4,800
	10	2,500	10,000

Hit Frequency:	6.47%	Hit Frequency:	6.47%
Payback Percentage:	46.85%	Payback Percentage:	187.42%
Total Hit Frequency:	6.47%	Total Payback:	93.90%

Most intriguing about this pay table are the enormous payback percentage contributions of the power hits. As you can see, most of them are well over 200 percent in payback percentage, with only the 10-spot being slightly below that. Conversely, you will notice how tiny the payback is on the base pay table. This is because a balance needs to be struck between the enormously high pays when the power number is hit and the standard nonpower pays. Without this, the game couldn't exist. No casino would have a game that pays back more than 200 percent, and no manufacturer would be able to sell it. As players, we would love such a game, but as much as we would like to see games that always make us winners, there is an underlying fiscal reality in everything. If the company you work for didn't make a profit, do you think they would be able to give you a paycheck? I don't think so—unless you're in a nonprofit company, of course, or perhaps in Congress! Anyway, the truth is that with all bonus games, something has to give in order to accommodate that big win. In this *Super Keno*™ game, that power hit is what makes the game. That power hit is also what contributes the majority of the overall game payback percentage.

This is somewhat similar to the *Caveman Keno*® game, with all those dino eggs. Although I didn't show them, there are individual pay tables for each of the bonus features for that game as well. There's a pay table for a hit with one dino egg, another for a hit with two dino eggs, and another for three dino eggs. Similarly so with *Cleopatra*® *Keno*, where we have another pay table to account for the two-times bonus pay. I have chosen to show this particular bonus pay schedule for the *Super Keno*™ game because it is very similar in principle to the "Hot Ball" in Bingo. When the last number drawn makes you a Bingo—or in the case of *Super Keno*™ makes you a winner, or a bigger winner—you get paid something really nice, as a bonus. In Bingo, these bonuses are paid for by extra money paid by players who wish to participate in such hot-ball games. In Bingo that's called "validation." In Video Keno, you pay for this in a similar manner, by giving up some of the regular pays and shifting the majority of your payback to those hits that happen with the power ball. The concept is identical. This particular version of *Super Keno*™ is so ideally suited to show this that I have used it as an example. Just so that you know, the actual breakdown of all the video keno games and their various pay tables, each with the corresponding payback percentage, runs into many, many pages. I have a calculation of more than sixty pages, closely typed, containing well over 100,000 individual calculations pertaining to just some of the video keno games available in the *Game King*® machines. I could easily fill up a book twice this size with nothing but numbers and breakdowns of pays and payback percentages, but not many people are interested enough in these calculations to demand such a book. Those sections that I am including here are enough to show just how varied · the video games can be, and are designed to give you a heads-up about the game. With this knowledge you will be far better equipped to make educated decisions regarding your play, and to make those powerful profits that Video Keno can so frequently provide.

TOP AND BOTTOM KENO

This is a popular game, one that got its video version inter-est from the lounge keno version. In Lounge Keno, there are two versions of precisely this same game. The original one was the classic top/bottom ticket, wherein a player bets on how many numbers will appear either at the "top" of the ticket—the "top" numbers 1 through 40 as shown on the ticket layout—versus the "bottom" portion of the ticket, showing the numbers 41 through 80, as printed on the keno tickets, and as being displayed on the keno board, and also on video keno screens. The second version is a derivative called "left/right ticket," wherein the player wagers whether the majority of the keno numbers drawn will be either on the left side of the keno board, or on the right. Basically, this is the simplest use of "patterns" play, and I will discuss more of that as it applies to Video Keno a little later on. On both versions of this ticket, it doesn't matter whether the num-bers hit either top or bottom, or left or right, because as long as the player bets both sides, he gets paid whether a lot of the numbers show up, or not many at all. You see, these tickets pay for hitting a lot of numbers, but also for *not* hit-ting numbers. This makes the tickets hugely popular, partic-ularly with people who don't know much about Keno, but know that non-hits happen a lot on their tickets. They play these tickets primarily because they feel that they will get paid even if they don't hit anything.

The video keno version of these tickets never quite caught on in the same manner as the lounge keno versions. There are only the top/bottom video keno versions of this game, and they work on a very simple principle. You bet ei-ther on the top 40 numbers, or on the bottom 40 numbers. That's it. Afterward, the game plays. If more than 12 num-bers are selected by the machine among the 40-section you picked, then you will get paid the minimum pay, usually

even money—1:1. The more numbers you hit in your selected half of the keno board, the more you get paid. Conversely, however, if you hit only 7 numbers, then you get
paid 2:1 on that "non" hit. In this case—without you having
to move your selections—the *fewer* numbers you hit, the more
you will be paid, so, you have two chances to win: One, the
more numbers you hit, the more you get paid. Two, the *fewer*
numbers you hit, the more you get paid.

Sounds good? Well, it is, but there is a catch—you don't
get paid anything for hits of 8, 9, 10, and 11 numbers, or
non-hits of more than 7 and less than 12. These four number groups combinations—8, 9, 10, and 12 numbers—are
the most common hits on this game. Therefore, you will not
get many of those really juicy hits. In reality, this game
looks better than it is. Overall, the best version of this game
pays back about 94.323 percent, and that's not too bad. I
have played this game many times, and the best pay I ever
got was a non-hit, where I caught only 2 numbers out of the
selected field of 40, and this paid me $500 on this particular
machine and game. There are many versions of this game
available, but the best one is the IGT top/bottom video keno
game with the 94.323 percent payback. The chart opposite
shows the pay table and payback schedule for that game, for
coins 1 through 4.

As you can see, this can be an intriguing game, particularly when you either hit—or don't hit—the higher-paying
combinations. I have only seen one event where the top
award was hit, and that was on a game in one of the off-
Strip casinos in Las Vegas. The man playing won $50,000
on a dollar version of this game by *not* hitting any numbers
among his selected 40—which was the 0-out-of-40 hit
shown at the top of the pay chart. Such wins are very rare,
but the game can be lots of fun. Most of the time you will
receive enough of the smaller pays to keep you going for
quite a while, and it can be a nice relaxing means to enjoy-

Pay Table Chart for Top-Bottom Keno with 94.323 Percent Payback Average

(starts with minimum 40 spots selected—either top or bottom)

SPOTS HIT	PAYS	HIT FREQUENCY (%)	CONTRIBUTION TO PAYBACK (%)
0 of 40	12,500	0.000004	0.05
1 of 40	5,000	0.000149	0.74
2 of 40	558	0.002502	1.40
3 of 40	180	0.024798	4.46
4 of 40	32	0.162476	5.20
5 of 40	12	0.748691	8.98
6 of 40	3	2.519634	7.56
7 of 40	2	6.345744	12.69
8 of 40	0	12.153233	0.00
9 of 40	0	17.880619	0.00
10 of 40	0	20.324303	0.00
11 of 40	0	17.880619	0.00
12 of 40	1	12.153233	12.15
13 of 40	2	6.345744	12.69
14 of 40	3	2.519634	7.56
15 of 40	12	0.748691	8.98
16 of 40	32	0.162476	5.20
17 of 40	180	0.024798	4.46
18 of 40	558	0.002502	1.40
19 of 40	5,000	0.000149	0.74
20 of 40	12,500	0.000004	0.05

ing your casino visit, with a potential for some very good hits. This game is, however, passive and doesn't allow you too many choices, nor does it allow you to practice much of any kind of skill in keno play. The previously shown versions of Video Keno, and those that follow, are usually better bets because they allow you not only to choose your numbers, but also to choose your groups, and to change those as you wish. Therefore, these games offer much more flexibility.

SUPER WAY KENO®

This is one of several different video keno versions of keno "way" tickets, such as those I have shown you in part one. Making these kinds of tickets available on video keno machines has been difficult, not only because of the complexity of programming the computer to make such a game—with so many variations—but primarily because of the lack of expertise on the part of the players. Even regular keno players are often befuddled by way tickets, although playing Keno with such tickets is not only profitable, but easy. Such play is also easily learned, and with experience even more easily exploited for good pays. Unfortunately, many people simply find any kind of thinking a problem when it comes to Slots, and that's why so many people play even Reel Slots so badly and lose so much money in the process. Video Keno way tickets require forethought, understanding, and a good dose of skill. Playing any gambling game well, and hence profitably, requires more than just the passive handing over of your money to the machine and then waiting to find out if you won. There are many skills involved, and even the most basic of passive games—such as plain Reel Slots—requires selection skills and some kind of a strategy.

Making a video keno game attractive to enough players so that they would play it, and still make a game that at least mirrors some of the way ticket options available in the live lounge keno game, has been a problem. To solve this, and still have a game that is reasonably good, IGT made a game called *Super Way Keno®*. This is basically a combination of a 2-spot, 3-spot, 4-spot, 5-spot, 6-spot, 7-spot, and a 9-spot. The game requires you to select three groups, marked "A," "B," and "C." Each group of numbers you select is identified on the game screen by the corresponding letter. For example, all the numbers selected for group "A" will be marked on the game's video screen with the letter "A." All the numbers marked in group "B" will be marked with the letter "B," and all those you mark in group "C" will be shown as marked by the letter "C." It's easy to understand the basic concept. Don't worry too much about the pays, because they combine, and the pay schedule may look a little complicated on the game's pay table, but you'll get the idea pretty quickly once you start playing. Just remember that the machine will automatically add the various pays together and show you the total of what you have won. It's that easy to get started.

In this game, group "A" must consist of 4 numbers together. Group "B" must have 3 numbers together, and group "C" must have 2 numbers together, making 9 the total number you can pick. That's why this is often called the "video keno 9-spot way ticket." There are many hits you can make on such a ticket. Each time you hit your 2 numbers in group "C," you get paid for a 2-spot, as well as all of the 2 out of other numbers in their combinations. Each time you get all 3 numbers in group "B," you will get paid for a 3-spot, as well as all of the 3 out of all the other number combination pays. Each time you hit all 4 of the numbers in group "A," you will be paid for the 4-spot, as well as all the pays for all the possible combinations of 4 out of the other number picks. Of course, once you start combining these hits, that's where the big money is. If you combine the group "A" 4-spot hit with the group "C" 2-spot hit, you have a solid 6-spot hit, as well as all the other pays combined, and so on, for all the possible combinations of all these various other hits. As with all video keno games, the various combinations are complex, as are the pay tables. Suffice it to say that the game comes in several configurations, with pay tables ranging from 94 percent payback to as low as only 88.2 percent. The chart below lists the pay table for the 94 percent payback game; you can use your own skills to compare it with others.

Pay Table Chart for *Super Way Keno*® with 94.00 Percent Payback Average

Starts with minimum 2 spots selected

Hit frequency and payback shown for solid hits only

SPOTS MARKED	HITS	PAYS
2	0	0
	1	1
	2	10

Hit Frequency: 43.987%

Payback Percentage: 98.101%

— — — —

SPOTS MARKED	HITS	PAYS
3	0	0
	1	0
	2	2
	3	50

Hit Frequency: 15.263%

Payback Percentage: 97.128%

— — — —

SPOTS MARKED	HITS	PAYS
4	0	0
	1	0
	2	2
	3	5
	4	100

Hit Frequency: 25.895%

Payback Percentage: 94.785%

— — — —

SPOTS MARKED	HITS	PAYS
5	0	0
	1	0
	2	0
	3	3
	4	12
	5	825

Hit Frequency: 9.667%
Payback Percentage: 92.049%

― ― ― ―

SPOTS MARKED	HITS	PAYS
6	0	0
	1	0
	2	0
	3	3
	4	4
	5	68
	6	1,600

Hit Frequency: 16.158%
Payback Percentage: 91.579%

― ― ― ―

SPOTS MARKED	HITS	PAYS
7	0	0
	1	0
	2	0
	3	1
	4	2
	5	20
	6	400
	7	7,000

Hit Frequency: 23.658%
Payback Percentage: 91.579%

― ― ― ―

SPOTS MARKED	HITS	PAYS
8		

There is NO 8-spot available in this "way" ticket configuration.

▬ ▬ ▬ ▬

SPOTS MARKED	HITS	PAYS
9	0	0
	1	0
	2	0
	3	0
	4	1
	5	6
	6	44
	7	326
	8	4,700
	9	10,000

Hit Frequency:	15.305%
Payback Percentage:	91.469%

▬ ▬ ▬ ▬

SPOTS MARKED	HITS	PAYS
10		

There is NO 10-spot possible in this game, because 9 numbers are the maximum that can be selected with this way-ticket combination.

As you can see, many of these pays are quite generous, especially when compared with some of the other pay tables for the previously shown games. However, you should always be aware that each of these games is *different*. Just because they are all generically "Video Keno" doesn't mean that they are identical. As with the other games, I have shown you the best pay table available for this game. Be aware, however, that your casino may not necessarily have this version of the game and that other versions may not pay nearly as well. To find out if you have the better game, look at the pays for the 2-spot, 3-spot, 4-spot, and 5-spot. If the solid hits on these are listed as 9, 44, 80, and 800, respectively, instead of the 10, 50, 100, and 825 as shown on the better pay table I have shown you here in detail, then you don't have the best available version of this game. This particular version, with that pay table, is only an 88.20 percent payback game, so you can easily see the big difference between them and just how important the very small alterations in the smallest pays really are.

Be aware, however, that as I have said in Part One about Lounge Keno, the same also applies here—playing "way" tickets is a lot better than playing only straight up tickets. With Video Keno, you may be limited only to the preformatted selections that the programmers have given you, but this is still a good way to explore and exploit the game. Its biggest drawback, however, is that you can often only bet one coin for each of the groups, for a total of seven coins maximum, and this limits your pays to only the one-coin payoffs. This is the biggest issue I have with all of these various versions of video keno "way" tickets—a factor that significantly detracts from them and therefore from my wholehearted endorsement. Nevertheless, they are better than nothing and can be played to good advantage, particularly in the better payback pay tables, and if played with limited bankrolls and for longevity at the game. I am disappointed that these games are not available with the options to wager maximum coins on each combination, or for selections that allow the *player* to determine how much to wager on which group. This modification would go a long way toward making these limited video versions of keno "way" tickets far more attractive, particularly for a regular video keno player. But that shouldn't keep you from trying this game or any of its variations. Some versions of these games can provide good enough wins even within the limitations of their design and programs. Some of these now follow.

3-6-9 WAY KENO

Among keno players, this ticket and game are known as "the three-way kiss." It is another version of the 9-spot way ticket that I have just shown you. On this ticket, however, you can only pick three groups of three numbers, making a total of three 3-spots, three 6-spots (although it really should be six 6-spots), and one 9-spot. Therefore, on the pay table there are only three possible winning combinations, and these are pays for the 3-spots, 6-spots, and the 9-spot. The chart below shows how such a pay table breaks down.

Pay Table Chart for 3-6-9 Way Keno with 94.00 Percent Payback Average

Starts with minimum 3 spots selected

Hit frequency and payback shown for solid hits only

SPOTS MARKED	HITS	PAYS
3	0	0
	1	0
	2	2
	3	48

Hit Frequency:	15.263%
Payback Percentage:	97.350%

— — — —

SPOTS MARKED	HITS	PAYS
6	0	0
	1	0
	2	0
	3	3
	4	4
	5	75
	6	1,600

Hit Frequency: 16.158%

Payback Percentage: 91.220%

— — — —

SPOTS MARKED	HITS	PAYS
9	0	0
	1	0
	2	0
	3	0
	4	1
	5	6
	6	44
	7	340
	8	4,700
	9	10,000

Hit Frequency: 15.305%

Payback Percentage: 92.300%

— — — —

As with all variations on the video keno game, this game also comes with different pay tables and payback percentages. The chart I have shown you is the best one available, with an average payback of 94.00 percent. Several other versions don't pay back nearly as well, so you should check to see which game you have by looking at the pay table variations. For example, a version of this game is available with only an average of 88.01 percent payback. This game only pays 2 and 44 for the 3-spots, instead of 2 and 48; only 54 for the 5-out-of-6 pay, instead of 75; and only 38 for the 6-out-of-9 hit, instead of 44. Again, these apparently tiny alterations in the pay table have a huge impact on the overall payback percentage.

2-4-6 WAY KENO

Finally, there is a version of the 3-6-9 keno game that uses the very same principles, but instead of playing for 3-spots, 6-spots, and a 9-spot, this game only plays for 2-spots, 4-spots, and 6-spots. Each of the three possible groups—A, B, and C—are marked with only two numbers, each such group of two numbers forming each of these three groups of two. Keno players often call this game the two-ABCs game. On this game, you can only hit 2-spots, 4-spots, and a 6-spot. Otherwise, the game plays exactly like the 3-6-9 way keno we just discussed. See the chart below for the best pay table for this game—paying back 94 percent.

Pay Table Chart for 2-4-6 Way Keno with 94.00 Percent Payback Average

Starts with minimum 2 spots selected

Hit frequency and payback shown for solid hits only

SPOTS MARKED	HITS	PAYS
2	0	0
	1	1
	2	10

Hit Frequency: 43.987%
Payback Percentage: 98.101%

— — — —

SPOTS MARKED	HITS	PAYS
4	0	0
	1	0
	2	2
	3	6
	4	74

Hit Frequency:		25.895%
Payback Percentage:	91.145%

— — — —

SPOTS MARKED	HITS	PAYS
6	0	0
	1	0
	2	0
	3	3
	4	4
	5	58
	6	1,700

Hit Frequency:		16.158%
Payback Percentage:	90.243%

— — — —

As you can see, there are some slight alterations in this pay schedule to account for the more frequent occurrence of solid hits. As with the earlier games, this one also comes with different paybacks. This pay table is the best, with an average payback of 94 percent. Some casinos may have games that don't pay as well, with some games paying back as little as 88.23 percent. To find out which game you are considering, look for these differences: the solid 2-spot should pay 10, and not 9 or less. The 3 out of 4 and the solid 4 should pay 6 and 70, respectively, and not 5 and 70, or less. The 5 out of 6 and the solid 6-spot should pay 58 and

1,700, respectively, and not 48 and 1,500. For this game, as well as every other video keno game—and indeed for all other machine games—these differences in the small pays account for the majority of the percentage payback drop you will encounter as you make your choices among the various casino games.

And this now brings us to the last few games in this chapter. First, I will show you the pay tables for the regular, standard video keno game, known as *Spot Keno*™. This is the game upon which all of the others are based. I have left it for the end of this chapter because I first wanted to show you all the variations on the basic principle of the game, so that when you finally look at the basic video keno game you will already have become accustomed to seeing, and understanding, the various pay table and payback differences. This is important, because the basic Spot Keno game is offered in so many varieties and incarnations that you have to be very vigilant to make certain you are playing one of the better payback versions, instead of one of the worst.

The next game I will show is the 10-coin Spot Keno game, and that is the principle behind *Four Card Keno*™. By being able to show you all these variations, and now the various differences in the basic video keno game you will be ready to play multi-card video keno games like *Four Card Keno*™, which are based on the 10-coin *Spot Keno*™ pay table. And that will then lead us into the discussion of best games, and, finally, on to strategy.

SPOT KENO™

The granddaddy of them all, this is the standard, the very basis of all video keno games. Although just about everybody calls this game *Video* Keno, its "industry" name has always been "spot" keno, because of the marking of the "spots." If you look again at Photo 4, on page 170, you will see that the old-style video keno machines were much more like "spot" Keno. You had to use a "wand," touch it over the number you wished to select, and therefore "spot" the number. It doesn't really matter what the "industry" name for this game is, these days it's all Video Keno. On the modern machines the screen looks a lot different from those older machines, but the principle is still the same.

Photo 8 shows what *Spot Keno*™ looks like on the newest *Game King*® machines; this is what the video keno game will look like to you after you select the "Keno" icon from the on-screen game menu. Nothing in the menu will actually identify this game as *Spot Keno*™, because it is mostly referred to simply as "Keno." If it is a plain, simple, "spot keno" game, then all you will see in the on-screen

Photo 8. The look of the modern *Spot Keno*™ game screen for *Game King*® touch screen machines.

menu is an icon that says "Keno." If you touch it, the machine will take you to the standard video keno game—the one called *Spot Keno*™—and *that's* the game I am discussing now.

As with all of these video keno games, *Spot Keno*™ comes with many different pay tables and payback programs. Which one you get in the casino where you happen to be depends on the casino and how liberal they think they should be with their customers. Most of the time, the casinos in Las Vegas will have the best pay tables and payback percentages, with the locals' places off the Strip having the better of the mix. There are, however, many casinos nationwide that also carry the better payback games, so you will simply have to look closely at the pay tables and find out for yourself which game you are about to play, and how good it actually is. Generally speaking, the traditional single-screen *Spot Keno*™ is not among the overall better-paying video keno games, because many of the newer versions of Video Keno—such as the games I showed earlier, and those that follow—pay a few percentage points more in some versions. The most liberal of the standard Spot Keno programs pays back at about 93.99 percent, making it just a tad over a 6 percent house withholding percentage game. This isn't bad, considering that Roulette holds 5.6 percent, and many blackjack players who play the game badly face more than a 6 percent house edge. Many reel slot machines don't even pay back this much, particularly those outside of Nevada. So you see, even though this traditional video keno game may not be as good as some of its more recent versions, dismissing it as a "bad" game is unfair and gives the game an unnecessarily bad rap. Nevertheless standard, plain *Spot Keno*™ isn't as exciting as it once was, and certainly not so much fun as some of its various derivatives. But since the principles of this game are the core of all such video keno games, it is essential that we know about it and what it means to us. All of the other pay tables and payback percentages, as well as our ability to make selections based on our understanding of the pay tables, are based on this game. Once you learn to understand this game, and how to look for the differences in the various pay tables and what they mean to your profit potential, you will be more able to pick the better games among the others. This becomes even more important when you get into *Four Card Keno*™, and *Multi-Card Keno*™, both of which are based on the *Spot Keno*™ pay tables. By learning what they are here you will be better able to gauge the potential profitability of playing the other games. Among the various paybacks for *Spot Keno*™, the variations are too numerous to list; I can, however, give you some parameters.

The chart below offers a listing of the top eight of the most common payback programs for regular Video Keno, known as *Spot Keno*™.

SPOT KENO™ PAYBACK	PERCENT
Best	93.99
Next best	92.43
Third best	91.97
Fourth best	89.65
Fifth best	88.19
Sixth best	87.61
Seventh best	85.34
Eighth best	85.02

Again, and also as we have seen earlier, there is a vast difference between how these games are offered. Some casinos may have the better game, at the top of this list, that holds only 6.01 percent for the house. Some casinos may wish to take in more money, and so offer the worst pay table—the one at the bottom of the chart—holding a huge

14.98 percent for the house. And some casinos may have games that are somewhere in the middle of all of this; it is left up to you to figure out which. To help you with these decisions, I will first list the best pay table for the 93.99 percent payback Spot Keno game, and then show you what to look for if you are about to play one of the not-so-good payback games—perhaps one in the chart.

Pay Table Chart for *Spot Keno*™ with 93.99 Percent Payback Average

Starts with minimum 2 spots selected

Hit frequency and payback shown for solid hits only

SPOTS MARKED	HITS	PAYS
2	0	0
	1	0
	2	15

Hit Frequency: 6.01%

Payback Percentage: 91.19%

— — — —

SPOTS MARKED	HITS	PAYS
3	0	0
	1	0
	2	2
	3	48

Hit Frequency: 15.26%

Payback Percentage: 94.35%

— — — —

SPOTS MARKED	HITS	PAYS
4	0	0
	1	0
	2	2
	3	5
	4	100

Hit Frequency: 25.89%

Payback Percentage: 94.78%

SPOTS MARKED	HITS	PAYS
5	0	0
	1	0
	2	0
	3	3
	4	14
	5	838

Hit Frequency: 9.67%

Payback Percentage: 94.95%

SPOTS MARKED	HITS	PAYS
6	0	0
	1	0
	2	0
	3	3
	4	4
	5	75
	6	1,660

Hit Frequency: 16.16%

Payback Percentage: 94.99%

SPOTS MARKED	HITS	PAYS
7	0	0
	1	0
	2	0
	3	1
	4	2
	5	22
	6	422
	7	7,000

Hit Frequency: 23.66%
Payback Percentage: 94.92%

— — — —

SPOTS MARKED	HITS	PAYS
8	0	0
	1	0
	2	0
	3	0
	4	2
	5	13
	6	100
	7	1,670
	8	10,000

Hit Frequency: 10.23%
Payback Percentage: 94.90%

— — — —

SPOTS MARKED	HITS	PAYS
9	0	0
	1	0
	2	0
	3	0
	4	1
	5	6
	6	44
	7	362
	8	4,700
	9	10,000

Hit Frequency: 15.31%
Payback Percentage: 93.60%

SPOTS MARKED	HITS	PAYS
10	0	0
	1	0
	2	0
	3	0
	4	0
	5	5
	6	24
	7	146
	8	1,000
	9	4,500
	10	10,000

Hit Frequency: 6.47%
Payback Percentage: 93.20%

▬ ▬ ▬ ▬

If you can find a video keno game with this pay table—one that is the traditional *Spot Keno*™ and not one of its derivatives—then you have one of the better paying video keno games now available. However, watch out for the small changes in the pay table, because they significantly alter the game's overall payback percentage and your ability to make profits as well as the costs involved in playing, such as the size of your session bankroll. Watch for the following indicators of a lower-payback program:

- If the game pays 14 for a 2-out-of-2 hit, instead of 15
- If the game pays 40 for a 3-out-of-3 hit, instead of 48
- If the game pays 3 for the 3-out-of-4 hit, instead of 5
- If the game pays 2 for the 3-out-of-5 hit, instead of 3
- If the game pays 2 for the 3-out-of-6 hit, instead of 3
- If the game pays 15 for the 5-out-of-7 hit, instead of 22
- If the game pays 348 for the 6-out-of-7 hit, instead of 422 (or at least 400)

- If the game pays 1 for the 4-out-of-8 hit, instead of 2
- If the game pays12 for the 5-out-of-8 hit, instead of 13
- If the game pays 3 for the 5-out-of-9 hit, instead of 6
- If the game pays 3 for the 5-out-of-10 hit, instead of 5
- If any game pays less than 10,000 for the solid 8, solid 9, and/or solid 10 hits.

Whenever you see a game that has any pays similar to these, as compared with the best, this is not the best video keno *Spot Keno*™ game available. Look carefully at the various differences in the pay table structure to see precisely which pays have been reduced. Remember that it does *not* matter what higher pays there may be; making the game "top heavy" is a favorite trick for casinos who want to get more of your money, by reducing the very frequently occurring pays and "loading up" on the top pays that are so much harder to hit, and don't hit very often. Any change in the pay table for the *smallest pays* is usually a clear indicator that this game is not among the best paying *Spot Keno*™ games. Sometimes you can find better versions of *Spot Keno*™ even in the same casino. Often a casino will have some of their *Spot Keno*™ games with the lower pay tables, but elsewhere in the same casino they may have the same game—one that looks identical to all the other *Spot Keno*™ games but with the better pay table and payback. There is nothing wrong with this kind of a varied game mix. This is the same principle often used by supermarkets, as well as any other retailer. Some of the large stores can easily have the same product with different prices in different locations, either within the same store, or among their other stores. It simply depends on the "smarts" of the shopper to find this out if they don't want to pay the higher prices. The same applies to casinos, casino players, and casino machines. It's up to you—the "customer"—to find out if you are paying a premium price a game that actually pays you back a whole lot more than something else that looks identical, but "costs" more. Take a few seconds to look at the pay table on your *Spot Keno*™ game and compare it with the one listed here. If it's the same, or is very similar overall, then you have one of the better games. If not, you have one of the not-so-good games that will cost you more to play. Your choice, your "smarts."

And so we come to the 10-coin *Spot Keno*™ game, which I will use as a model for the *Four Card Keno*™ games I like so much. In fact, I will refer to this as the *Four Card Keno*™ game, because most of these games are the 10-coin-type video keno games, and their pay tables and payback percentages reflect those for the 10-coin *Spot Keno*™.

FOUR CARD KENO™

This is currently my all-time favorite keno game, and the one on which I have won the vast majority of my most recent video keno jackpots. I have hit numerous 8-out-of-9 hits on this game, for $4,700 plus all the other pays, as well as solid 9s for $5,000 pays (2 coins) plus all the other pays in the "wheel," many, many 8-out-of-10 hits for $500 (2 coins) and $1,000 (four coins), plus all of the many other pays this provided for the combination hits. I have also hit 9 out of 10 for anywhere from $4,500 to over $5,500, and also solid 10s for pays over $5,000 each (2 coins), and more. Plus, of course, many more hits and pays for all the possibilities in between all these huge hits. These are huge wins when considering that Video Keno is a negative-expectation game, always having a comparatively high house edge. The payback programs in most of these *Four Card Keno*™ games average about 91.97 percent, which means that these games hold about 8.03 percent for the house. I have actually seen the on-screen in-game payback figures from the game's own progressively tallied payback percentage readout screen, accessible from on the floor by the floorperson with the turn of a special key and the selection of an icon from the "secret" menu that the players never see. On that I was able to see that the various cards not only have their own individual payback percentages, but that they combine to form the actual average overall payback percentage for the game as a whole. Some of the cards in *Four Card Keno*™ pay back at about 88 percent, others as high as 97%. It all depends on what numbers were marked and hit and how often any one of the four cards has hit, and what the pays were. Each such value varies as the game is played, with some cards hitting more and others hitting less. This averages to the machine's overall average payback in the end, and this is usually around 92 percent, give or take a few tenths of a percentage point.

The main advantage of *Four Card Keno*™ is that you can play more than one keno card at the same time. This is similar to the "way" ticket concept in Lounge Keno, and is better than the "way" ticket style video keno games, because on those you can only play the combinations the machine allows you to pick, and not those you want to play—including those you may wish to play that could be to your better advantage. In *Four Card Keno*™, you can "wheel" your numbers, which means you can combine several "core" numbers to be the same on all the four cards you can play. By doing this, each time you get a paying hit on the core numbers, you immediately get that pay four times, including any of the other pays you may get by having these core numbers the same among all of your four cards. This often results in very large pays, not only because the pays themselves combine, but because when you hit your core numbers this also usually means that you will have hit one or more of your other numbers on the other cards, and these combine to get you really large pays. All of this will become a lot more obvious to you once you see the actual game, and are able to play it.

Playing *Four Card Keno*™ is quite easy, but many players are confused by what appears to be a very complex screen. First, the screen is divided into four squares, each "lettered" with "A," "B," "C," and "D." These letters designate the game screens available in this game. Each of the individual game screens looks almost identical to the regular video keno game screen, such as the one shown earlier in Photo 8, on page 223. The main difference is in the main screen, which combines all four cards. There you will see four cards, each with the designated letter identifying it as either Card A, B, C, or D. Although you can play any one, two, or three of these cards, either individually or together, the main advantage to playing this game is that *you can play four cards all at the same time.* Trying to play this game *without* playing all the four cards is *not* a good idea; you should *never* do this because you will not be getting the best value for your play. If you don't wish to play all four cards, don't play this game. Play the standard *Spot Keno*™ instead, or perhaps some of the other video keno games I have mentioned previously. Your advantage in playing *Four Card Keno*™—and later the even newer and better *Multi-Card Keno*™—is precisely in your ability to play ALL the cards at the same time. It's silly to play a game that gives you the chance for multiple winners when you aren't playing it in a manner that allows you to *get* those multiple winners.

As surprising as it may seem, thousands of players look at this simple game and are completely befuddled by it. They try to play one card out of the four, or make a wager and then don't know what is happening, and then make other silly mistakes and wonder why the game isn't playing or paying. All they have to do is touch the icon on the game that says "pays," or the one that says "help," and the machine will explain how to play it. Of course it will only tell you how to play, and not how to play well and for powerful profits, but that's all you need to start. I understand that gambling machines and games can be confusing to people who don't know anything about them, and that's why I always try to explain everything as simply as possible, even though I realize that many readers may already know some of this. So, if you already know about *Four Card Keno*™, bear with me a while as I try to explain the game as simply as possible.

First you find a *Game King*® machine, and look to see if it has *Four Card Keno*™ in its game menu. Look again at Photo 2, on page 164, to see what such a multi-game machine looks like. In that photograph you can clearly see the game menu, where there are many games. If this machine has the *Four Card Keno*™ icon, simply touch it and the game will take you to the game screen. There, you will see four keno cards divided, as I have explained previously, with the A, B, C, and D cards. Now comes the part that confuses most players: how to bet, what to bet, and how to get all the cards to work together. It's actually simple, but the game doesn't immediately display this method, and so it may take a little time. The first thing you must do after you have this four-card main game screen in front of you is to make a wager. You must make a wager on *all* the cards before you can go to any one of them individually. If you wish to play, for example, one credit per card, push the game's credit button four times, once for each card. Now you have wagered four coins (credits), and you have bet one credit on each of the four cards. Once this is done, you have activated all four cards, and you can now proceed. Remember, however, that you *must* make at least this minimum wager, because otherwise you will *not* be able to play *all* the four cards, thus defeating the purpose of playing this game in the first place.

Assuming you have made at least the minimum wager of one credit for all the four cards, for a total wager of a minimum of four credits, you can proceed to selecting your numbers. First, touch the on-screen icon marked as "Card A,"

located at the top far left. This will take you to the Card A
screen. Once there, touch the "erase" icon, and then select
your numbers by touching the game screen over each of the
numbers you wish to pick, using the tip of your finger. Each
number selected will become marked on the game screen
with the letter "A." You can select from a minimum of two
numbers to a maximum of ten numbers per card. Once you
have completed the selection of your numbers on Card A,
touch the icon marked "switch," located at the top left of
the game's screen. This will take you back to the main four-
card screen. Alternatively—and primarily to save time—you
can go directly to the next game screen simply by touching
the next card's icon, in this case Card B. The machine will
then display the game screen for Card B, and you can mark
your numbers using the same procedure you used to mark
the numbers for Card A. You may—if you wish—mark the
same numbers as those you have selected for Card A, but
the point of this game is that you don't have to. Pick other
numbers, perhaps some that are the same as those on Card
A, but others that are different. Once you have completed
the selection of your numbers for Card B, touch the icon at
the top of the game screen identified as Card C, and this will
take you to that game card. Again, erase and mark the numbers you want. When you are finished, touch the icon
marked as Card D, and this will take you to the last card—
card four. Again, use the same procedure as before, and
mark your numbers. Once you are finished, you have successfully marked all the numbers you wanted on all the four
cards. Now you can either touch the icon "switch," which
will take you back to the four-card screen, or you can simply begin the game by touching the button (or icon) marked
"play." The machine will now play a game using all four
cards, with your numbers as you have marked them. To
help you understand all of this, Figure 16, on page 236,
shows an example of the game's four-card screen.

Thereafter, if you wish to play the same numbers all the

time—or for as long as you want to play these numbers, and for the same wager—you can simply keep touching the "bet" button, which is often called "re-bet" or "play" button or icon. Each time you touch this button or icon, the machine will play the next game with the same wager and the same numbers, for as long as you wish to keep playing it this way. If at any time you wish to change either any of the numbers, or the size of the wager, simply repeat the wagering and number selections procedure—however, do *not* attempt to go directly to each game screen without first going to the main four-card screen by touching the "switch" icon and then first making the bets, as described previously. Each time you want to change either the size of the wager, or any numbers on any card, *always repeat the entire proce-*

Switch   Card A   Card B   Card C   Card D

1	2	3	4	5	6	7	8	9	10
11	12	13	14	15	16	17	18	19	20
21	22	23	24	25	26	27	28	29	30
31	32	33	34	35	36	37	38	39	40
41	42	43	44	45	46	47	48	49	50
51	52	53	54	55	56	57	58	59	60
61	62	63	64	65	66	67	68	69	70
71	72	73	74	75	76	77	78	79	80

1	2	3	4	5	6	7	8	9	10
11	12	13	14	15	16	17	18	19	20
21	22	23	24	25	26	27	28	29	30
31	32	33	34	35	36	37	38	39	40
41	42	43	44	45	46	47	48	49	50
51	52	53	54	55	56	57	58	59	60
61	62	63	64	65	66	67	68	69	70
71	72	73	74	75	76	77	78	79	80

1	2	3	4	5	6	7	8	9	10
11	12	13	14	15	16	17	18	19	20
21	22	23	24	25	26	27	28	29	30
31	32	33	34	35	36	37	38	39	40
41	42	43	44	45	46	47	48	49	50
51	52	53	54	55	56	57	58	59	60
61	62	63	64	65	66	67	68	69	70
71	72	73	74	75	76	77	78	79	80

1	2	3	4	5	6	7	8	9	10
11	12	13	14	15	16	17	18	19	20
21	22	23	24	25	26	27	28	29	30
31	32	33	34	35	36	37	38	39	40
41	42	43	44	45	46	47	48	49	50
51	52	53	54	55	56	57	58	59	60
61	62	63	64	65	66	67	68	69	70
71	72	73	74	75	76	77	78	79	80

Figure 16. An example of the *Four Card Keno*™ main game screen format and layout.

dure from the start. If you don't, the machine may take that as another event and not play the other cards, and you may lose the numbers on the other cards and not have the cards marked as you first started. You must remember that each time you do anything, to the machine this is a "user command," and it will do what it's programmed to do with such commands. Unless you start from the beginning, the machine won't "know" you only wished to make *one* change. It will take that as a "new event," and if you don't start at the beginning, nothing you had been playing before will remain. This becomes even more important when it comes to making wagers, because many people habitually change one card or another, forget to go through the procedure from the start, and then wonder why the machine either doesn't play, or somehow doesn't play all the cards or numbers they had previously marked. Each time you make *any* change to *Four Card Keno*™—no matter what it is—*you must always start from the beginning*, from the "switch" menu, and always start by first making a wager on all four cards. If you make this a habit, you will never have problems, you will never become confused about what is happening, and you will always be able to preserve your numbers and your game just as you want it.

This issue is the most common problem experienced by players of *Four Card Keno*™, because they only think of one card at a time, instead of the four cards as a total unit. By making changes individually—by jumping from Card A, to B, to C, to D, then back to B, then to C, and so on—they think of each card as a single game, when it is only one-fourth of the game, because this game is *Four Card Keno*™, and the four cards *together* are the game. Any change to any one of those four cards must always be done from the beginning, with all wagers properly made first, and only then go to any of the individual cards to make your changes. This is the simplest means of playing this game, and if you do this every time you want to make any changes to your cards or wagers, you will never forget any cards or become confused.

For those players who are familiar with the game and more sophisticated in playing it, there are other ways to make changes to the cards. Each card can be accessed individually, and so changed, but to do so you must always be able to make a wager first for each such card, and then go through all the other cards and re-make the wagers for all of them and re-mark the numbers there as well. If you don't, the machine will only register your actions as a selection of only that one card on which you made the change. Let's say, for example, that you want to change the numbers on Card C. To do this properly, you would first touch the "switch" icon, go to the main four-card screen menu, then make the proper wagers, touch the Card C screen icon, and then erase and re-mark your new numbers on that card only. By doing this in this manner, your other three cards are preserved, and only the change on Card C will be made. However, many players who wish to make such a change first immediately go to Card C and then try to make the change. It won't work. The machine won't let you—unless, that is, you first make a wager on that Card C (in our example, and so on for any of these individual cards). But, if you make a wager on Card C (as in our example) and then make your changes to that one card only, and do not go to all the other cards and re-bet and re-mark your numbers there as well, the machine will now think that you want to play *only* Card C, and it will only play that card and wipe out the other three. Players become incredibly frustrated at this, because they can't figure out why the machine won't let them make the changes they wish, or if it does, why it won't play the other cards or why it wipes them out. This is not the fault of the machine. It's the fault of the player who can't remember that this is a **Four** *Card Keno*™ game, and that *all four cards therefore work together as a single game.*

To avoid confusion and to save yourself from many such

problems, remember to treat *all* four cards as *one game*. Each time you want to make any changes to any cards, simply go to the main four-card menu by touching the "switch" icon, make all four wagers again, and then make whatever number changes you wish on any of the cards. You can then go back to playing through the re-bet button or icon indefinately, until the next time you wish to change something. It's easy to do, as long as you realize that the machine will only know what you want it to do if *you* know what to do in the first place.

Later, as you master these multi-card games, you will come to realize that you can also make different-sized wagers on each of the individual cards, similarly so to the split-rates tickets we discussed in Lounge Keno. Many of the newest multi-card video keno games have twenty cards, each identified with a letter just like *Four Card Keno*™, and on these it may be possible to vary your wagers on specific number combinations. I always play maximum coins for all four cards in *Four Card Keno*™ and only reduce my wagers to no less than two coins per card if I am playing in the higher-denomination games. I always play the same number of credits on all cards, and I never vary this. The advantage of this game lies solely in the ability to combine your hits on more than one card, and through the addition of other numbers as a core, and as a wheel, and often also in groups of duplicates. This assures you of larger wins when you get them, as well as many more frequent wins. My simplest strategy advice is to play the same credit value on all your cards, play a core with a wheel, and set a duplicate pattern for all cards. While it is possible to make various "refinements" to this kind of multi-card keno game, it is not to your advantage to futz around with fractional wagers on different cards. It is far better to focus more on the number selection and patterns, as well as cores, wheels, and duplicates, because these are the strategy keys that will help you make your powerful profits from this game.

So, now for the 10-coin pay table. I'm using a 10-coin pay table because many of these *Four Card Keno*™ games have a maximum of 10 credits per card wager, with a total maximum wager of 40 credits (coins) per all four cards. In some machines—those that are multidenominational—these credit restrictions may not be the same. Some machines may allow you to wager up to 100 credits per card, for a total of 400 credits for all four cards. Other machines may limit you to merely 16 credits total, with a maximum wager of merely 4 credits per card. These limits vary considerably from machine to machine and game to game, as well as casino to casino. Mostly, for games that use 1-cent, 2-cent, 5-cent, and 10-cent credits, the maximum will be 10 credits per card, with a 40-credit maximum for all four cards. For denominations of 25 cents, 50 cents, $1, and higher, the limits may be 4 credits per card, with a maximum of 16 credits for all four cards. Whatever this may be, the chart below shows the pay table most commonly found on these *Four Card Keno*™ games. It is a 91.97 percent payback pay table—not necessarily the best there is, but it's the best most commonly available among these kinds of machines. And although it's not the best video keno pay table possible, remember that here in this *Four Card Keno*™ game you have the ability to win many more times than just on a single pay table, which allows you to make more money even against a pay table with a relatively high house edge. Overall, all matters considered, even this pay table—one that can easily be looked at as "bad" if viewed merely singly, rather than in the combination in which it truly functions—makes the game worthwhile. By looking at the pay table, and comparing it with the one that you may find on your machine, you will be able to gauge whether your game is better, or worse, than what it generally should be.

Pay Table Chart for Four Card 10-Coin *Spot Keno*™ with 91.97 Percent Payback Average

Starts with minimum 2 spots selected

Hit frequency and payback shown for solid hits only

(averages are for the total combination of all cards)

SPOTS MARKED	HITS	PAYS
2	0	0
	1	0
	2	15

Hit Frequency: 6.01%

Payback Percentage: 91.19%

— — — —

SPOTS MARKED	HITS	PAYS
3	0	0
	1	0
	2	2
	3	46

Hit Frequency: 15.26%

Payback Percentage: 91.58%

— — — —

SPOTS MARKED	HITS	PAYS
4	0	0
	1	0
	2	2
	3	5
	4	91

Hit Frequency: 25.89%

Payback Percentage: 92.03%

— — — —

SPOTS MARKED	HITS	PAYS
5	0	0
	1	0
	2	0
	3	3
	4	12
	5	810

Hit Frequency: 9.67%
Payback Percentage: 91.93%

— — — —

SPOTS MARKED	HITS	PAYS
6	0	0
	1	0
	2	0
	3	3
	4	4
	5	70
	6	1,600

Hit Frequency: 16.16%
Payback Percentage: 92.67%

— — — —

SPOTS MARKED	HITS	PAYS
7	0	0
	1	0
	2	0
	3	1
	4	2
	5	21
	6	400
	7	7,000

Hit Frequency: 23.66%
Payback Percentage: 92.44%

— — — —

SPOTS MARKED	HITS	PAYS
8	0	0
	1	0
	2	0
	3	0
	4	2
	5	12
	6	98
	7	1,652
	8	10,000

Hit Frequency: 10.23%
Payback Percentage: 92.31%

— — — —

SPOTS MARKED	HITS	PAYS
9	0	0
	1	0
	2	0
	3	0
	4	1
	5	6
	6	44
	7	335
	8	4,700
	9	10,000

Hit Frequency: 15.31%
Payback Percentage: 92.00%

— — — —

SPOTS MARKED	HITS	PAYS
10	0	0
	1	0
	2	0
	3	0
	4	0
	5	5
	6	24
	7	142
	8	1,000
	9	4,500
	10	10,000

Hit Frequency: 6.47%

Payback Percentage: 92.55%

— — — —

Four Card Keno™ has a strategy all its own, as is the case for the multi-card keno games that will soon be available (by the time you read this book, the new *Multi-Card Keno*™ should be out in the casinos). I will discuss the finer points of such strategy play in chapter 11 on strategy, but for now, just remember the simple advice I made previously: play core numbers in a wheel, and make them duplicates, or play duplicate cards for twice the win. Now I'd like to move on to *Multi-Card Keno*™—the next generation of *Four Card Keno*™.

MULTI-CARD KENO™

Four Card Keno™ has been a huge success, converting even those slot players who previously shunned Video Keno into avid fans of this game. It's easy to see why: you can play more cards and increase your wins. You can also interlace (i.e. where you weave your numbers together) and cross-bet your groups (i.e. where you stack one group over another), and by so doing increase the wins when your core numbers hit. There are so many ways to make this game profitable and entertaining that players who overcome the initial confusion become great enthusiasts of the game. If you have played any kind of Video Keno before, how many times have you seen numbers similar to your groupings appear elsewhere on the keno board? Everyone who has ever played Video Keno knows this frustration. Thousands of times, when I played single-screen standard Video Keno, I heard players say: "Oh, look! My numbers all came up just *next* to where I marked them!" In the first generation of these Multi-Card Keno games—the *Four Card Keno™*—this was overcome to a certain extent by the ability to play four cards. With this flexibility, it became easy to mark numbers in groups and selections that also included those nearby. This eliminated the problem faced by so many single-screen keno players, because now if the numbers hit "just next to the ones marked," this was still a winner and that player could mark those "nearby" groups. In addition, by using the core and wheel strategy, players of *Four Card Keno™* were able to increase the value of their wins, thus compensating for the increased "cost" of playing the four games at the same time. Nevertheless, there was still one major problem—there simply weren't enough available game screens to mark all the possibilities, or at least more than just the four. This is about to be overcome by a terrific new game called *Multi-Card Keno™*.

Multi Card Keno™ is the next evolution of *Four Card*

Keno™. In *Four Card Keno™* the player only has the possibility of marking four cards, indicated by the alphabet letters A, B, C, and D, but with this new *Multi-Card Keno™* one can play up to twenty such cards at the same time. These are marked as cards A through T, twenty in all. Of course you don't have to play all of these cards, in the same manner as you don't have to play all of the four cards in *Four Card Keno™*. As in the earlier game, however, the advantage will lie directly in being able to do so, although with twenty cards your strategy will also come into play as this applies to the selection of the number of cards you wish to play. On some combinations of numbers, patterns, or groups, it may not be necessary to play all the cards. The jury is still out on much of this, though, because the game is not yet widely available. Nevertheless, I have decided to include some description of the game because *Multi-Card Keno™* will soon be available in most casinos. At this writing, it is still undergoing its lab and field trials before it can be made available to the casinos at large. I was able to obtain a picture of the game screen, and you can see what it looks like in Photo 9.

If this lives up to its potential, it will be a terrific game. If you have played *Four Card Keno™* before, you know that the greatest frustration among players who know how to play this game well is the lack of available cards to make all the patterns and groups pay off. Many times, as I have played that game, I wished I had the opportunity to add other groups and combinations, so that I could cover the majority of the options for the game and selections, because such would have constituted many more pays. With *Multi-Card Keno™*, this will now become a reality. Of course, we will have to wait and see if this new game will include all of the possibilities and will come with payback programs that make it worthwhile to play. The actual payback percentages are not yet known, and therefore I am not able to show them here, but

Photo 9. The *Multi-Card Keno™* game screen, similar to that seen in the popular *Four Card Keno™*.

the pay table for the *Four Card Keno™* ten-coin *Spot Keno™* example I used in the chart on page 241 will serve as a good gauge. If you see this new *Multi-Card Keno™* game in your casino, check out the pay tables and compare them with the one shown here. If it is close to it, the game should be a reasonable bet. Pay close attention to the changes in the smallest payoffs. Any such small changes will result in very large differences in payback percentage, so we will all have to do a little research before playing. However, I have high hopes that this will become one of the best gambling games available, regardless of its "bad" rap as a "house game." Even if the overall payback program is going to be only around 91 to 92 percent, or fractionally higher or lower, the game will allow the smart player to make the most of it. Playing Video Keno smartly is similar to the skills required in Lounge Keno. It's not just the dumb game many people think it is. This will become even more important with *Multi-Card Keno*™, because here you will have to do some serious thinking before you commit your money.

In the *Four Card Keno*™ game, your base wager is increased four times. Therefore, in order to play all four cards, you must wager at least the minimum of 1 credit on each card. This means you will have the minimum cost of 4 credits per game. With *Multi-Card Keno*™, the more cards you choose to play, the more costly it will become. If you choose to play all 20 cards, your cost will be the minimum of 1 credit per card, times 20—20 credits per game. Since the game is multi-denominational—as indeed most of the *Game King*® machines already are—you will be able to select the value of your credits, but even at 1 cent per credit per card, this now becomes a 20 cents per pull game. This is not the best way to play, because at such low value your reward when hit won't be enough to overcome your losses as the cost of the game increases through non-hit events, or events that constitute a win, but not enough of a win to overcome the cost of the total wager, all cards combined. You will also have to possess increased fiscal skills, not only to calculate your relative costs to win ratio, but also the value of the wins relative to the value of the expense.

These considerations will have to become part of your knowledge reservoir, and actually should already be there. Thousands of players will probably flock to this game, make large wagers, and win nothing because they might not properly investigate the possibilities and therefore make silly wagers rather than knowledgeable ones, while many more thousands will play only 1-cent credits at 1 credit per card, or 2-cent credits at 1 credit per card, or even 5-cent credits at 1 credit per card, and lose hundreds of dollars without realizing any significant wins. This is what will pay for the game, and why casinos will have the game on the floor. Few of us—those who have learned something about these video keno games—will be able to take this game to the level at which it can perform, and play it to the hilt.

Of course, the main detractor from this game will be the increased cost of play and therefore the larger required bankroll. However, just as when we discussed the "smart" use of "way" tickets in Lounge Keno, similarly a player will here be able to play this game in a manner that will allow for most of the replays either to pay for themselves or allow one to play the next game at a reduced cost. For example, if all 20 cards are played at 5-cent credit value, at a wager of 2 credits per card, that will be a cost of 10 cents per card, times 20 cards, which equals 40 credits—a total cash value of $2 per game. This may sound like a lot to wager, especially on what can easily be considered as a "nickel keno" game, because the base credit unit value is a nickel. However, compare this with the standard Video Slots, most of which take 45 credits to play all the lines and pays. At the base credit unit value of a nickel—which most of these machines are—this is a total wager of $2.25. So, playing this Multi-Card Keno game at the same unit credit value of a base of 5 cents, and using 2 credits (10 cents) as the per-card investment, the total "cost" of each game would be $2—25 cents less than the comparable "cost" of a game on most video slot machines. Therefore, playing *Multi-Card Keno*™ is practically the same as playing the video reel slot machines, in terms of the overall per-game cost factors.

In Video Keno, however, and unlike in most Video Slots, *you* can affect your ability to win, or at least your ability to minimize the replay cost of your game. Just as using "way" tickets and "kings" smartly in Lounge Keno can reduce the cost of the replay of such tickets for the next game, so this new *Multi-Card Keno*™ will also make this possible. This is already possible in *Four Card Keno*™, but not nearly to the extent that this new *Multi-Card Keno*™ will allow. By using the wagering methods that I will describe in more detail in chapter 11, you will be able to use the game to help you overcome the inherently negative expectation of the game and allow yourself the best possible chance to win. Furthermore, by utilizing your session playing skills, you just might be able to overcome the negativity altogether. At the very least, by using this game to cross-bet and offset your groups, and using core numbers and multiple wheels, you will reduce your re-bet costs remarkably, and thus be able to play the game for higher win values than the base game allows. And that's how you can turn even a "house" game such as Video Keno into one that makes you powerful profits.

Although these are not the only methods that can be used, they are among the most workable in the real world, in the very real short-term slice of your exposure to the game and the experience of playing it. By using your "smarts," you can play a $2 game, but know that the vast majority of the time it will cost you much less than that to replay the game, with many such events actually paying out a positive winner. Thereafter, knowing when to quit, and actually going home with the profit, will differentiate you from the losers. You will always be a winner, regardless of what the game's actual payback percentage may be—although I still strongly advise you to make sure *before* playing that the game's pay table is at the very least identical to, or better, than the one shown in the chart on page 241 for the base 10-coin *Four Card Keno*™. Knowing how much to bet, relative to the overall cost of the games, mindful of selections that allow for reduced-rate playback, and knowing how and when to leave with a profit are some of the most important skills you will need to ensure a win.

Strategies for Video Keno

While writing this book, I spoke with dozens of slot and keno players, and casino players in general. Over my twenty years or so in the industry—in one incarnation or another—I have spoken to tens of thousands of players of all kinds of casino games, and all kinds of people. It always surprises me how many of them think of Slots and Keno as completely passive games where no strategy is possible. Naturally, table game players think of themselves as the only "true" gamblers. Remarkable to me was that slot players and keno players *themselves* thought of their games in these terms. Almost all of these players thought of themselves as passive participants when playing Keno—kind of perennial victims to the fortunes of pure luck.

When I first encountered this phenomenon, it was a wakeup call for me. At that time I was also one of those players who found more fun than substance in these games. But I asked myself, "Is this really so?" It took about five years to find the answer. As I became more interested in Video Keno, as well as what I now call Lounge Keno, I found that people who play Slots also tend to play Keno and Video Keno but none of these players seemed to have any notion of "skills" in the game, much less anything that could be called a "strategy." Among those few who did have some inkling about being more interactive with the games were the "way" ticket players in Lounge Keno, and the "pattern" players in Video Keno. The original video keno machines were very strange looking at the time, as you can see from the example of that older style machine shown in Photo 4 on page 170. They also had some very interesting quirks. For example, long before "quick picks" became part of the on-screen menu choices for modern multi-game touch-screen machines, these older-style games were able to pick a selection of numbers in a really odd manner. By taking the wand and touching it in certain portions of the topmost video monitor, the one that displayed the pay tables, a player was able to get the machine to make the number picks for him. This "quick pick" existed long before anything even closely resembling it was part of the computer programs, which had the effect of making the machine pick the numbers. Many times, that resulted in an immediate major win, and countless times I was able to get a big win by doing precisely that. Other players also began to find this out.

Other strategies revolved around "patterns," such as groupings of three numbers side by side, making a 9-spot in a square block. Other popular patterns were the 10 numbers forming the bottom row, from the number 71 through number 80. Many players—myself included—quickly found out that the bottom row on these older machines hit winners a lot more often than any other, or so it seemed. This was the very row on which I hit my very first 9-out-of-10 and 10-out-of-10 hits. A player's club even formed in Las Vegas, called—appropriately—"the Bottom Row Club." As far as I know, it still exists and comprises video keno players who only play that bottom row. Whether this was an actual strategy or not is debatable. The fact remains that the programs of video keno machines are random, or should be. However, many of the patterns, plays, and groupings that I used on these games—and which other successful players also used—were possibly due to some of the "quirks" that these machines most certainly did display. I don't think it would have been possible to win as much, or as often, otherwise.

Nevertheless, many players still considered that far from any "strategy." Rather, they thought it was more like finding a group, spot, or pattern, that the machines would hit more often, and sticking to it. However, it *was* actually a strategy, based on observation and skilled play resulting from observations acquired from direct experience. Machines aren't perfect, nor is anything else made by human hands. These games appeared to have these quirks, and exploiting them for profits was, in actuality, a strategy. This was one of the revelations I experienced after several years of playing the games just like that—as well as in other formats that proved not to be nearly as successful as those where I used these "strategies."

It took a decade or so before Video Keno underwent any change. This happened as computer technology advanced and was first manifest in video keno games in the touch-screen machines. Now the big and bulky old machines were gone, replaced by faster games on smaller screens wherein the player could make selections simply by touching a finger over the desired numbers. These early touch-screen machines seemed to have the same computer program that ran the game as in the older machines, because the same playing principles applied. Some of the earliest of these machines were at a well-known casino in Las Vegas where I used to play frequently—until the management changed all the payoffs and reduced the payback so much that playing there was like throwing money away.

I used to play there a lot, and on those very same new

video keno machines. I used several patterns on those that had proved themselves successful on the older-style tall and bulky machines, and they worked just as well on the new ones. I had many great and glorious hits on those machines and games. Then, it all changed. Suddenly, a newer crop of video keno machines came out, and the old strategies and patterns didn't seem to work as well. Was this simply a fact of the randomness of the numbers, making up for the apparent anomaly of so many wins in previous years—or was it something else? Was it a change in the program? Was it a "better" randomizer? Well, as far as I can tell, it was a combination of all of these factors, but mostly it was a result of better technology. Computer speed, storage, memory—all those things that make computers so fast and so good these days—were just new discoveries then, and this allowed for more and more combinations to be increasingly better randomized.

The effect was that the older "strategies" did not work as well on these newer games. New methods needed to be found. For this, we had to wait for the next generation of video keno machines, such as those now found in the *Game King*® platform from IGT, and other video keno games such as *Four Card Keno*™ and the still-to-come *Multi-Card Keno*™. Once these were available, a whole slew of new strategies became possible. Now these games can yield very nice profits for a relatively small investment.

VIDEO KENO STRATEGY

I have said previously that the word "strategy" will sound odd to those people whose understanding of casino games is vested purely and only in mathematics. To those readers, I wish to categorically restate that I understand that video keno games are negative-expectation games—meaning they are games with inherent programming that does not allow them to mathematically perform at a higher payback level than that which the program dictates. Therefore, if a video keno machine is set to pay back 91.97 percent, this also means that—mathematically speaking—it will always hold 8.03 percent for the house (i.e., the house edge on that game). It is not my intent to dispute this, as long as we are discussing these games from "inside that box"—meaning from within the understanding only of mathematical concepts and parameters. For any video keno player, a game that is said to "hold" 8.03 percent for the house also means that the game must *pay out* 91.97 percent. It's that old principle of the glass half full of water: The mathematicians in this case will see the glass as half empty, and the players will see the same glass as half full. It's a good analogy and a nice way to explain why some of us will never understand how Video Keno can make us profits, while for others it will seem easy and natural.

What the mathematicians often fail to understand is that we who wish to play Video Keno for profit do not play the game either to validate the statistics they have created or because we wish to "buck the odds." We play the game because we know that even a negative expectation game such as Video Keno with an 8.03 percent house hold must pay out 91.97 percent of the time—a pretty solid fact that even the math people will accept. The difference is that the math people will always say something like this: "A machine that holds 8.03 percent for the house means that you will be losing $8.03 from each $100 you play in the machine." Fine. We understand that. It's a good way to get the machine licensed, a good way to explain to the casinos what they are likely to make on the game, and it all fits nicely within the parameters of that very comfortable box called "mathematics, probability, and odds." Basically, what this means is that if you play any such game for, say, fifty-five years or so, it is likely that you will lose an average of close to $8.03 out of every $100 you spend.

Notice, however, *how* the mathematicians tend to explain such events. They use terms such as: "will most likely lose," and "an average of close to," and so on. These are indefinables and are so used because not even the most exhaustive mathematical analysis of such protracted events can take into account the infinity of the events themselves. What if the 10 million events that went into these calculations were actually an anomaly? What if the reality of a billion times more of these events were to prove that the reality is actually nothing like these tests? Therein lies the major fallacy of mathematical thinking—it can't be proven to be accurate for all infinite events. Of course, "proving" something in numerics and physical sciences is apparently extremely important to those who do this, and therefore in the absence of any such "proof" one has to be made up to look reasonably like a "proof," at least something on which others who also think this way can agree. So, they all get together, run millions of events, and when they get tired of it they call it a day—hence we have our physical proof, and we can get the game licensed and sold. So far so good. But does that automatically mean that no players can ever win on that game? Well, of course not. If no player ever won on the game, why make it? No one would play it. If such a game holds 8.03 percent for the house, therefore, and pays back 91.97 percent, why would we automatically accept the pseudo-logic of the math experts because they say we can't win? Can't we? Let's see now—the game won't pay anything for 8.03 percent of the time, but will pay something 91.97 percent of the time . . . hmm, is there anything mathematically important here?

Okay, I know I'm poking fun at the math people and many of my friends and fellow gaming authors who write about the stats for gambling games. It's not my intent to lambaste them. I simply wish to point out that while mathematics is a very useful and wonderful *guide* to the video keno games—and all other casino gambling games as well—it doesn't provide *all* the answers that make up the success in playing them. I actually enjoy talking about odds and percentages. I realize how useful they are in understanding the games and how important they are in the overall game acumen and strategy for any gambling game. I also understand how useful mathematics is to the explanation of the games and how crucial it is for the games themselves. I do not dispute any of this—just the parts that say, "Don't play this game because—" followed by a string of "bad" games with high house withholding percentages. Although I tend to look for games whose programs allow for the games to pay back more than others of their kind, this is simply good common sense. The same applies to the other games in which skills allow one to reduce, or eliminate, the house edge. But that isn't all there is to the strategy, or to the play of it. Overall success in the game is a combination of understanding, skills, bankroll, time at the game, ability, luck, and all of the other factors and Keys to Winning that I have told you about. It is the entire, overall, package of *you* as the knowledgeable, smart player that accounts for your success—or failure—in the casino.

Video Keno is not among the best games that may be available, but it isn't one of the worst either. Many video poker versions, for example, have worse payback percentages than those in Video Keno, while the odds of winning something are thousands of times longer than their comparable cash-equivalent wins in Video Keno. No matter how "bad" the game may appear from the mathematical perspective, even a game that holds 8.03 percent for the house—or whatever such a house hold percentage may be—it also has to pay out 91.07 percent of the money cycled through it (or whatever that percentage may be on the game, comparatively speaking). Although it is always better to look for and play games whose programs allow them to pay back *more*, it isn't the only factor to consider in any strategy. Nothing in such programs excludes the possibility, or the viability, of actually having a strategy. Anyone who says that there can't be any strategy for negative-expectation games isn't wholly able to grasp the big picture and is mired in a singularly limited and highly dogmatic *mis*-understanding of the objectives of gambling games. The two objectives of all gambling games are: to have fun and to make money. That's it. One doesn't necessarily exclude the other, although either can be practiced without the other. Consequently, strategies for casino games whose in-built house withholding percentages are inflexible—such as machine games in which the programs are not manufactured with the possibility of more than 100 percent payback based on skills, of which all video keno games are such a version—such strategies must be based on the exploitation of short-term slices of the overall game reality and the ability to maximize profitable yield and limit the exposure to losses. Such strategies are possible even for games whose basic programs don't allow them to "pay back" equally, or greater than 100 percent. These games are not "unfair" games, they are simply casino games designed to produce revenue for the owners. Players, therefore, must be able to play such games in short bursts—relative to the life of the machine's program—whereby the player can use and exploit some of the oddities of anomalous behavior of random events. Video Keno offers perhaps the clearest example of such oddities, which produce financial results over and above the general negative-expectation nature of the game.

For Video Keno, the strategy that can be exploited most frequently for financial profits is pattern recognition and group play. Although there aren't any such things in the world of math as "groups" or "patterns," the simple fact remains that in nature, as well as in Video Keno, patterns do happen, as do groups. Group and pattern theory are actually parts of some studies of mathematics, although such thinking is mostly relegated to the philosophical discipline of theoretical logic. A programmer of video keno games may say there aren't any such events as "patterns" or "groups," because all the numbers have an equal possibility of being selected during any one drawing of the video keno game. That may be true, as understood from the randomness model of these events, but the truth is that these events *do* happen in patterns and groups.

Human beings have the ability to so recognize such patterns and groups, and although they cannot be mathematically identifiable within the statistical randomness model of the event trigger, the outcome is plain to see. In Video Keno, numbers *bunch*. Numbers run in *sequences*, either across the line, or top to bottom. Numbers run in *groups*, either squares, lines, or rectangles. They run in groups that form a 6-number "T" formation, or a "cross." They run in a five-star formation, or a sideways cross, for 5- and 6-number groups, respectively. They run in blocks of 6, 8, and 9—even blocks of 10. Some rows and columns appear to be hit more often than others, and that's not merely an idle comment. For some twenty years I have seen this in many different versions of Video Keno. Whatever the theory of the randomness of numbers may be, the fact remains that in the reality of the game as it exists on the casino floor *wins happen*, and can happen more frequently to you as the player if you follow some of the patterns that show up seemingly more often than others, and much more often than a pure random distribution of binary events triggered by a bit register.

Figures 17a through 17j, on pages 261 to 267, show some of the most commonly occurring patterns in Video Keno. These patterns show up more often than any others, or any other arrangements, grouping, or other distribution of numbers. These are the patterns and groups I play myself, and on which I have frequently hit very large wins. I will show you the general areas on the video keno board where these patterns happen to hit more often than in others. These are my personal observations based on two decades of playing Keno. There are no mathematical "facts" that can prove, or disprove what you see here. There is no way to quantify it. It happens, and using these methods and patterns as part of your overall strategy helps to make powerful profits, to which I can attest through documented wins. Whether they will happen to you, or as frequently, I can't say. I can say, however, that if you play Video Keno with these patterns and groups, you will have more success than you would without them. Later, as you get better acquainted with the game, perhaps you will find your own groups, ones that work for you as well as these have for me.

Figure 17a shows a classic video keno "box" 6-spot. The one shown here consists of the best placement for this group, because it tends to hit there more often than elsewhere. In addition, this same group of six numbers can also be played similarly well in the same grouping by placing these in the top left, or the bottom right, of the video keno screen number layout.

Figure 17b shows a classic video keno "columns" 8-spot. This one happens to be the row of tens, meaning it is the last row to the right side of the video keno screen. This is also one of the rows that appears to hit winners frequently. The opposite side, which is the first row, can also so be successfully used.

Figure 17c shows a classic video keno "cross" 6-spot. This can be used effectively by placing its center number on either the number 36 or the number 38. It also seems to work well when the center number is either 15 or 16 (as shown in the illustration), as well as either 18 or 19. This pattern also often hits in the lower portions of the video

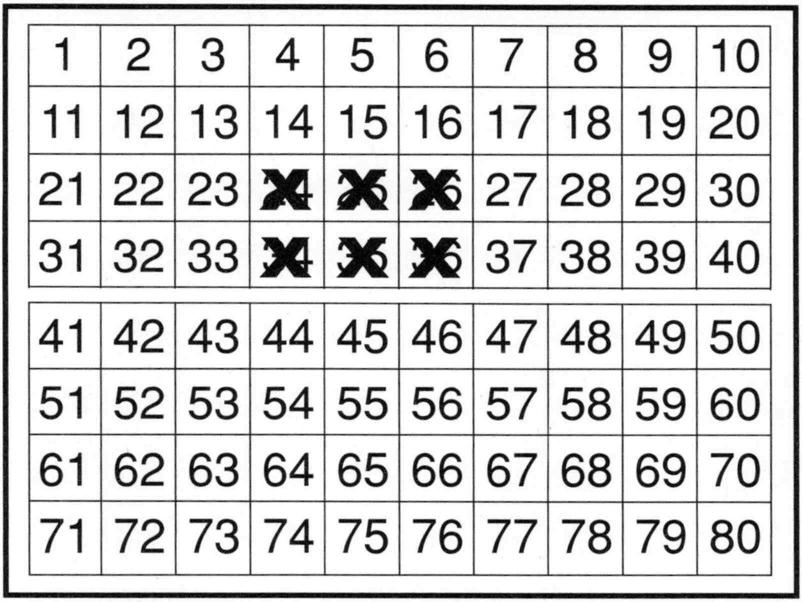

1	2	3	4	5	6	7	8	9	10
11	12	13	14	15	16	17	18	19	20
21	22	23	✖	✖	✖	27	28	29	30
31	32	33	✖	✖	✖	37	38	39	40
41	42	43	44	45	46	47	48	49	50
51	52	53	54	55	56	57	58	59	60
61	62	63	64	65	66	67	68	69	70
71	72	73	74	75	76	77	78	79	80

Figure 17a. A classic video keno 6-spot group.

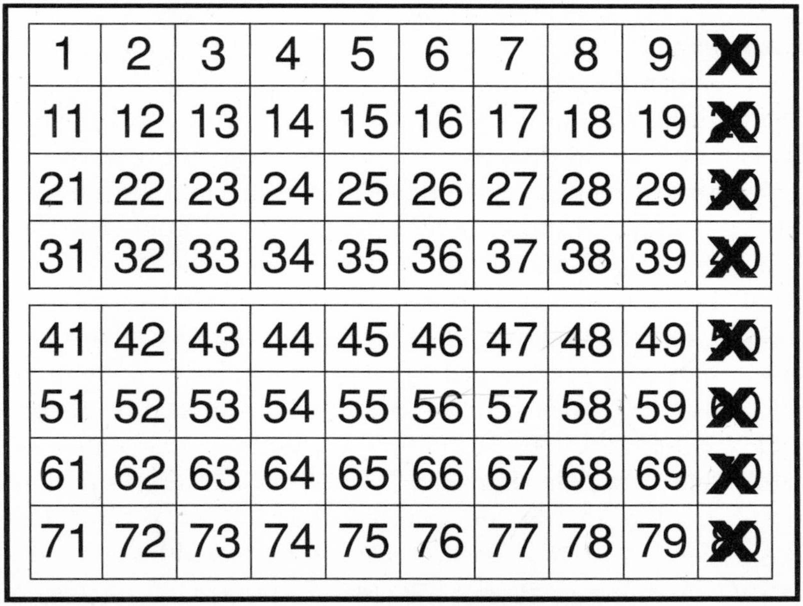

1	2	3	4	5	6	7	8	9	✖
11	12	13	14	15	16	17	18	19	✖
21	22	23	24	25	26	27	28	29	✖
31	32	33	34	35	36	37	38	39	✖
41	42	43	44	45	46	47	48	49	✖
51	52	53	54	55	56	57	58	59	✖
61	62	63	64	65	66	67	68	69	✖
71	72	73	74	75	76	77	78	79	✖

Figure 17b. A classic video keno 8-spot "column" group.

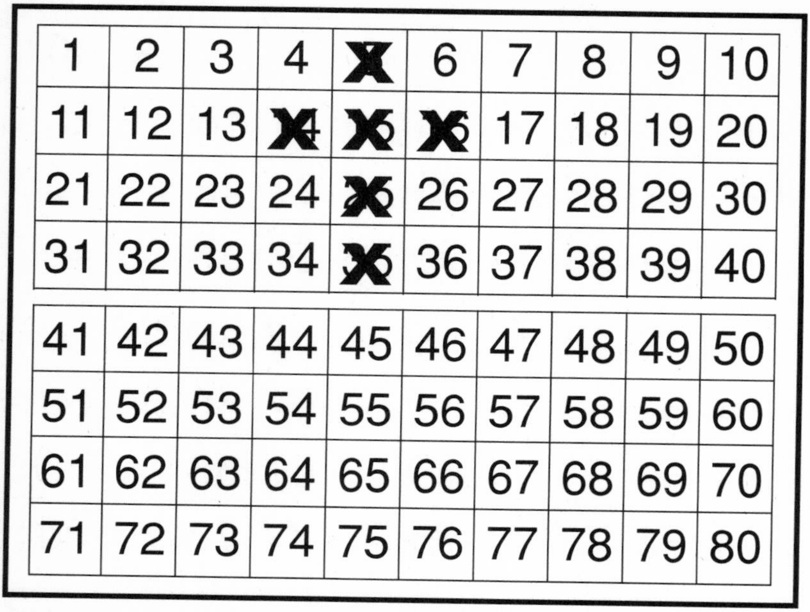

1	2	3	4	✖	6	7	8	9	10
11	12	13	✖	✖	✖	17	18	19	20
21	22	23	24	✖	26	27	28	29	30
31	32	33	34	✖	36	37	38	39	40
41	42	43	44	45	46	47	48	49	50
51	52	53	54	55	56	57	58	59	60
61	62	63	64	65	66	67	68	69	70
71	72	73	74	75	76	77	78	79	80

Figure 17c. A video keno "cross" 6-spot group.

keno screen, such as when the numbers 55 or 56 are used as the center number.

Figure 17d shows a classic video keno "star" 5-spot. This can be used effectively on all of the combinations for the "cross" 6-spot, simply by eliminating the extra number at the bottom of the long side of the "cross" pattern, thus making it into the "star" shape seen here.

Figure 17e shows a classic video keno "sideways cross" 6-spot. This can be played in all combinations that are also used for the more standard "upright cross" pattern, by using the same core number in the center of the cross, but instead of extending the shape vertically, it is now instead extended horizontally, to the right-hand side (never to the left). This combination can also be used as a derivative of the "star" 5-spot, and it can also be successfully extended by one number farther across to make a "cross" 7-spot.

1	2	3	4	5	6	7	8	9	10
11	12	13	14	15	16	17	18	19	20
21	22	23	24	25	26	27	✗	29	30
31	32	33	34	35	36	✗	✗	✗	40
41	42	43	44	45	46	47	✗	49	50
51	52	53	54	55	56	57	58	59	60
61	62	63	64	65	66	67	68	69	70
71	72	73	74	75	76	77	78	79	80

Figure 17d. A video keno "star" 5-spot group.

1	2	3	4	5	6	7	✗	9	10
11	12	13	14	15	16	✗	✗	✗	✗
21	22	23	24	25	26	27	✗	29	30
31	32	33	34	35	36	37	38	39	40
41	42	43	44	45	46	47	48	49	50
51	52	53	54	55	56	57	58	59	60
61	62	63	64	65	66	67	68	69	70
71	72	73	74	75	76	77	78	79	80

Figure 17e. A video keno classic "sideways cross" 6-spot group.

Figure 17f shows a classic video keno "vertical box" 8-spot. This can be played very successfully anywhere, but mostly it works best in the top-left corner of the video keno screen, the top right, bottom left, and bottom right. Also the two row boxes directly next to each of these, as well as those in the exact middle of the screen, using the 4, 5, 6, and 7 rows at the top, and bottom, to make these patterns.

Figure 17g shows a classic video keno "horizontal box" 10-spot. This is a pattern of two rows each comprising five numbers, one on top of the other to make this pattern. It works best when placed in the top left corner, bottom left corner, bottom right corner, or the 2s and 3s rows flush left, as shown in the illustration.

Figure 17h shows a classic video keno "square box" 9-spot. This is the 3-by-3 pattern used in the 3-6-9 Way Ticket video keno game I discussed previously using three

X	X	3	4	5	6	7	8	9	10
X	X	13	14	15	16	17	18	19	20
X	X	23	24	25	26	27	28	29	30
X	X	33	34	35	36	37	38	39	40
41	42	43	44	45	46	47	48	49	50
51	52	53	54	55	56	57	58	59	60
61	62	63	64	65	66	67	68	69	70
71	72	73	74	75	76	77	78	79	80

Figure 17f. A classic video keno 8-spot block.

1	2	3	4	5	6	7	8	9	10
11	12	13	14	15	16	17	18	19	20
X	X	X	X	X	26	27	28	29	30
X	X	X	X	X	36	37	38	39	40
41	42	43	44	45	46	47	48	49	50
51	52	53	54	55	56	57	58	59	60
61	62	63	64	65	66	67	68	69	70
71	72	73	74	75	76	77	78	79	80

Figure 17g. A classic video keno 10-spot block.

1	2	3	4	5	6	7	8	9	10
11	12	13	14	15	16	17	18	19	20
21	22	23	24	25	26	27	28	29	30
31	32	33	34	35	36	37	38	39	40
X	X	X	44	45	46	47	48	49	50
X	X	X	54	55	56	57	58	59	60
X	X	X	64	65	66	67	68	69	70
71	72	73	74	75	76	77	78	79	80

Figure 17h. A classic video keno 9-spot block square.

groups of three numbers, each vertically arranged (or horizontally since this is a square), to make a 9-spot pattern in a square shape. Using this pattern in the 3-6-9 video keno game will help make you a more frequent winner on that version of Video Keno, but it can also be used very effectively in standard Video Keno, the game most often referred to as *Spot Keno™*. This pattern works best if placed in the top-left corner of the bottom-40 number grid, starting with the numbers 41, 42, and 43, then 51, 52, and 53, and finally 61, 62, and 63, as shown in the illustration. This same pattern is also successful in the bottom right, as well as one row up from that placement, and also similarly in the top left and top right of the screen. It can also be used well in the 5s block in the top middle, and also in the 40s and 70s block at the bottom middle.

Figure 17i shows the classic video keno "bottom row"

1	2	3	4	5	6	7	8	9	10
11	12	13	14	15	16	17	18	19	20
21	22	23	24	25	26	27	28	29	30
31	32	33	34	35	36	37	38	39	40
41	42	43	44	45	46	47	48	49	50
51	52	53	54	55	56	57	58	59	60
61	62	63	64	65	66	67	68	69	70
X	X	X	X	X	X	X	X	X	X

Figure 17i. The "bottom row" classic video keno 10-spot row pattern.

10-spot. I have used it here as the example of the bottom row because that's what is often called the "locals' special," as well as being the principle behind the Bottom Row Club I mentioned earlier. A row such as this can be used effectively on any of the rows available on the video keno screen, although the bottom row, the row of 30s, and the topmost row from 1 though 10 are the most often hit. In *Four Card Keno*™, it is often also advantageous to use the 60s row as well.

Finally, Figure 17j shows a classic video keno "side wrap" 6-spot. This is often used in multi-pattern games, such as on *Four Card Keno*™, but can be effectively used by itself for a 6-spot hit. It is best used in the top-right corner, bottom right, and sometimes top or bottom left, although it is better used in the top or bottom right. Some machines will also hit this in the 5s and 6s row as well, but this pat-

1	2	3	4	5	6	7	8	9	10
11	12	13	14	15	16	17	18	19	20
21	22	23	24	25	26	27	28	29	30
31	32	33	34	35	36	37	38	39	40
41	42	43	44	45	46	47	48	✗	✗
51	52	53	54	55	56	57	58	59	✗
61	62	63	64	65	66	67	68	69	✗
71	72	73	74	75	76	77	78	✗	✗

Figure 17j. A video keno "sideways wrap" 6-spot group.

tern seems to work best only in the top- or bottom-right corner placement.

Well, there you have the most common and most popular patterns for video keno strategy play. These are by no means all the patterns that can be played, and not the only ones that video keno regulars play exclusively. However, from my experience of playing straight, standard Video Keno, these are the combinations that work the best and hit winners most often. Following are some general hints for standard video keno play:

• Pick a group, and play it where you put it without changing it—or the placement of it—unless you choose to leave and play another machine.

• Don't "chase the numbers" (changing your patterns and "chasing" what appear to be similar such patterns appearing elsewhere on the screen). Video keno machines often appear to be "teasers," meaning they will "show you" your patterns, but elsewhere on the screen. When you see this happen, it's a warning sign. Take your money and find another machine and start over.

• If you decided to stay with the same machine, stay with your group—your pattern—and don't change your numbers. Changing your numbers is suicide, because the more you do this the more you will likely become a victim to the "chasing numbers syndrome" (see above). There are, however, some exceptions. As you gain expertise, you may be able to continue with the same machine and play a different selection, but generally it is a better bet to simply stick to what you pick, lest you become victim to the numbers chase.

• Be patient. If you play on a session principle, limit your exposure to 100 events. After that, take stock of where you stand, financially, and then decide if you want to continue the next session on the same machine or move to another machine and start over. This applies only to session-strategy players, such as those who adapt my 10-session-block strategy*, and apply it to Video Keno. For others, your limitations should be whatever it is you select as your win goal and win expectation, as based on your other skills in general gambling (see the Keys to Winning).

• Don't habitually mark, erase, and re-mark your numbers. Some writers claim that this somehow "resets" the machine, but this is bogus. There is nothing in the machine's program, or quirks, that allows for this to be so. In order for you to be able to erase the previous numbers, you first must make a wager. At the very microsecond you make that wager, the trigger signals the bit register to select the winning events. These are cast in iron and will not change for the duration of that game, no matter how many times you mark, erase, and re-mark the numbers. Just because on a few occasions it seems that you hit a big winner immediately after you mark, erase, and re-mark your numbers, this has nothing to do with the game. This is only in your mind, and does nothing to help you or make you win. This has happened to me several times, but it is merely a plain accident of just getting really lucky in that instant. Most of the time, the longer you play the same numbers, the greater the probability that some will hit for a winner, and that you will get a bigger winner. In fact, my experience has been the direct opposite to that recently being propagated by some writers. I have found, over some twenty years of playing, that *staying* with your numbers *unchanged* produces *more winners* and more regular winners with far less stress and work than erasing and re-marking numbers constantly after each three pulls. To make sure that I am not being arbitrarily antagonistic to this concept, I tried it myself over many thousands of real in-casino events. It simply doesn't work.

*See *Powerful Profits from Blackjack.*

The machine's program knows only the trigger that causes it to stop scanning and picks the bits that it tells the graphics program to display for you to see. Habitually erasing and re-marking your numbers will only get you tired and frustrated. Just do what I do—pick your numbers and stick to them for whatever duration you have allocated to your session, as based on your time, bankroll, win goal, win expectations, and objectives. Using this approach, along with the patterns I have outlined, will make you more comfortable and more at ease with the game, and a winner much more often and with less stress and frustration than using the method of constantly futzing with your selections. (I have more to say about this in Chapter 12.)

• Always remember that *you* are the human being and the machine is the machine. Don't *blame* the machine. It doesn't know that the numbers it picked looked to you like being "right *next* to the ones I picked," as so many frustrated video keno players say constantly. Pick your groups, stay with them, be patient, allocate your proper session time and bankroll, and in the end you will not only win more and more often, but you will also be much happier about it and never frustrated.

• Finally—know when to quit. To make powerful profits from Video Keno, you must not only know the game and how to play it well, but also know not to put back what you have won. Making profits from a game that holds around 8.03 percent for the house also means that any time you beat it, to continue to beat it you must know when to stop trying and leave with the profit. Many people become winners playing Video Keno, only to put it back and then start chasing the money and the numbers. *Stop right there.* If you lose your session money, remember that in all gambling losing is inevitable, no matter how good you are. Even players who play mathematically perfectly on only positive expectation games also lose. It happens to everyone, all the time.

The difference between those who are winners in the end, and those who aren't, is mostly in the simple fact that the winners leave when they are winners, and the losers put back their wins and try to get their money back by playing more, faster, and in a tailspin. Set reasonable win goals and win expectations based on your knowledge of the game, its expected "costs," and your time, bankroll, and skills. Then, when you win, be happy. Wins taken home add up to bigger wins. Wins not lost back also add up to bigger wins. Wins upon wins also add to more wins and bigger bankrolls.

It's easy to say, but hard to do. I know that too. But it is possible, and in Video Keno, it is essential. What if you win $5,000? Is that enough? Well, if you hit that with a 50-cent bet—as I did many times—I think so. Take 10 percent to play back, and if you lose it, leave with the win. There will always be a next time. The fastest road to a gambler's ruin is to win big and then go gambling big without a plan, and recklessly. Such gamblers abound, and you can find many of them in history's past and present. Any time you have a big win—whatever "big" may mean to you—if you wish to play again, or continue playing afterward, take 10 percent of that amount, and no more, and see if you get lucky again. Nothing wrong with that at all—it's called "parlay." A good gambler always knows when to parlay, but he or she also knows when to go home with the money. That's the best advice I can give you for any kind of gambling.

DERIVATIVE VIDEO KENO GAMES STRATEGY

By "derivative" I mean those games that are some kind of a "bonusing" video keno game, such as *Cleopatra® Keno*, *Caveman Keno®*, and the *Super"Power" Keno™*, which I discussed previously. *Four Card Keno™* and *Multi-Card*

Keno™ are also derivatives in the pure sense of the term, but these last two are so different from the basic video keno game that they really belong in the "multi-game" category rather than within the video keno game derivatives. The term "derivative" is better suited to games that are basically the same as the standard video keno *Spot Keno*™, but offer something else, such as the bonus pays for the last number hit, or free games, and so on. I will, therefore, use these differences to classify the games separately into "derivatives" and "multi-game."

Earlier in the book I discussed the standard video keno game strategy for the game most commonly known as *Spot Keno*™. The next step in the natural evolution of any such video keno strategy is to touch briefly on the derivatives. These are all games that play almost identically to the standard *Spot Keno*™, but with two main differences:

- Their basic pay tables have a reduced pay schedule and a reduced payback percentage.
- The majority of the game's payback percentage, and value in playing, is in the "bonus" hits.

The reduced pay table and primary game payback percentage are necessary to allow for the increased pays on the bonus events. Therefore, these games are often referred to as being "top heavy," meaning they vest most of their player benefits in the harder-to-achieve hits. Consequently, your desired objective on these games is to go for the highest-value bonus hits possible. This requires a change in the way you approach standard Video Keno. In regular Video Keno, marking—say—a 6-spot produces many more wins relative to potential losses. There are only three ways to "not hit"—which are the 0, 1, and 2 out of the 6. But the video keno 6-spot pays for hits of 3, 4, 5, and 6, so there are four ways to hit. This makes the 6-spot a most attractive proposition among the better tickets for standard Video Keno. However, the majority of the value in this ticket is that it begins its pays at 3:1, meaning 3 quarters for 1 quarter wagered in most pay tables. Therefore, any paying hit on a 6-spot immediately gives a profit at a pretty good ratio. On the derivatives, this same approach is not advisable, largely because of the huge reductions in the small pays at the bottom or middle payouts of the pay table schedule. This is the area of the pay table from which the majority of the machine's payback contribution stems, and it is therefore here that the alterations generally are made to reduce the basic payback, to allow for the increased payback on the bonus hits. When accounted, all of this combines to provide the overall payback averages as shown in the pay tables I have detailed previously, for those derivative games I have shown.

In the same manner as these bonusing games are a "derivative" of the basic *Spot Keno™* game, so the strategy needs to be tweaked to take this into account. Realizing that the smaller—and more frequently occurring—pays have mostly been reduced in value (as well as some of the intermediate and perhaps even top pays on some such games) means that your approach to playing the game should be for the biggest bang you can get for your buck. That means *not* playing these games in the same manner as you would approach the standard *Spot Keno™*. By this I mean that while in the standard Spot Keno games the better bets may be in the 6-spot, 7-spot, and 8-spot play options, in these bonusing games it's exactly the opposite. On these games you should *never* play anything lower than a 9-spot, and I would even say never play anything lower than a 10-spot. This is because the pays for the 9- and 10-spots are usually left untouched when the programmed paybacks are changed, and the pays are lowered on all the other spots. It is a known fact that most players will play these bonusing games in the same manner as they would play the standard *Spot Keno™*

games, and therefore play the "fewer numbers the better" strategy. This is *not* the best manner to play these derivative bonusing games. Here the value of the game lies directly in the game's top-heavy structure, whereby the bonusing event is that which triggers the majority of the game's payback. To get the most value out of these games, you should forgo the smaller number combinations, forget the "fewer numbers the better" strategy (because it does not work on these games), and instead focus on playing the one or two combinations whose basic payback is usually largely preserved and whose hit frequency will more than offset the game's increased hit volatility index. By so limiting your game play to only the 9- or 10-spots—with my preferred recommendation being only the 10-spot—you will also give yourself many more opportunities to catch that last number, and on these games it is usually that last number—and that last number alone—that triggers the bonusing event and gives you those big pays. This is by far the best strategy for these games, and should so be used almost exclusively—unless you take into account other games, or game derivatives that you yourself judge to require a different approach. This you will be able to do for yourself as you become more experienced in the game and better able to make such decisions and judgments.

FOUR CARD KENO™ STRATEGY

Of all the innovations in Video Keno, and all the derivatives, *Four Card Keno*™ is by far the best. (It will be surpassed only by *Multi-Card Keno*™ as soon as it is available.) This is the game I now play almost exclusively, and I will only "graduate" from it to the *Multi-Card Keno*™ games if these prove to be as good as they appear to be. The current game of *Four Card Keno*™ runs circles around any other video keno game. It can be highly profitable if played well and if you follow the advice and gambling principles I have outlined in this book and in my other books. What makes *Four Card Keno*™ such a good game? The main reasons are as follows:

- You can play more than one game at once. It's just like playing four machines at the same time, except you don't have to keep moving from machine to machine to make this possible.
- You can "wheel" your numbers.
- You can use the "core" numbers strategy to maximize winning hits.
- You can vary the size of your wagers on different cards, if you so wish and are experienced enough to understand why this may be to your advantage, and when.
- You can "overlap" your groups, to get twice the win for one times the bet, such as when you play lower-denomination games but make two cards the same. Although the base wager may only be 25 cents per card, you get paid for a 50-cent hit each time two of the cards match.
- You can play four *different* cards, and even play them with different bets, when you choose not to wheel or overlap them, thereby covering a wider range of the possibilities.
- You can create "cross-bet groups," whereby you cover a specific area of the video keno screen and then over-lay your numbers groups in patterns over each other, so that any time you get a hit you get paid something and thus maximize the jackpot hits when most or all of the numbers hit your group.

These are just some of the many means at your disposal to maximize the win value of this game. *Four Card Keno*™

makes it possible for you not only to gain more winners more often, but also to last longer with your bankroll, even though the actual costs of the game are four times higher than the single-screen single-event games, like standard Video Keno or the single-game derivatives. What this means is that most of the time you get paid at least something, and that reduces the cost of the next event. For example, if you wager a total of $1, with a wager of 25 cents per each of the four cards, most of the time you will get at least some pays, such as a pay of 25 cents, or 50 cents, or 75 cents, or your money back—the whole $1. So, if you bet like this, each time you hit a 25-cent pay, your next game cost is *reduced by that amount.* Although you did not gain a winner—because overall you lost 75 cents on that event—the next event will not cost you the full $1 to replay, but will be reduced in overall cost by the pay you did get, namely that 25 cents. So, in this example, your next wager will replay the game at the $1 full value, but your real out-of-pocket cost is only 75 cents, because on the previous event you received a 25-cent pay. While this still places you in an overall "loss" position over these example events, the point here is that *the next event did not cost you the full replay amount value*, even though you are still getting the full win value from it.

This concept of diminished risk is often ignored and glossed over in gambling texts. If we were to look at all gambling merely as a single event, whereby we make one wager and never make another, then the calculations would be relatively easy: either that wager produced a win, in which case we would have walked away a winner and have defeated the game for far more than its available payback percentage, or we would lose, in which case we would walk away a loser and have lost far more than the game's overall payback percentage indicates we should have lost. Both cases are extremes and are based on the erroneous assumption that all events are, and will always be single, and understood merely as single occurrences. But that is not true in the real world. While some players will fall smack into these extremes—people who will come to a casino, make one bet, win or lose, and then leave and never make another—this is not the case for the vast majority of gamblers. Most people come to casinos to play at least a little, and this necessitates more than a single event. Therefore, allowing for the sequence of several such events being made by the player, each cannot be viewed singly as an independent event, because it is the *protracted series* that eventually consists of that player's win-loss value. As a result, looking at the "costs" of each event separately from the sequence is to misunderstand and misuse not only the statistics of the game, but the point and purpose of playing.

Whenever a player makes more than one bet on the same game, this constitutes a sequence. As a direct result, that player's "costs" of that sequence are not the "costs" of each event, but the overall "costs" of the entire sequence of events, whatever that may be. In the example of the series of two events, the "cost" of the first one may be that $1 (as in the example I used just a moment ago), but if that event produces any kind of a return on the investment—such as that 25-cent win— then the next event does not "cost" the same as the initializing event. That second event's "costs" are reduced by the factor of the previous event's return value, and, therefore, that next event is wagered at full win value, but at a 25 percent cost reduction in outright expenditure. Therefore the concept of diminished risk also must take into account the protracted sequences that apply to the overall cost value of the player's events, as well as the comparative replay value of the previous win events, applied within the diminished risk capacity model.

Each time you play more than one game on Video Keno, you have committed to a sequence of events. The initiating

factor is the "cost" of that first event. Thereafter, each additional event played can "cost" no more than the initiating
value, unless you have chosen to change that initiating
value, in which case a new sequence begins with that new
starting value. Assuming you do not make such a change in
the initiating value of the beginning event, each subsequent
event within these same parameters will result in no additional cost value, while each "win" will result in the diminished "cost" of each subsequent replay value. The effect of
this is that although you are wagering more to initiate
games in *Four Card Keno*™—and it may look as if you must
bet four times the amount you would otherwise have to
wager when playing a single-game Video Keno—this seemingly "extra cost" is more often than not offset by the reduced replay cost value of your sequence of repeated
events. What this means is that although you gain the opportunity to play more cards, and even though it looks like
it costs more, the fact remains that as long as you play a sequence of events you will actually be able to make your
bankroll last longer than it would in other games where the
same bankroll amount would be played at one-fourth of that
value, *but singly on just one-card games*. Even more simply
put, you are getting *four* chances to win something, while
your bankroll does not require a four-times increase because of the frequency of wins upon successive repetitious
events.

Naturally, this presupposes that you play *Four Card
Keno*™ well, and that you use the core numbers wheel and
overlay principles of play, as well as make the same-value
wager on all four cards. Although you can play *Four Card
Keno*™ in many different ways, there is really only one successfully profitable manner of playing this game—by following these three Powerful Profits Keys to Winning at *Four
Card Keno*™:

- Always use a "core numbers" strategy.
- Always use a "wheel" strategy with your core numbers.
- Always use an "overlay pattern" to your core and wheel strategy.

This works just as well for Lounge Keno, except that in Lounge Keno you will have to use more than one "way" ticket to accomplish this. In Video Keno, on the Four Card Keno game, this is much easier to do because the game allows you to do it very well and very easily. Of course, you may be wondering what these three strategies mean, so a brief description follows.

What Is the Core Numbers Strategy?

Simply put, this means to pick a series of numbers in a pattern that will be repeated on all subsequent tickets. For example, look again at Figure 17a, on page 261. This is the classic box 6-spot. Let us assume here for the sake of this example, that you have decided to play these exact numbers as part of your *Four Card Keno*™ game. Therefore, these will be your "core numbers" because each such subsequent ticket on the remaining three cards in *Four Card Keno*™ will have these *same exact numbers* as part of their ticket combinations. Such a strategy simply means that these numbers are the foundation of all other selections, and whatever other combinations you pick will always include these very same six numbers in exactly this form and format. For example, let's say you wish to play a 6-spot, a 7-spot, a 9-spot, and a 10-spot on a *Four Card Keno*™ game, by using the core numbers strategy for all these four cards. Well, first you would mark Card A with the 6-spot, as shown in Figure 17a.

Then you would mark Card B with the same 6-spot, but add one more number to it to make a 7-spot. Then you would mark Card C with the same 6-spot, and add the same number that made the 7-spot, but now also add two more numbers to make this into a 9-spot. Then you would mark Card D with the same 6-spot that is your "core," then add to it the same number that made this into a 7-spot on Card B, then add to that the same two numbers that made this into a 9-spot on Card C. Now you will add that one last number that will make all these numbers into a 10-spot on Card D. You now have all four cards marked, and you have used the core numbers strategy to full effect. Figure 18 shows exactly what I have described.

Switch   Card A   Card B   Card C   Card D

Card A

1	2	3	4	5	6	7	8	9	10
11	12	13	14	15	16	17	18	19	20
21	22	23	⊠24	⊠25	⊠26	27	28	29	30
31	32	33	⊠34	⊠35	⊠36	37	38	39	40
41	42	43	44	45	46	47	48	49	50
51	52	53	54	55	56	57	58	59	60
61	62	63	64	65	66	67	68	69	70
71	72	73	74	75	76	77	78	79	80

Card B

1	2	3	4	5	6	7	8	9	10
11	12	13	14	⊠15	16	17	18	19	20
21	22	23	⊠24	⊠25	⊠26	27	28	29	30
31	32	33	⊠34	⊠35	⊠36	37	38	39	40
41	42	43	44	45	46	47	48	49	50
51	52	53	54	55	56	57	58	59	60
61	62	63	64	65	66	67	68	69	70
71	72	73	74	75	76	77	78	79	80

Card C

1	2	3	4	5	6	7	8	9	10
11	12	13	14	⊠15	16	17	18	19	20
21	22	23	⊠24	⊠25	⊠26	27	28	29	30
31	32	⊠33	⊠34	⊠35	⊠36	⊠37	38	39	40
41	42	43	44	45	46	47	48	49	50
51	52	53	54	55	56	57	58	59	60
61	62	63	64	65	66	67	68	69	70
71	72	73	74	75	76	77	78	79	80

Card D

1	2	3	4	⊠5	6	7	8	9	10
11	12	13	14	⊠15	16	17	18	19	20
21	22	23	⊠24	⊠25	⊠26	27	28	29	30
31	32	⊠33	⊠34	⊠35	⊠36	⊠37	38	39	40
41	42	43	44	45	46	47	48	49	50
51	52	53	54	55	56	57	58	59	60
61	62	63	64	65	66	67	68	69	70
71	72	73	74	75	76	77	78	79	80

Figure 18. An example of a *Four Card Keno*™ "core numbers group" overlapping patterns.

This brings us to the concept of the "wheel". You have not only used the core numbers strategy, but you began to use the concept of the wheel strategy.

What Is the Wheel Strategy?

Making a "wheel" and using the wheel strategy is a little different from the core numbers concept, but the two work together. With the core numbers strategy you are using the same set of selected numbers (and patterns) in all your cards. This means that whenever you gain a hit on the core numbers, you are far more likely also to gain a winner on one or more of the other cards, including the possibility of a combined big win. Of course if you hit your entire core numbers set, you get a very large win, because even if you don't hit any of the other numbers at all you will still get paid for four times the win over all four cards, since these first set of core numbers are duplicated in all of the other cards. This is the principle behind using the core numbers strategy successfully. If you look again at Figure 18, you will see a pattern of core numbers very similar to the one I used when achieving precisely such a core numbers hit. In my case, I used a somewhat more sophisticated core numbers set, along with the wheel strategy and the overlay pattern principle. I used a core set of a block of six numbers (as shown in Figure 18) but I also had an offset 7 top and bottom, all in a four-way 9-spot. This kind of play is actually easy to show, but hard to explain. Suffice it to say that the final pattern looked very much like the one shown on Card C in Figure 18, except that these were four 9-spots overlapped and inverted. I hit my solid core of top and bottom 7s, along with an 8 out of 9, so that I received a whole bunch of 6-out-of-9 pays, 7-out-of-9 pays, and a single 8-out-of-9 pay, for a cumulative huge jackpot. It is precisely this kind of play that allows even "house" games like Video Keno to provide you with powerful profits, especially on games like *Four Card Keno*™.

Wheeling numbers can also be used in such plays, although a numbers wheel can be successfully used by itself as well. In the wheel numbers strategy, you are using a series of numbers based around an overlay concept. In order to use the wheel numbers strategy successfully, you must first learn how to use the wheel to calculate your groups and then select the groups you wish to play. To help you with such a guide, please look at Figure 19.

This is an easy guide to using the wheel numbers strategy, by first understanding how to calculate your wheel number groups. This example happens to be the row of 10 numbers along the 40s row on the video keno screen. As

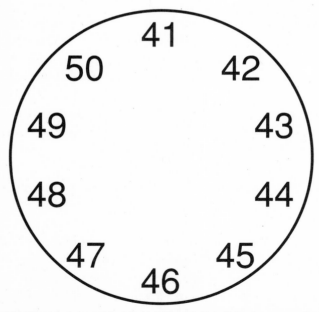

Figure 19. The classic guide for making a "wheel" for keno number patterns, useful for both Lounge and Video Keno.

you can see, it looks kind of like a wagon wheel, with numbers around it in a circle. Starting with the number 41, which in this example is our first number, we wheel around to number 50, and this completes the 10-number spokes of this wheel. You can easily make such a wheel for yourself, simply by drawing a circle and then marking whatever number of numbers you want around the inside of the circle, as shown in Figure 19. Such a wheel guide can contain any number of numbers—as many as you want and as many as can reasonably be used in Video Keno. This concept can also be used to calculate wheels for Lounge Keno, especially for games in which you can use interlaced multiple wheels over way tickets. If you want an easier example, look at your watch: You have numbers from 1 through 12. Use that to help you make a multitude of wheel ticket combinations almost instantly, containing any number of number groups from a mere 2-number group to as many as a 12-number group, and all possibilities in between. For Video Keno, using the simple 10-number wheel, as shown in Figure 19, or an 8- or 9-number wheel, is sufficient to take into account all of the best possible plays that we can reasonably use for *Four Card Keno*™. Later on, in *Multi-Card Keno*™, we can use a more sophisticated and complex wheel to account for the majority of the available options, while still using the same principles behind such tickets as those we are learning here for *Four Card Keno*™.

Let's say, for example, that we want to play four 7-spots on the wheel numbers strategy principle, and that we have noticed that many times numbers in Video Keno tend to show up along the eight possible rows of 10 numbers. We want to maximize our win yield and minimize our costs per game, as well as our replay costs, but we also want to take a more aggressive approach by limiting the variety of number selections and instead targeting a specific close combination to make the strongest possible wheel.

First, we select 7 numbers as each of our wheel groups. So, the first group on our wheel will be the 7-numbers group starting with 41 through 47. Our second 7 numbers group will be the numbers 42 through 48. Our third will be the numbers 43 through 49, and our fourth and last group as available in the Four Card Keno game will be the numbers 44 through 50. This, therefore, is an overlay core wheel 7-spot. As you see, in this example the numbers 44, 45, 46, and 47 are your core numbers, because they are the common numbers to all cards. Therefore, if you hit all of these four numbers, you will get the 4-out-of-7 pay on all four cards. Naturally, if this happens, most of the time you will get at least one number somewhere else to make this into a bigger pay, but the point of understanding here is the application of the core numbers strategy to coincide with such a wheel numbers strategy as shown and described here. In addition, numbers 43 and 48 are also common to three of the four cards, and numbers 42 and 49 are common to two of the four cards. This leaves only the edge numbers, 41 and 50, as part of only one card each. A play strategy using the core and wheels in this manner also includes the overlay principle, because these are groups over groups in cores and wheels. As a result, anytime you get a winner anywhere on this line, you will get at least some pays, with many times more pays the more numbers that hit. It offers numerous possibilities for major wins. Its most valuable product is not only the frequent reduction on replay "costs," but the simple fact that this Four Card Keno ticket entails within its very concept maximum win-value yield.

There are, of course, many other possible ways in which such a 7-spot wheel can be used to great effect on this row, any other row, or in whatever number combinations you happen to select. When *Multi-Card Keno*™ becomes more widely available, being able to use all twenty cards to expand such a wheel and also to include many of the other available combinations will mean that smart video keno players will be able to hit huge jackpots at a very low relative cost-per-event ratio. If you learn to do this well, and play wisely, you will never suffer great defeats, but you will always maximize your great successes.

What Is the Overlay Numbers Concept?

As simply as I can put it, the overlay numbers concept is the intelligent application of the core numbers strategy along with the wheel numbers strategy to arrive at a series of *intercalated* groups of numbers that can produce frequent "small" winners to allow for reduced "costs" of replay, while at the same time allowing for the maximum win-yield value when the higher-paying-number combinations hit.

This principle—now available only for use in Video Keno on the *Four Card Keno*™ game—will also be highly productive when applied to *Multi-Card Keno*™ games. It can be used in Lounge Keno, and you can put it to good and profitable use in all such casino keno games, particularly when you also use way tickets in such combinations as I have shown earlier. The easiest way to visualize the numbers overlay concept is to think of a multilayered cake—like a wedding cake. The bottom layer is your core numbers set strategy; the middle layer is your wheel numbers strategy, because it also sits on and combines with the base layer; the topmost layer is the overlay principle, because that layer lies over all the others and combines with them all to produce that wonderful effect. Playing in this manner is simply the best and most profitable way to make powerful profits from Keno.

MULTI-CARD KENO™ STRATEGY

This is short and sweet. When you are able to play *Multi-Card Keno*™—once it becomes universally available—use the strategies and playing principles you have learned in this book, specifically those shown for *Four Card Keno*™. Everything you have learned thus far can be used to even greater effect on the *Multi-Card Keno*™ games, because these will allow you to play such patterns, groups, cores, wheels, and overlays to much more profitable effect just by the availability of the twenty cards. This results in the smart keno player's ability to do much more than just blindly bet a bunch of loose numbers on many cards. I am very excited about this game, and as soon as it becomes available I will make it my most treasured casino game. It will be a highly profitable game for those who know how to play it properly.

As this book goes to press the game of *Multi-Card Keno*™ is not yet available, and I have not yet been able to play it. Therefore, I base my recommendation only on knowing what the game is *supposed* to be, based on the information from the game's manufacturer. If the game that makes it to the casino floor is exactly like the one that I have seen in tests—the same game whose game screen I have shown you in Photo 9 on page 247—then this will be by far the best casino video game ever made or offered. It will be hugely profitable when played as I have indicated.

FINAL TIPS FOR VIDEO KENO PLAY

Finally, some words of wisdom for any kind of video keno play. These apply to any individual game, and any of the specific strategy recommendations I have made for video keno games. None of these items are mutually exclusive, and many work in concert. You will need to adapt them as they apply to whatever game you happen to be playing, or thinking about playing.

- *Be patient.* I've said this before, but it bears repeating. Video Keno can be a slow game, so don't play it if you don't have patience.
- *Pick numbers wisely.* Pick your numbers in bunched groups, or horizontal lines, vertical lines, or boxes as shown in my examples in Figures 17a through 17j.
- *Don't habitually mark and re-mark your numbers.* The theory behind this is that it somehow "re-sets" the machine, but it's not so. Anyone hitting any winners by doing this is merely lucky *in that instant.* Machines pick number groups in bits.
- *Play 100-event sessions.* If you practice the session play principles, 100-event sessions should be your guideline.
- *Bring an adequate bankroll.* Don't play short changed. This is a prescription for disaster and the fastest road to a gambler's ruin. Pick a bankroll adequate to your win goal and win expectations, time and game, and how well you think you know to play. Then stick to it.
- *Walk away a winner.* If you hit a win, either leave immediately, or if you wish to continue playing, allocate only 10 percent of the total win value to your continued play. If you hit again, continue with this principle, but if you don't—well, don't chase your money for more wins. To be a winner you must learn to leave a winner.

Video Keno Myths and Superstitions

This short chapter is important, because so much wrong and downright erroneous information has been circulating about Video Keno, that we must try to dispel these myths and superstitions. In order to accomplish this with as much accurate and factual information as is possible, I called the company that makes these video keno machines—IGT of Reno, Nevada. I spoke with the supervisor of the firmware engineers—the actual technicians who make and write the programs that run the video keno games. Although I was already aware that much of what has become common folklore in Video Keno isn't reality, but merely players' superstitions, I nevertheless proceeded with the often embarrassingly simple questions that video keno players ask so often. Even though these questions are real to the players, to the firmware engineers who write and create these mathematical programs that run the games they seem entirely silly. The computer technician knows that the program that runs Video Keno doesn't "know" what the numbers are, but the players think they "know" that the machine is "out to get them," and "pick only those numbers I didn't pick."

These and other such problems have plagued video keno players for as long as there have been video keno machines and games. Players just can't believe that the number events are entirely random, and firmware engineers just can't believe that players don't understand that. So, to resolve these matters once and for all, I decided to write this chapter in which I will—I hope—put these myths and superstitions to rest once and for all. Wherever possible, I will use the actual words of the firmware engineers to whom I spoke about these issues, and to whom I posed the exact questions you will see here. What follows are direct quotes (in quotation marks) as well as my personal observations (**Translation**).

I began my investigation into these common myths and superstitions by asking some of the most frequently asked questions (FAQs) that video keno players ask. My friend Ron, the firmware engineer, answered simply, to the point, and as generally as possible.

"The simple answer to all these questions is that all currently approved *Game King®* games—including all video keno games—exhibit random outcomes by utilizing a code-based random number generator that has been rigorously tested and approved by numerous independent testing and regulatory agencies." **Translation:** Video keno machines are computers that contain a software program that picks a series of number combinations totally at random, and there is nothing else in the program that would cause the game to exhibit or draw out anything other than a totally random combination of numbers.

"The 'details' of the random number generation algorithm is a secret code, and these details—for obvious security purposes—must remain confidential. Needless to say, however, the methodology of the creation of these programs and codes has undergone close scrutiny and has been approved, meeting all statistical and randomness tests and requirements." **Translation:** The programs and the codes that make them possible have been tested as much as possible, and that as far as anything humanly made can be random, these number generators are so.

"Since, therefore, the actual generation of random numbers is not in question, the question remains as to how we ask for numbers for each game and how these numbers are actually utilized in each game. For Keno, the answers are more appropriately in the realm of human behavior, not engineering. The underlying rule behind the numbers chosen for game outcomes is that they are random occurrences. There are no patterns or knowledge of player actions." **Translation:** The machine or its program doesn't "know" what the results are, and it doesn't "know" that it is generating numbers that have any "meaning" to a human player. The machine just picks out sequences of binary numerals that are then translated into graphic representations that—in the case of Video Keno—happen to look like the numbers we are all familiar with seeing and understanding. The machine doesn't "know" that from the pool of 80 available numbers, it happened to pick just precisely *these* 20—whatever these 20 numbers may be—and it also doesn't "know" that it did, or did not, match any of those to any of the ones you happened to pick for your game. The machine simply cycles billions of bits, and at the trigger point—which traditionally is the insertion of the coin or the activation of the first credit—it then stops that scan, and whatever outcome of those randomly assembled numbers is in that instance, those and only those will be "displayed" on the machine's monitor for that current game. Even though to you—the player—it may seem like several seconds have passed as the viewing monitor displays the keno numbers (or balls) as being drawn out one by one, to the machine this is simply the process of displaying an event that already happened several seconds before you actually see it on the game's monitor. Just because on the game's monitor it looks like the numbers are coming up one after the other, this is only the "display" part of the graphic interface that translates the machine's binary numeral events into pictures that human players can understand and to which they can relate.

This is the same for all video slots, and video poker machines. The event that determines the win or loss for that game happens in a microsecond and several seconds before you ever get to see it on the monitor. The "display" you see can be cards (as in Video Poker) or cherries, bars, fruits, or whatever (as in video slots) or Arabic numerals (as in Video Keno), which happen to be the "numbers" as we understand them. The actual pictures—the "display"—has no bearing on the game. Only the pure, simple, dry, and uninteresting mathematical random distribution of binary numerals matters, as scanned and stopped by the program at the point of the trigger. After that, if this was a winning event, the machine's program instructs the credit meter to be awarded the appropriate amount of credits, or currency, and the game is over. If this is *not* a winning event—as programmed in the machine's computer software that recognizes what are, and what are not, winning events—the machine will simply display the words "Game Over," and that's it. Now the random number scan will continue undisturbed until the next trigger, and the process is repeated. And so on, for all such events, for all video and computer-based slot machines, of which Video Keno is one.

Of course, it wouldn't be interesting if all we ever saw were strings of binary numerals, like so much math spaghetti all running across our screen. Although that is precisely what Video Keno really is—as indeed all slot machines—this would be interesting only to the programmers and mathematicians. Casino players wouldn't find this exciting at all. That's why there are pictures on Slots, cards in Video Poker, and numbers in Video Keno. These "pictures" are the graphics that represent the random number events. By being able to see these familiar pictures, we, the human players, become interested in playing the games and find enjoyment and excitement in so doing. That's why slot machines have pictures and themes.

The following are the most commonly asked questions from among video keno players.

Why does the machine always pick the numbers right next to mine?

Answer: It doesn't. The machine doesn't "know" it did this. Only you, the human player, think this is so. People like to see patterns, even where patterns do not exist. "In a standard keno game, the player can choose up to 10 spots to play out of a possible 80 spots numbered 1 through 80. When the game actually needs to choose the final 'keno balls' for the game after the player hits the 'start' button, the actual call to the random number generator goes like this (anglicized to explain what is happening): 'Get me 20 random numbers.' To the machine this command means: 'Choose 20 random balls within the range of numbers 1 through 80.' First, we have already established that the process of choosing random numbers is indeed a valid and approved process, so we are guaranteed 20 random balls. Second, the call to get these numbers is simple and does not possess any knowledge of the numbers the player has chosen. In other words, the outcome is random." **Translation:** The machine has no idea that you—the human player— happen to have selected the numbers you picked. There is nothing in the machine's program that somehow "tells" or "informs" the machine that you picked those numbers, nor is there anything in the machine's program that in any way tells the machine to "not pick" those numbers. The machine's program *has nothing to do with the picks you make* as a player of Video Keno. It will only display the numbers it drew randomly, and then show them to you on the screen. If they happen to match yours, you win. If they don't, you lose. That's all there is to it.

Why does the machine pick the same group I am playing, but always right next to where I have it marked?

Answer: It doesn't. Again, the machine doesn't "know" you happened to have picked *that* group, and it doesn't "know" its selections happened to be displayed in the same pattern and shown next to where you happened to have picked it. "If the player chooses a number with eight surrounding unpicked numbers, the chances are high that one of those unpicked numbers will be chosen as compared with the picked number by 8-to-1. It's perception, not anything actual." **Translation:** If you pick a number that has eight other numbers around it, the odds are significant that some of the randomly drawn numbers will be displayed as being "next to" the one you picked. Similarly so for whatever you think of as a "pattern." The machine doesn't know it "picked a pattern," and it doesn't know it happened to show that pattern "right next to the same kind" you picked. So, if you play a block of nine numbers, and the machine picks a block that looks exactly like the one you picked, and shows that block right next to yours, or above it, or below it, it doesn't do this because it somehow "knows" it is the same pattern as that which you played, nor does it do this because it somehow "knows" that it placed this "next to" what you picked. Furthermore, there is nothing in the machine's program that "tells" it to so "tease" you. It's only in your mind. People see patterns—clouds in the sky that look like bunny rabbits, for example. Machines see nothing, know nothing. They only generate random numbers as they are programmed to do, and then "show" what they picked by means of a graphics interface that then represents these selections in a manner that you can understand and recognize. Just because you see a bunny rabbit in the clouds doesn't mean that the clouds somehow "know" they made such a pattern. Same for video keno machines, and all slot machines that run on these programs.

Marking, erasing, and then re-marking the same numbers "re-sets" the machine.

Answer: No. Wrong. It doesn't. This has NO effect whatsoever on the game. Please understand this clearly. There has been a lot of literature and much exposure recently given to proponents of a "theory" that when you play numbers that don't hit a winner for two or three games, you should then erase them and re-mark the same numbers again, because this has the effect of "re-setting" the machine. This is such bad advice, and such a hugely misleading superstition that it is a great pity it is finding acceptance among players, and in some major publications. Nothing could be further from the truth. This is about as bad as a superstition can get. If you believe this, you have been misled. It is wrong and untrue. "The game has no knowledge of the current picks by the player or any previous picks by the player when it calls for the next set of 20 random numbers. The numbers chosen are random as described above." **Translation:** Whenever you trigger the stop of the random scan, such as when you press the first credit or insert the first coin, those results and those results only are those that the machine will display. At that instant, the message "Get me 20 random numbers" has already happened. No amount of work or effort on your part of marking, erasing, and then re-marking your numbers will have any effect whatsoever on those 20 picks the machine already made a long time before you ever get to the marking, erasing, and re-marking procedure.

All this will do is make you tired. It will NOT help you win any more, or more often. "Each game chooses 20 new random balls from a field of 80 choices with no knowledge of the current or prior player choices. There is no validity to the 're-pick' suggestion."

Why is it that the game picks numbers in clearly defined patterns?

Answer: It doesn't. The human mind cannot keep track of 80 numbers at once, so it makes the comprehension possibility easier by combining them into what we call "patterns." "There are no 'real' patterns, just *player perceptions* of patterns. Take a simple example: A player notices that 6 of the 10 numbers in the first row of the keno board were chosen in a game. A few games later, the player notices again that 6 of the 10 numbers in the first row are again chosen. The player has just seen a pattern. If, however, in these two occurrences of 6 out of 10 were played on another board where the numbers 1 through 10 were scattered randomly over the board, and not in the same regular orientation, no pattern would be perceived. The same sets of random numbers would appear differently to the player, who cannot comprehend all 80 numbers simultaneously. Any weak alignment of objects quickly becomes a 'pattern' that the human mind can comprehend." **Translation:** What you see is what only YOU see—not what the machine actually does. Machines have no concept or understanding of "patterns"—they simply generate numbers. Only YOU, the human player, make something out of it. And that, dear friends, is the truth behind all those players' myths and superstitions about Video Keno.

Okay, now we have heard the engineer, and we have understood the failures that are part of what we are—human beings. We aren't perfect. We can't comprehend the number theories that the machines understand and generate and operate by. We *can* understand that the machine knows nothing about what we think we are seeing, but we also know that machines don't perform as human beings can. Indeed, we also know that machines are made by human beings, as are the programs that run them. Indeed, the programs that test the programs within the machines are in themselves made by human beings. **Question:** True or False—Everything made by humans is always perfect. **Answer:** No. Human beings make mistakes. We use human skills to make choices and decisions that machines can't. While a machine cannot "understand" patterns and cannot perform an educated and meaningfully applied pattern recognition choice, we as human players *can*. We can do something the machines can't— we can observe, adapt, and make playing choices based on what we have seen, learned, experienced, and adapted. Regardless of how "random" anything may appear, the "appearance" of such in itself is a "pattern." Patterns abound in nature, as they do in gambling games. Machines that are programmed to randomly select events may do so perfectly and without mistake, fault, or error, but the pure natural fact remains that no matter how this may be in theory, in the reality of the short-term slice of the events you will experience playing the machine—in these precise small slices of the overall random reality—you *will* see patterns, and they will repeat. Therefore, as a human player—rather than a machine—you will be able to exploit these situations to your financial profit on these gambling games if you learn to play in accordance with your human abilities.

This is why gambling strategies and powerful profits are possible even on games whose very nature is not to make you a long-term winner, because of the lower than 100 percent payback in all negative-expectation machine-based games. Even a perfect machine will at some point display what we perceive as patterns, and display results in extreme ranges of probabilities. These are also accounted for in the mathematics of the game's program; they are called "statistical anomalies." It is because these statistical anomalies are in fact possible—in nature and in all things, gambling machines included—that we can make them pay. This is so for any human endeavor, be it Slots, Blackjack, Craps, Roulette, the stock market, or political pundits. Or for survey results, so popular with all players, stock analysts, and computer programmers. We, the human beings, can do something that machines can't. We can observe, learn, adapt, and wager accordingly because we know our end-result purpose is to win money. The machines have no knowledge or concept of "money," or of "winning" or "losing." None of these are part of the machine's "understanding." The machine simply sits and generates numbers. When a human player triggers the machine to stop the scan, the machine then shows the player what the result of that event was. It is then up to the player to make something out of it, and that's where skill in play comes into full focus. There is more to winning in Video Keno then to just sit and watch the results of the random events. "There is *skill* in them thar machines, and gold in them thar hills, pardner." You just gotta know how to find it and how to dig it out.

Postscript

Live Keno and Video Keno are two distinct games. Although they share the same principles, they are not identical. Most of the time the payback percentages on video keno games are much higher than on virtually all live keno games—those games played in the keno lounge that I have dubbed Lounge Keno. The most liberal payback lounge keno game I know of is played at the Silverton Hotel Casino and RV Park, on Blue Diamond Road just off the I-15 freeway, just a shade outside of the southernmost end of the Las Vegas Strip. This game pays back just a tad over 80 percent, and that's huge for Lounge Keno. Most of the other casinos in and around Las Vegas pay back only around 75 percent, and that's good for Lounge Keno. To most casino players—especially those immersed in the mathematics of the games—this kind of a huge house edge appears overbearingly daunting. They therefore immediately dismiss this game as "stupid," and "unbeatable," and refer to anyone playing it as "ignorant casino fodder." Keno has always been thought of as a lousy game from the player's perspective, and a true "house game" from the casino's view.

While I agree that games with a tiny house edge, or no house edge at all, are generally better to play than games with a large house edge, this doesn't mean that those games are somehow inherently bad, or that they never produce winners. The greatest misconception on the part of those who consider casino games only from inside the "box" of mathematics, odds, and probabilities is that they don't take into account that even "lousy" games can make *financial winners* for their players. So what if the game is a 25 percent house hold game. Is it your purpose to play the game for fifty-five years so that in the end you can validate the math, and say: "Yup, after fifty-five years of playing, I can surely say I lost 25 percent of all the money I played." How terrific. What exactly did this do for you while you were in the casino today? Or yesterday? Or tomorrow? Or on your next trip? Did any of this have an impact on your play for the one or two hours you will be sitting in the keno lounge? Or the forty-five minutes you will be playing while waiting for your dinner? What about regular players—does this have some kind of an impact on them? Although regular players are exposed to greater fluctuations in the game's statistics, these are not nearly as wide or volatile as the overall math would tend to indicate. It is simply not true that regular players will always lose $25 out of each $100 they wager on Lounge Keno. While I have no intention of disputing that a regular player may indeed prove to be a 25 percent loser over a lifetime of playing—provided he or she plays only in accordance with the single-ticket test case theory—it is a fallacy for anyone to claim that just because of that perspective Mr. or Ms. Keno Player won't win anything. Remember—even statistically "bad" games produce winners!

Unfortunately, too many experts have lambasted Keno as a bad game. The casinos themselves do not seem to understand their games, or their proper marketing—and certainly have almost no clue as to *why* people play the games they do. I have spent ten years as a casino consultant, analyzing everything casinos do from the ground up. I have been to every casino region in the United States and to every casino in Nevada throughout the 1980s and 1990s, and these issues linger and aren't resolved. Even when casino executives are clearly informed about what is happening, they tend to ignore Keno because it doesn't appear to be a priority. As a consequence, casino keno brochures show only the bad "way" tickets, and not the good ones, and don't promote understanding of the game from the player's perspective. This leaves the players largely to themselves, with not much to go on. I hope that I have helped to overcome that problem in this book and have provided you with a clear overview and understanding on how keno can be played for profit. Intelligent use of way tickets, combinations, core strategies, wheels, and so on, all combine to make keno a good game that can be fun to play and profitable.

Video Keno has been more successful, largely because it is a simple slot machine and people aren't afraid to play a slot machine, especially one that is as simple as this one. Put in your quarter, mark your numbers, push "play," then wait to see if you won something. That was the principle behind the video keno games introduced to the casinos some twenty years ago, when the computer revolution was just beginning to take hold. These days video keno games and machines are far more sophisticated. The greatest advance in the game was the speed, especially those games that have a speed control button. If you like a fast game— which I do, because I hate to sit and wait for the game to display a result that I know was already determined many seconds ago (as soon as the machine's trigger stopped the binary numerical sequencing algorithm scan)—then the speed control button, or icon, is a blessing. Prior to this, players had to sit and wait for the silly machine to chime away and display the numbers, and some of these games took forever to do this. Most of the new machines will display the speed control icon on the screen as soon as you insert your currency. If your machine doesn't show this on the video keno screen, simply switch to any video poker program on the machine's main menu, locate the speed control there, set it to "fast," and return to the video keno game. Conversely, if you enjoy playing a slow game, you can use this same procedure to slow down the game's speed. It's yet another aspect of the control that you can now exert over a game that was previously only a very passive game, whereby you were merely the spectator to someone else's preconceived design about how the game should play, or how fast or slow.

This single fact of the speed of the game contributes directly to the machine's overall better payback percentage, and resultant much lower house edge. Video Keno becomes a slot machine that can be played to good effect, often with programs that pay back upward of 94 percent. Many casinos around the United States have slot machines whose payback percentages are below 92 percent, so even this "bad" video keno game is quite a few percentage points better than such machines in those casinos. Video Keno is, therefore, not nearly as "bad" a slot machine as many people claim—players and experts alike. Furthermore, with the advances in computer technology, we now have games like *Four Card Keno*™ and *Multi-Card Keno*™. These games allow us to use many of the strategy principles I have outlined in this book to play this game for truly powerful profits. Other than skill-based games, such as Live Poker, or perhaps Blackjack, Video Keno offers the knowledgeable player the best opportunities to play a slot machine with a playing method that can, and does, result in protracted and frequent profits. How much profit? Well, that depends on the same set of factors and your personal circumstances as any other casino game. How much is in your dedicated bankroll. How well can you play? How *long* can you play? How well can you manage your money? These "skills" are part of all gambling, not just Keno or Video Keno. If you can do all of those well, and you learn to do what I have shown here in this book, then you have the wherewithal to make Keno and Video Keno into a profitable game. Keno, Video Keno in particular, are my favorite casino games. Only Live Poker is better in my opinion, but Live Poker is not a casino game in the truest sense of the word, because it is not a house-banked game (people play against each other, not against the casino).

I wanted to write a book about Keno and Video Keno because I like these games, and because I have never seen a book that takes the game seriously, tries to explain it equally seriously, and treats it as a serious casino game that can be played profitably. Several books on the market deal with casino Keno, and even Video Keno, but not many tell the whole story—at least not in the way that I have tried to do here. If I have succeeded in showing you how to play Keno and Video Keno better, or at least made you interested in discovering the game for yourself, then I am happy. If I have also succeeded in making Keno a profitable experience for you, I will be happier still. Whatever value I was able to provide for you in this book, I hope it was entertaining and informative. That is all that any gaming author can ever seek to achieve.

Finally, I would like to finish with a story. It is a fable, but as far as I know, it is true. Way back when, in the days when computers were the size of a two-story house and most casino players had never heard of one, there was only Lounge Keno, and no video machines of any kind. It was a game whose tickets were marked with a messy black ink, a game played in large smoke-filled rooms with old leather lounge chairs, in one of the classic casinos of Las Vegas. This lounge is actually still there, and I have been in it many times. It is like stepping back in time some forty years. Back then, Keno was mostly played by elderly players—people who enjoyed a quiet and relaxing game. It was also an extraordinarily slow game, because the tickets had to be marked twice, first by the player and then by the keno writer in that messy black ink, and everything else had to be done manually. Even the flashboard was controlled manually, by an employee punching the drawn numbers onto an electronic board with switches that lit up the corresponding numbers on the flashboard. Often something went wrong—the switch wouldn't work or the lightbulb would burn out. The game was so slow that it was said that the players could be seen aging between games.

Many of the regulars back then used to play for many hours, and sometimes many days. Casinos would serve drinks and meals to any player anywhere. It was a far friendlier atmosphere and much more relaxed than the frenzied pace of the casinos today. In this particular casino, there was an elderly man who would play every day, and often stay for long periods of time. He would always play the same ticket, playing for the big jackpot of $25,000, which was at that time the maximum limit allowed. Many times he would win small hits, and even bigger hits, and he would grumble about not hitting the big one. Although he was always pleasant when spoken to, most of the time he kept to himself, not wanting to be bothered by other players and particularly the casino and keno staff. He eventually became known as "the grouch," and sometimes "Groucho." This wasn't quite fair, because the few people who knew him well always knew he was a true gentleman. But, true or not, the moniker stayed and he became known as "the resident grouch."

One day he died right there in the leather lounge chair in the keno lounge, and no one realized it for three days.

Everyone in the casino had learned to leave him alone, and they were so used to seeing him there, sometimes for several days in a row, sometimes asleep in his chair, that it simply didn't occur to anyone that he was dead. He looked like he had fallen asleep, and since shifts change each eight hours, no one noticed that the old grouch had died. Eventually, of course, they found out. When the police arrived, they lifted up his head as best as they could to see if he was truly dead. There he was, sporting a huge smile on his face, looking more pleasant than anyone had ever seen him. A little more investigation produced a keno ticket that he was still holding in his hand. After getting the ticket out of his fingers, they checked the game and found out that the ticket had won the big jackpot! Finally, after all those years, he had won the big one.

Well, it seemed that when he saw the numbers come up he got so excited that he suffered a stroke and died right then and there, his happy smile forever frozen to his lips. The old gent was removed and buried, but the ticket was never paid because, by the law of the time, the winning tickets had to be collected immediately after the end of the last game. The grouch hit his several days before he was discovered, and so the ticket was ruled void. After the funeral, the police went to the man's house, since no relatives could be found. His was an old house, and it looked kind of dilapidated. As they were searching the meager furniture and skimpy belongings that were left behind, one of the old floorboards cracked. There, hidden underneath the floorboards of the house, the police found $16 million in cash, neatly stuffed into bags and boxes.

The point of this story is—don't judge a man by his appearance, and don't judge a player's choice of game based on what *you* think his goals and objectives may be. For old "Groucho," all he wanted was to hit the big jackpot, even though it was peanuts compared with the money he had stashed. It was his moment of happiness. So for you, your choice of Keno may just be one such moment of happiness, no matter what others may think. And this, dear friends, is about as much of a story as I am allowed to tell in a book like this.

Acknowledgments

First and foremost, I wish to thank my dear mother, Georgina S. Royer, for her lifetime of help, guidance, and assistance. She is a remarkable lady who fully deserves notice for her tremendous abilities and steadfast faith in me.

I also wish to thank my literary agents, Greg Dinkin and Frank Scatoni. Greg is an accomplished author in his own right, and Frank a widely respected book editor. Through their agency, Venture Literary, they recognized the value of what I had to offer as an author of books on casino games and gaming. Without their efforts, this book, and the others in this series, would never have come to exist.

My thanks also to Bruce Bender, at Kensington Publishing Group, who has published this book and this series. He recognized that this book, and this series, offers valuable insight into the casino games as they really are, and that this book will enable almost all players to finally realize a happy and profitable casino experience. I thank Bruce, and the staff of Kensington, for their help in this process, and in particular to my editors, Richard Ember and that wonderful lady Ann LaFarge.

I extend my gratitude and thanks to my long-time friend Tom Caldwell for the many things he has done to help me, and to enrich my life. I also send my thanks to Norreta, Sean, and Brent, for reasons they all know.

My sincere thanks also to Bob Dempsey, and his company in Las Vegas, Dempsey Graphics, for his help with many illustrations in my books. Bob, thanks also for making that video tape for me for Jay Leno and the *Tonight Show*.

I would also like to acknowledge www.thegamblersedge. com and www.14g.com, two Internet sites that proved very informative about the history of Keno. I used these to complement my other historical research and used portions of that research in illustrating the origins and history of Keno, especially as played in the United States. I also wish to acknowledge www.wizardofodds.com—Michael Shackleford— a brilliant statistician whose site provides many interesting items pertaining to gambling odds. I used it as a reference point for comparison to the stats that I obtained directly from the games' manufacturer.

To all my other friends and associates in the gaming business, from owners, managers, senior executives, to hosts and supervisors, you all know who you are, and I thank you.

My friends in Australia: Neil and his family, Lilli and little MRM (Mark); Ormond College, University of Melbourne; the governor of Victoria and my former master, Sir Davis McCaughey. Also his Proctorial Eminence R. A. Dwyer, Esq. (I still have the Swiss knife you gave me more than twenty years ago), the Alumni Association of the University of Wollongong, NSW, Department of Philosophy, and Professor Chipman. Also to the executive, editorial, and display advertising staff of *The Age* newspaper in Melbourne, Australia, and to Fairfax Press in Sydney, with whom I had the pleasure of being associated at one time.

I also extend my grateful appreciation to Laurence E. Levit, C.P.A., of Los Angeles, who has been my steadfast friend, accountant, and adviser for two decades, and whose faith in me and my work has never faltered. A truer friend a man rarely finds. Also to Michael Harrison, attorney at law in Beverly Hills, California, whose expertise and help have made my life more secure.

To the folks at International Game Technology (IGT): I wish to single out Ed Rogich and thank him for his foresight, and his much appreciated assistance, during the process of writing this book. I also wish to thank my long-time friend, Rick Sorensen for all his help. Both Ed and Rick were directly instrumental in providing me with the kind of information I needed. They provided the photographs of those many IGT multi-game and video keno machines, the games I like so much. Thanks also to Cynthia White for her support, as well as Connie Fox, Dawn Cox, Robert Lightfoot, Todd Brown, Joe Kaminkow, and Harold Shotwell. Without the support of all these people, and their valuable help and assistance, it would have been much more difficult to tell you about the games I wanted to write about—the ones I have played and wanted to showcase in this book. My thanks also to all the staff, executives, and officers of International Game Technology, of Reno, Nevada.

Finally, to all those whose paths have crossed with mine, and who have for one reason or another stopped a while and visited. I may no longer remember your names, but I do remember what it meant to have those moments.

Thank you!

Copyright and Trademark Notice

Throughout this book, I mentioned several machines and games that are products either owned by, or often based upon registered, copyright, and trademark ownership of either IGT or third parties. All are used herein by permission. The following information acknowledges such ownership of these products, images, logos, and other distinctive features as indicated.

IGT® AND THIRD-PARTY TRADEMARK LISTS

The following are registered, copyrighted, and/or trademarked by International Game Technology (IGT), of Reno, Nevada, used by permission:

Game King®
Spot Keno™
Caveman Keno®
Cleopatra® Keno

Super Keno™
Power Keno®
Four Card Keno™
Multi-Card Keno™
Cleopatra® Video Slots
Leopard Spots® Video Slots
Cleopatra and *Leopard Spots* are trademarks of IGT.
Caveman Keno, Game King, and *Keno Deluxe* are trademarks of IGT.

Index